EDITIONS SR

Volume 6

Averroes' Doctrine of Immortality
A Matter of Controversy

Ovey N. Mohammed

Published for the Canadian Corporation for Studies in
Religion/Corporation Canadienne des Sciences Religieuses
by Wilfrid Laurier University Press

1984

Canadian Cataloguing in Publication Data

Mohammed, Ovey N. (Ovey Nelson), 1933-
   Averroes' doctrine of immortality

(Editions SR ; 6)
Bibliography: p.
Includes index.
ISBN 0-88920-178-1

1. Averroës, 1126-1198. 2. Immortality.
3. Scholasticism. I. Title. II. Series.

B749.Z7M63 1984   129   C84-099253-X

© 1984 Canadian Corporation for Studies in Religion/
   Corporation Canadienne des Sciences Religieuses

84 85 86 87 4 3 2 1

No part of this book may be translated or reproduced in any form, by print, photoprint, microfilm, microfiche, or any other means, without written permission from the publisher.

Cover design by Michael Baldwin, MSIAD

Order from:
Wilfrid Laurier University Press
Wilfrid Laurier University
Waterloo, Ontario, Canada   N2L 3C5

Printed in the
United States
of America

ACKNOWLEDGEMENT

This book has been published with the help of a grant from the Canadian Federation for the Humanities, using funds provided by the Social Sciences and Humanities Research Council of Canada.

TABLE OF CONTENTS

INTRODUCTION	1
The Background	1
The Medieval Reaction to Averroes	4
The Medieval Reaction Reconsidered	10
The Modern Reaction	15
The Problem of the Immortality of the Soul in Averroes	22

CHAPTER

I. THE ANTHROPOLOGICAL BACKGROUND OF THE AVERROISTIC CONTROVERSIES … 29

  The Qur'anic Anthropology … 29
  The Christian Anthropologies … 40
  The Aristotelian Anthropology … 53

II. AVERROES ON REASON AND REVELATION … 60

  Reason and Revelation in Islam Before Averroes … 60
  Reason and Revelation According to Averroes … 67
  Reason and Revelation According to Aquinas … 82

III. THE IMMORTALITY OF THE SOUL … 84

  Soul and Intellect in the Commentary on the *De Anima* … 84
  Soul and Intellect in the *Tahafut al-Tahafut* … 104
  Life After Death … 107

IV. THE NATURE OF MAN'S BEATITUDE … 115

  Averroes' Theory of Intellection … 115
  Man's Perfection as Union with the Agent Intellect … 121
  Reward and Punishment … 128

V. CONCLUSION … 131

NOTES

  Introduction … 143
  Chapter I … 149
  Chapter II … 157
  Chapter III … 164
  Chapter IV … 168

Chapter V	170
BIBLIOGRAPHY	172
INDEX	195

INTRODUCTION

The Background

Mid-way through the twelfth century, as the Latin West was introduced to a wealth of previously unknown scientific and philosophical literature through translations from the Greek and Arabic, a new chapter in the history of Christian philosophy began. This chapter might well have been entitled: "Aristotelianism and the great turning point of Christian thought."

During patristic times, Plato had exerted much more influence on Christian philosophy than Aristotle; of all of Aristotle's works, only his logic was then known. Two Christians, Marius Victorinus and Boethius, had transmitted the logic to the Middle Ages as the instrument of philosophy and theology. It was only about 1128 that James of Venice translated the two <u>Analytics</u>, the <u>Topics</u>, and the <u>Sophistics</u> from Greek into Latin. These became known as the <u>logica nova</u>, in contrast to the <u>logica vetus</u> of Boethius, which included the Categories and <u>On Interpretation</u>. Through these translations, the cultural horizon of the medieval world was suddenly broadened, and the scholastics were exposed to the breadth of the philosophic genius of Aristotle. For the first time, they were confronted with a philosophy that relied on reason to an unprecedented degree. Plato, for instance, for all his dependence upon the devices of human reason, was heavily influenced nevertheless by such factors as Orphism and Pythagorean religiosity. To be sure, Plato was a "philosopher." But he was, of course, hardly a philosopher in the sense of the term that corresponds to the practice of philosophy since, say, the age of Descartes. This is not, on the other hand, to take away the "theological" import of the work of Aristotle. It is simply to remember that there is a vast difference between the empirical attitude reflected by the philosophical activity of an Aristotle -- an attitude that ultimately became normative of the philosophical orientation -- and the philosophical yet intuitive, aprioristic, and mythological procedures of a Plato. This difference is worth recalling because it was, to a large measure, on account of it that the Middle Ages were eventually confronted with a serious problem concerning the relationship -- and more particularly, the possible conflict -- between faith and reason. Plato had never posed quite the same sort of difficulty for earlier Christian thought.

If the introduction of Aristotelianism into the West may be truthfully described as the introduction of a ferment, however, it may equally be spoken of in terms of conflict, disruption, and turmoil. Because of Aristotle, certain Christian authors felt inspired to create some of the most impressive achievements of a Christian intellect that knows itself to be activated by its Christian belief. Others, however, found their most cherished beliefs challenged by the new world view, which they deemed almost entirely at variance with their Christian faith: in not a few quarters the reaction to Aristotle was from the first one of distrust. Thus, in 1210 the Provincial Council of Paris forbade the public or private teaching of Aristotle's writings on natural philosophy or commentaries on them in the schools. In 1215, Robert Courson, the papal legate in Paris, extended the prohibition to include the metaphysics or commentaries on them. Yet such prohibitions, renewed in 1231 by Pope Gregory IX, did not prevent the growing popularity of these works.

In the light of the eventual vogue of Aristotelianism in Catholic intellectual circles, the initial and long-held suspicion -- mixed, to be sure, with equal parts of fascination -- with which it was received in the Christian world requires some explanation. Part of the reason has to do with the nature of Aristotle's own doctrine. For example, the doctrine of creation is unsuspected by Aristotle; indeed, it is foreign to his mind. The reconciliation of Aristotle and the Christian faith required a transformation of Aristotle, rather than a simple acceptance of him. However, part of the explanation has to do with the historical context and the circumstances of Aristotle's reception in

Introduction

the West, and, in the first place, with the fact that the Arabs were one of the channels of the Aristotelian philosophical heritage for the Latin West.

The vicissitudes of the works of Aristotle after the closing of the Academies by Justinian in 529 need not be recounted here. Suffice it to recall that by the ninth century, while Aristoteles Latinus comprised no more than the logica nova, the Aristotelian corpus was known and preserved in the Arabic-speaking world almost entire, together with the pseudo-Aristotelian treatises as the Theology of Aristotle and the Liber de causis. As is well known, though the latter works were ascribed to Aristotle, the first was really an excerpt of the Enneads of Plotinus, and the second was taken from the Element of Theology by Proclus. This probably explains why the Aristotelian philosophy of Al-Kindi (ca. 800-70), Alfarabi (875-950), and Avicenna (980-1037) in the Islamic East is highly Neoplatonized. Aristotelianism proper developed in the twelfth century in Spain, where the effort was made to cleanse Aristotle's doctrines of the Neoplatonic accretions, and where it reached its climax in the Islamic West with Averroes (1126-98). Thus, when the Aristotelian corpus was translated into Latin from Arabic and Greek, in the twelfth and early thirteenth centuries, the Christian interest in Aristotle created a simultaneous interest in the philosophical writings of Arab Aristotelians, which had also been translated and circulated at the same time. Indeed, because of the profundity of Aristotle's thought, the medieval scholastics sought instruction in Aristotle's meaning from Averroes, the most celebrated of his non-Christian interpreters. In short, the great turning point in Christian thought may be defined as that period of Christian intellectual history when Christian scholars were exposed not only to the philosophy of Aristotle, but also to the commentaries of Averroes.

Averroes' commentaries on the writings of Aristotle were made known to Christian Europe in Latin translation through the work of the court of Frederick II of Sicily and Archbishop Raymond's school of translators at Toledo,

Spain. Among the best-known translators were: Adelard of
Bath, Herman the German, Dominicus Gundalissalinus, John of
Spain, Gerard of Cremona, and Michael Scot. It has been
well established that Averroes' commentary on the De Anima
of Aristotle was among the works translated into Latin by
Michael Scot at the court of Sicily from 1227 to 1230. It
was made available to a number of universities by Frederick
II in 1231. In any event, by the middle of the thirteenth
century there was a tendency for the doctrine of the Philosopher to be identified with that of the Commentator, as
Averroes soon became metonymically known: Aristotle meant,
for some, neither more nor less than the Commentator and
his interpretations. Thus, the name of a Muslim philosopher became bound up with the efforts of the medieval scholastics to establish a stable synthesis between the Christian faith and the Aristotelian science that so seductively
appealed to the human reason. The reason was that, if
Aristotle by himself appeared to resist the reconciling
efforts of Christian scholars, Aristotle as interpreted and
complemented by Averroes seemed to make the task an impossible one. Of all those positions of Aristotelianism intrinsically least easy to harmonize with Christianity, his
doctrine of the soul was prominent. More particularly, it
seemed to many Christians that Averroes' teaching -- and,
therefore, supposedly Aristotle's -- that there is one intellect for all men demanded a denial of the spirituality
and immortality of the soul.

The Medieval Reaction to Averroes

The theologians were quick to react. St. Bonaventure in his commentary on the Sentences,[1] composed about
1250, was the first to criticize Averroes' theory of the
intellect, which to him meant that mortal man cannot attain
immortality. His In Hexaemeron of 1273 witnesses to the
bitterness of his opposition to Aristotle and the Latin
Averroists.[2] In 1256, Albert the Great wrote his De
Unitate Intellectus Contra Averroem[3] at the request of Pope
Alexander IV. Following the current method of the philosophers, in contrast to that of the theologians, Albert pre-

Introduction

sents his thought on the immortality of the soul in syllogisms. He offers thirty arguments for the survival of only one soul after death and thirty-six arguments against it, in support of the survival of each human soul. To Albert the doctrine of the unicity of the intellect seems pernicious, pessimistic, and very improbable,[4] but he admits and maintains that there must be unity of knowledge.

The position of Aquinas in this matter is much more complex than that of most of his contemporaries. On the one hand, Aquinas must be said to have been, in some reasonable and recognizable sense of the term, an Aristotelian. This is not to dispute the view that Aquinas transformed, and did not merely reproduce, the doctrine of Aristotle. The point is rather that in certain key respects Aquinas based himself upon the doctrine of Aristotle, as understood by him. On the other hand, Aquinas clearly shared with the anti-Averroists the view that the incompatibility of Christian belief and the doctrine of Averroes is beyond reasonable doubt. Thus, in the <u>De Unitate Intellectus Contra Averroistas</u> of 1270, Aquinas states that his refutation of the Averroistic doctrine of the unicity of the intellect is based upon a faithful understanding of Aristotle.[5] Aquinas, thus, was one of the principal sources of a historical trend that eventually resulted in placing upon Averroes' shoulders the major burden of responsibility for the genesis of a doctrine that disrupted the intellectual well-being of Christian thought.

Aquinas' <u>De Unitate Intellectus Contra Averroistas</u> is devoted exclusively to the problem of the unicity of the intellect. He regards it as evident that Averroes' view of the intellect is contrary to the truth of the Christian faith. Yet Aquinas has a paradoxical relation to Averroes. He has great respect for him, and even honours him with the title "The Commentator."[6] However, he envisages Averroes as an antagonist, the exponent of an anti-Christian creed that he has to refute. Since Aquinas' analysis and refutation of Averroes was probably one of the most decisive and influential Christian reactions to "Averroism," perhaps we should examine it in slightly greater detail.

It is pertinent first to point out that Aquinas does admit two difficulties in writing against Muslims and Jews: his imperfect acquaintance with their views and the fact that the appeal to Scriptural authority cannot be used in controversy against Muslims, because they do not recognize the Bible as the final revelation of God.[7] In the circumstances, Aquinas argues in favour of the revelation of the Bible by claiming that its truth is authenticated by miracles and is of a supernatural character. He observes that the religion founded by the Prophet Muhammad can produce no such evidences.[8]

Now, Aquinas' argument is based on the consideration that, according to Averroes, every form of a body is completely immersed in matter and is consequently material. From this it follows that an immaterial substance cannot be the form of the body. Because man possesses a soul that is a material perishable form, the intellect cannot be a part of that soul but is somehow a separate unique substance. Aquinas accepts Averroes' theory of the universality of knowledge and the immateriality of the intellect. However, he rejects Averroes' conclusion that these characteristics necessitate a separate intellect for all men. On the other hand, he agrees with Averroes that matter is the principle of individuation in one and the same species. For Aquinas, the soul and the intellect are one, multiplied and individual, even though they are the perfection and form of the human body. Against Averroes he argues a Christian position: although man's existence is the existence of a composite, his existence is that of the soul in itself. The soul realizes its individuality from the body but is not dependent on the body for its existence.[9] According to Aquinas, Averroes' position would leave man without any incorruptible part of the soul; thus, there could be no personal immortality and, _a fortiori_, no reward and punishment in the afterlife.[10] But the human soul, Aquinas argues, must by its nature be, on the contrary, immortal and incorruptible.[11]

It may be relevant to recall in the present context that the Dominicans of the thirteenth century had set for themselves the objective of evangelizing Muslims and Jews. They even trained polemicists in Hebrew and Arabic with this end in view. Raymond Martin, for example, was an outstanding orientalist and, unlike his fellow Dominican, Aquinas, fully conversant with Islam and Islamic philosophy. His <u>Pugio Fidei Adversus Mauros et Judaeos</u>, completed in 1278, gives abundant proof of this. Like Aquinas' <u>Summa Contra Gentiles</u>, the <u>Pugio Fidei</u> is an attempt to argue for the truth of the Christian faith against non-Christian beliefs.[12] In this work Martin acknowledges that Averroes explains how his theory of the intellect is related to the subject of the soul in the <u>Tahafut al-Tahafut</u>, unknown in Latin translation at the time. However, in keeping with the apostolic nature of the <u>Pugio Fidei</u>, Martin summarily dismisses the explanation, calling Averroes' doctrine of the intellect Platonic, and his view of the soul the "nonsense of madmen."[13]

The feeling that the philosophy of Averroes, if not also that of Aristotle, posed a threat to the Christian faith was clearly growing stronger with the passage of time. Whatever the nature of the Islamic revelation, Averroes had made Aristotle highly respectable and, in the opinion of some, appeared to give a more systematic treatment of Aristotle's doctrine of the soul than Aquinas and other orthodox theologians. As a growing number of Christians chose to follow Averroes, the problem of reason and revelation deepened. The eventual result was that interesting, if somewhat elusive, phenomenon which has been abuilding since the middle of the thirteenth century: Latin Averroism. Maintaining that the intellect was one for all men, the Latin Averroists supported a view of human immortality incompatible with their religious allegiance. In the face of the obvious difficulty, they claimed that they were merely defending the position of philosophy, represented by Aristotle, and not denying the truth of the Christian revelation. Reason and revelation were in conflict, and the Latin Averroists could devise no better way to solve the conflict than to try to prevent it, that is, to introduce a radical separation of philosophy from revelation.

We have noted above some of the earliest condemnations of Aristotelianism between 1210 and 1231. This was hardly the end of the matter. In 1270, Etienne Tempier, bishop of Paris, found it necessary to declare anathema thirteen propositions bearing the name of Arabian authorship, and in 1277 these same views, along with others, were once more censured.[14] In addition, Giles of Rome included in his Errores Philosophorum of 1270 the errors of Aristotle and Averroes.[15] Tempier's condemnations were aimed at Siger de Brabant (ca. 1240 - ca. 1284) and Boethius of Dacia as propagators of the errors condemned. Bernier of Nivelles and Goswin of La Chapelle are other names usually associated with Latin Averroism in the thirteenth century.

Despite the refutation of Latin Averroism by Aquinas and other scholastics, and despite the official condemnations, Latin Averroism did not wither away and, indeed, in some respects gained ground. At the University of Paris, the complete Organon of Aristotle with Averroes' commentaries had been in use in 1255, and, by the fourteenth century, John of Jandun (1275-1328) was the best known Averroist in Paris. In England, John Baconthorp (1290-1348), though not an Averroist, wrote commentaries on Aristotle and Averroes that won the respect of Renaissance Averroists, and Thomas of Wilton (1288-1327) believed that human reason alone could not refute the doctrine of Averroes on the soul.

We know through Francesco Petrarch (1304-74), a violent critic of Averroism who complained that many scholars of the Renaissance honoured Aristotle in place of Christ and Averroes in place of Peter, that the Averroist movement had reached Italy in the fourteenth century. In the fifteenth century, the movement came to dominate the Italian universities, where it was stronger than in Paris, perhaps because the study of philosophy in Italy was associated with medicine rather than with theology. The Council of Florence and the fall of Constantinople in 1453 also brought many learned Greeks to Italy, and with them their interest in Aristotle's thought. Well-known Averroists in the fifteenth century are Paolo Veneto (1369-1428), Alexander Achillini (1463-1512), and Nicoletto Vernias (1420-99).

By the sixteenth century there were two rival camps of interpreters of Aristotle on the soul. According to the Averroists, the intellect was not individual but one for all men and immortal. Then there were those who, following Aquinas, made the possible intellect a power of each human soul, but who were dissatisfied with the proofs offered by Aquinas for the capacity of the individual soul to survive the dissolution of the body of which it was the form. These interpreters were known as Alexandrists, since their view coincided with that of Alexander of Aphrodisias.[16] They, like the Averroists, denied the personal immortality of the soul. They differed from the Averroists in thinking that the possible intellect was a power of each individual soul, and therefore mortal.

So influential were the positions of the Averroists and the Alexandrists that the Fifth Lateran Council condemned both on December 19, 1513.[17] The decree also ordered professors to refute those who taught the mortality of the soul as dangerous to the Christian faith. However, the decree did not have much effect in Italy, and, in 1518, Agostino Nifo (1473-1538) excused his interest in Averroes on the ground that he "is so famous in our time that no one seems to be a peripatetic unless he is an Averroist."[18]

Furthermore, in 1516, Pietro Pomponazzi (1464-1525), drawing support from Alexander of Aphrodisias, wrote his celebrated treatise De Immortalitate Animae[19] against the immortality of the soul. This aroused the opposition alike of both the orthodox theologians and the Averroists, whose favourite doctrine of the unicity of the intellect was denied. Pomponazzi wrote two apologies in defense of his view. The earlier of these is his Apologia of 1517 against Gaspar Contarini, afterwards bishop of Belluno. The other is his Defensorium of 1518 against Agostino Nifo, who tried to reconcile the doctrine of Averroes with that of the immortality of the individual soul in his own De

Immortalitate Animae. In both apologies Pomponazzi maintained that natural reason alone cannot prove the immortality of the soul, and contended that the doctrine of the mortality of the soul is the proper consequence of the doctrine of Aristotle and Averroes that the soul is the form of the body, though he did accept immortality as an article of faith.[20] His position reflects the dilemma of the Christian student of Averroes.

The Averroist controversy on the immortality of the soul faded away with the waning of interest in Aristotle in the sixteenth and seventeenth centuries. It faded with the Italian Renaissance, which was Platonic rather than Aristotelian. It faded with the Reformation in Germany, through Luther, who denounced the Aristotelianism of the scholastics. It faded with the growth of modern science, which sought to escape the medieval tradition to which Aristotle was yoked. Nevertheless, the impression tended to remain that the controversies between the orthodox theologians and the Averroists had rested on their correct interpretation of Averroes concerning the soul. In modern times, however, certain reasons have appeared that have made it reasonable to raise the question whether this assumption, long shared by historians of Christian thought, is correct: it may be that both the orthodox theologians and the Averroists misinterpreted Averroes' actual doctrine.

The Medieval Reaction Reconsidered

The first indication that this question may be raised is that the controversy at its height in the thirteenth century was conducted on the basis of Averroes' commentary on the De Anima, whereas the Tahafut al-Tahafut, in which he discusses how his theory of the intellect is related to his theory of the immortality of the soul, was not available in Latin until 1328, when it gained currency under the Latin title, Destructio Destructionum Philosophiae Algazelis. Moreover, this translation contained an incomplete text. The Tahafut al-Tahafut contains twenty disputations: sixteen disputations "In Metaphysicis" and four "In Physicis." Until 1527 the most widely available document, that of 1328, did not include the four disputations "In Physicis."

For the two principal translations of the Tahafut al-Tahafut into Latin, Christians are indebted to three Jewish scholars who, with striking coincidence, all bore the name Calonymos. The first of these was Calonymos, son of Meir, of Arles. He was asked by Robert the Good of Anjou to translate the work from Arabic into Latin. He accepted the assignment and completed it on April 18, 1328. The second Calonymos, a contemporary of the first, was a Judeo-Provençal translator. He translated the Tahafut al-Tahafut from Arabic into Hebrew sometime between 1318 and 1328. This was Calonymos, son of David, son of Todros or Calonymos ben David the Elder. The Hebrew translation is known as the Happalat-ha-Happala.

The Happalat-ha-Happala was translated into Latin in the sixteenth century by the third Calonymos, Calo Calonymos or Kalonymos ben David the Younger or Maestro Calo. It was this Latin translation, published in 1527, which contained the complete text of the Tahafut al-Tahafut. In the dedication of the work to Hercules Gonzaga, Calo Calonymos explains why he made a second Latin translation when that of Calonymos ben Calonymos of Arles already existed. As he puts it, there was a shortened version of the Destructio Destructionum, "especially lacking in the last four natural and principal disputations of great importance, but found among the Hebrews complete in all respects." "For this reason," Calo Calonymos continues, "I decided to translate the work from Hebrew into Latin."[21]

It was thus the text of 1328 that Nifo, for instance, the great and influential admirer of Averroes, used when he wrote his commentary on the Destructio Destructionum. Before he completed his commentary, Nifo, it appears, became aware that the disputations "In Metaphysicis" did not constitute the entire text. Nevertheless, it is significant that he evidently treated the document as if for practical purposes it were complete, that is, in the apparent expectation that the missing parts

would not affect his understanding of the true mind of
Averroes. His treatise ends with the following remark:
"And so ends my book on the "In Metaphysicis" of Averroes
which is called the Destructio Destructionum, begun in
1494 and completed on January 22, 1497."[22] An examination
of the Destructio Destructionum, however, which takes
account of the disputations "In Physicis" casts doubt on
the adequacy of Nifo's and earlier interpreters of
Averroes; for it is precisely in the last four disputations
"In Physicis" of the Tahafut al-Tahafut that Averroes discusses how his theory of the intellect is related to the
personal immortality of the soul. By the time that this
discussion had become readily available in Latin in 1527,
the Nifo-Pomponazzi controversy was already over. Indeed,
Pomponazzi, called "the last scholastic," was already dead.
He had died in 1525. And Aquinas had died in 1274.

However, it is not only a matter of the fuller
texts of Averroes as they later became available but also,
and indeed principally, of the way in which even the texts
known then can be read today. A second and, from the viewpoint of Christian scholarship, far more important reason
why it may be useful to reopen the question as to precisely
what Averroes thought about the nature and immortality of
the soul, without assuming that the interpretation of either the Averroists or the anti-Averroists is correct, is
that an examination of any of the texts of Averroes does
not at any point give an explicit denial of personal immortality: an understanding of the processes involved in the
Christian ascription to Averroes of the opposite opinion
may well be a most valuable aid towards an understanding of
the Christian mind and the history of Christian thought.
Indeed, if one reads the texts of Averroes mindful of the
absence of every explicit denial of the immortality of the
soul, one is led to ask whether such a denial can properly
be attributed to him at all. Aquinas and the other orthodox theologians were predisposed, of course, to attempt to
refute the illustrious Muslim. In the climate of the thirteenth century it was sufficient for them that the doctrine
of Averroes appeared to be in conflict with the Christian

faith. Furthermore, it could well be said that by their
insistence on the intellect being proper and individual to
every man, they were defending the integrity of the human
personality. Their position would naturally appear to them
as a corrective to the defective view of human personality
held by Averroes. But many modern scholars have indicated
that the unity of man has never been a point of interest in
the entire history of Muslim thought.[23] Medieval Christians may thus have taken for granted that Averroes shared
with them assumptions which may, in fact, have been exclusively their own.

   It is interesting to observe that the orthodox
theologians' insistence on the intellect being proper and
individual to every man is part of a Christian way of
thinking: that was is said of the intellect can also be
said of the soul, of which it is a power. This fact explains why the Latin Averroists thought that if all men
share in one intellect, they also share in one soul. For
them the spirituality of the intellect obviously established the spirituality of the soul. To separate the intellect from the soul was unthinkable. Hence they interpreted Averroes as teaching a doctrine of monopsychism, and
concluded that for him an impersonal but human immortality
was attached to the separate intelligence of the species
man.

   The inference drawn by the Latin Averroists is understandable since they, like the orthodox theologians,
were Christians. Yet we have some reason for questioning
whether they too, though believing themselves to be followers of Averroes, did not misunderstand his doctrine of the
soul. For Averroes was a Muslim, and the anthropology of
the Qur'an does not assume that what is predicable of the
intellect is predicable of the soul. Can we be certain
that his doctrine of the soul was monopsychist simply because he taught that there is one agent intellect for all
men? The answer may well be no.

   Furthermore, the orthodox doctrine of the immortality of the soul widespread in Latin Christianity should not
be formally so called, since it is really a doctrine of the

immortality of the subject of consciousness, or at least, of the subject of intellectual operations. It would seem that such a concept of the immortality of the soul had its origin in Greek philosophy when Plato transformed the primitive view of the immortality of the soul, that alien ghost within man, into the doctrine of the mortality of an alien body connected to the self. The transformation was effected through the identification of the soul with the principle of selfhood and consciousness that was capable of existing apart from the body. One may question if this Greek doctrine of the soul is compatible with the Christian revelation.

This brings us to a third consideration. No one denies the very close relationship of philosophy to religion during the Middle Ages. But if the relation of religion to philosophy depends in part on the philosophy involved, it depends also on the religion. We know that "the characteristic feature of much of medieval thought is its architectonic quality and systematic interconnectedness, so that theological commitments had their impact on philosophical subjects."[24] We should note, however, that if this is true for Christianity, it is equally true for Islam. Both Christianity and Islam are religions that are vitally concerned with the goals of human life in this world and the next. But the medieval Christian view of man is different from the Qur'anic. Transferred, as Averroes was, from the Arabic world with its Islamic background to the Latin world of medieval Christianity, it is no wonder that he evoked in the minds of his readers associations and meanings foreign to his thought. In sum, all these complications -- the difference in the doctrines of the two religions, the spurious interpretation of Averroes by the so-called Averroists, and the fact that only the Hebrew literature had fallen heir to the complete translation of the Tahafut al-Tahafut -- tended to hinder the Christian scholastics from understanding how Averroes' theory of the intellect could allow a personal immortality for man. It is no surprise, therefore, that for the Latin world Averroes was a naturalistic Aristotelian.

Introduction

The Modern Reaction

We today are in a better position to appreciate Averroes' view of the soul. The availability of the complete text of the Tahafut al-Tahafut, the discovery of his other works on reason and revelation in Arabic -- Fasl al-maqal and Kashf al-manahidj -- by M.J. Muller in 1859, and so unknown even to Munk and Renan, and the editing of the Hebrew text of his commentary on Plato's Republic by E.I.J. Rosenthal in 1956, permit us to improve our understanding of his doctrine of immortality.

This point has been recognized by twentieth-century scholars. From a reading of one or more of his treatises on reason and revelation, they have affirmed that Averroes does admit to an individual immortality for man. However, their inability to reconcile this finding with his theory of the intellect found in his commentary on the De Anima has given birth to new controversies. One approach to the question has been to attempt to deduce Averroes' position on the personal immortality of the soul in the light of his doctrine on the relation between reason and revelation. Among the scholars who have taken this approach, some have argued that Averroes was a fideist,[25] and that he accepted individual immortality, though this was contrary to the teaching of Aristotle. In 1904, Asín y Palacios went as far as to argue that "Averroes, far from being the teacher and patron of Averroistic rationalism, was its most irreconcilable opponent," so much so, that Averroes and Aquinas were in complete agreement in their theological doctrine on the relation of faith to reason.[26]

To substantiate his claim, Asín had made use of the Arabic texts of the Tahafut al-Tahafut and the Fasl al-maqal. But Mandonnet objected to this method of argumentation on the ground that Averroes was known to the Latin West through his commentaries on Aristotle. He even supposed that there is a difference in the views expressed in these commentaries and the Arabic texts used by Asín and went on to challenge Asín "to elucidate the antinomy, and if he could not do so, to establish which ... was the real thought of Averroes." Since Asín did not do so, Mandonnet concluded that the thesis of Asín was "flimsy."[27] Moreover, Mandonnet's reliance solely on the Latin texts of Averroes would mean by implication that the thought of Averroes expressed in the Tahafut al-Tahafut is different from that found in the Destructio Destructionum Philosophiae Algazelis, available since 1527, and more particularly, that the doctrine of the soul found in Averroes' commentary on the De Anima is different from that found in the Destructio Destructionum, which presumably he had studied. But there is no such antinomy, as we shall see.

In the last decade, however, Hourani, in his study of the Fasl al-maqal, has pointed out that Averroes does not regard Aristotle as another scripture, for occasionally he goes beyond statements of Aristotle.[28] And Fakhry, in his examination of the Kashf al-manahidj, the Fasl al-maqal, and the Tahafut al-Tahafut, claims that Averroes' doctrine on reason and revelation is that the truth of revelation is "not different in substance from" the truth arrived at by rhetorical, dialectical, and demonstrative argumentation. "Only the form in which they are expressed is different." Fakhry further explains that two circumstances enabled Averroes, as a philosopher of Islam, to defend his thesis on the parity of reason and revelation: one, it is a position "which the Koran itself (Koran, 3, 5) makes and which the commentaries from al-Tabari (d. 923) down had recognized;" and, two, there is no "teaching authority in (Sunnite) Islam upon which devolved the right to define doctrine."[29]

However, some scholars have considered Averroes a rationalist and have suggested that he supported an impersonal immortality for the human species,[30] in which case he adhered to Aristotle's position that the soul is mortal,[31] but advocated a belief in personal immortality for the "vulgar" based on religion. In 1909, Gauthier, for example, after analyzing the Fasl al-maqal concluded that this treatise is a work of "unreserved rationalism." He claimed that this treatise "does not contain a single word which indicates ... any subordination of philosophy to religion." Nonetheless, Gauthier is aware that there are passages in

Introduction   17

the Kashf al-manahidj and the Tahafut al-Tahafut that contradict his portrayal of Averroes as an "unreserved rationalist." In fact, he confesses his "bewilderment" at reading numerous passages in these two works in which Averroes "professes to believe in mysteries and miracles, to subordinate philosophy to religion." In spite of this admission, Gauthier holds that he has the right to portray Averroes as an "unreserved rationalist," since "the doctrine of the Fasl al-maqal is an unreserved rationalism."

Gauthier, as opposed to Fakhry, goes as far as to suggest that Averroes invented the doctrine of the three types of arguments to enable philosophers to conceal the truths of religion from "the vulgar crowd" by presenting them as mysteries.[32] Mandonnet, before Gauthier, had made the same accusation against Averroes. He claimed that Averroes taught that in cases of conflict between reason and revelation philosophers "ought to give a metaphorical interpretation of the revealed text, which is equivalent to saying" that philosophers "must reject its value while appearing to preserve it." He added that Averroes is careful to point out that philosophers ought to withhold this interpretation "from the ignorant masses incapable of penetrating these hidden meanings."[33] De Wulf, after Gauthier, went a step further and claimed that "More than one doctrine of Averroes goes counter to the Musulman religion;" and, like Mandonnet and Gauthier, he too suggested that Averroes' distinction "between the literal interpretation of the Koran, good for the illiterate, and its allegorical interpretation, accessible to the philosophers" was his device to appear orthodox before his contemporaries, since for him reason "alone gives access to higher truth."[34]

Gilson's position in the controversy is not wholly unlike Gauthier's. From his reading of the Destructio Destructionum, he concluded that, for Averroes, "the absolute truth was not to be found in any sort of Revelation, but in the writings of Aristotle." In Gilson's interpretation, "The more convinced Averroes was of the absolute superiority of philosophical knowledge, the more baffling must have been the existence" of the Qur'an.[35] Yet Gilson

is aware that Averroes never attacked the religion of the
Qur'an as such. His final conclusion is his inability to
solve the question: "What did the Commentator himself
really think? The answer is hidden in his most secret
conscience."[36] Gilson's admission that the answer is not
obvious is perhaps more prudent than the conjecture of
those authors who have interpreted the apparently blatant
self-contradiction of Averroes as betraying hypocrisy. As
Arnaldez has pointed out, with specific reference to
Averroes, it is methodologically unsound to resort to an
analysis of motives to solve an apparent conflict of
ideas. For Arnaldez, the intimate thought of Averroes does
not concern us, since "The historian of philosophy needs
only to interest himself in thought expressed, and we have
found nothing in the writings of this philosopher which
constrains us to accuse him of dissimulation."[37]

On the other hand, the mystery may not be quite as
impenetrable as Gilson finds it. The answer may not be
hidden in Averroes' "most secret conscience," though it may
be obscured by the assumptions that a Christian is most
likely to make, even when he is dealing with a Muslim
thinker. Many interpreters of the thought of Averroes seem
to be unaware that the notion of revelation is differently
understood in Islam and in Christianity: in Christianity,
revelation is usually understood as the system of right
beliefs found in Scripture to which man responds in faith.
In Islam, the view is more comprehensive, in that though
revelation contains the obligation of belief it is the legal code through which God legislates over all human affairs. It has the force of law rather than of belief, as
is the case in Christianity.[38] Taking this approach to the
problem, Rosenthal, in a more recent study of Averroes'
commentary on Plato's <u>Republic</u>, the <u>Fasl al-maqal</u>, the
<u>Kashf al-manahidj</u>, and the <u>Tahafut al-Tahafut</u>, finds that
Averroes resolved "the apparent conflict between reason and
revelation by his definition of revelation as prophetic
revealed law."[39] However, Rosenthal's claim is based on
the political thought of Averroes. He does not demonstrate
how this applies to Averroes' doctrine of the soul.

Other scholars who have written during the last twenty-five years or so have tried to resolve the controversy on the personal immortality of the soul in the thought of Averroes by actually re-studying his doctrine of the soul rather than by deducing Averroes' position from his general statements on reason and revelation. But they too have arrived at diverse conclusions. Sweetman states from his scrutiny of the Kashf al-manahidj that for Averroes "souls are the inner motive power of bodies but are separable from the body." Consequently, "there is a prima facie possibility of their surviving after the decomposition of the body." But he adds that, from his study of the Tahafut al-Tahafut, Averroes "makes it plain that immortality or resurrection is known not by philosophical proof but by revelation."[40] Tallon's study of the Tahafut al-Tahafut concludes that it does not contain a theory of the natural immortality of the soul. He attributes this finding to Averroes' defective exegesis of matter and form and to his inadequate concept of man. But Tallon's discussion is distorted by faulty citations from the text.[41]

In his study of the Kashf al-manahidj, Alonso notes that Averroes acknowledges that "some souls are happy and others unhappy in the future life," and points out that Averroes does recognize the teaching of the Qur'an that "man's immortality is not generic, but individual." He also notes that after death "the souls remain with very distinct characters," since "the grades of the state of salvation as well as those of condemnation" are proportioned to their distinct merit obtained "during their union with the body." But having acknowledged the individual immortality of the soul in the Kashf al-manahidj, Alonso now interjects that Averroes' difficulty as a philosopher is to explain the mode of existence of the soul without the body. In other words, since Averroes recognizes "the principle of individuation is matter," he is unable to explain how the soul exercises its faculties without the body when a man dies.[42]

It may be helpful to know that the Kashf al-manahidj is a work in which Averroes defends the external aspects of the Islamic faith revealed by the Prophet Muhammad against the unwarranted spiritual interpretations of some theologians. It is not a strictly philosophical treatise in which Averroes discusses his faith in Aristotelian terms. Furthermore, Arnaldez, from his study of the Tahafut al-Tahafut, says that Averroes' concept of the soul is Islamic, in which "there is discontinuity between this world and the other,"[43] that is, between death and the resurrection.

Teske, in his study of Averroes' commentaries on Plato's Republic and Aristotle's De Anima, finds that Averroes' theory of the intellect does not permit a "personal survival after death for the individual."[44] Yet the study of Nogales affirms that Averroes held a doctrine of personal immortality and tries to interpret the theory philosophically from the commentary on the De Anima, the Fasl al-maqal, the Kashf al-manahidj and the Epitome of the Metaphysics. However, while admitting that there is a difficulty in the use of soul and intellect in the commentary on the De Anima, since there exist "two general parts of the soul," one "to know all that is individual," and the other to know "that which is universal and, for this reason, it also has to be universal," his interpretation, like that of Alonso and Teske, regards the intellect as part of the soul.[45]

These scholars have uniformly overlooked, however, the Qur'anic anthropology. In an earlier generation, de Vaux was one of the relatively few scholars writing on this subject who did not do so. In 1918, in his study of the Tahafut al-Tahafut, he took account of the fact that in Islamic philosophy "the intellect and the soul ... are distinct": "The intellect alone seems absolutely free from matter; ... The soul is the energy that animates matter," and so distinct from the intellect. Consequently, he concluded, Averroes' theory of the unicity of the intellect does not in itself mean that he denied the personal immortality of the soul. De Vaux further acknowledges that, according to this distinction, philosophically the soul may survive and "remain individualized after the death of the body." For him, this "seems to be Averroes' point of view.... In the end, he leaves it to revelation to settle the question."[46]

The more recent study of Pegis of the commentary on the De Anima takes a position that is partly like de Vaux's: for Averroes, the soul and intellect are distinct, in that for him "To say soul is to say ... something material; to say intellect is to say something immaterial, in other words, something that in its very reality is separate from matter." But, unlike de Vaux, Pegis concludes that for Averroes the soul, far from being likely to survive the death of the body, as a form of matter, is perishable.[47]

Riordan, in a study of Averroes' commentaries on the De Anima, Physics, Metaphysics, and of his Epitome of the Metaphysics, concurs with Pegis that Averroes made a distinction between soul and intellect, and that for Averroes the soul is perishable. Riordan also thinks that it is because of this distinction that Averroes finds it "difficult to ascribe intellectual activity ... to the form which makes a man."[48]

However, the conclusion was drawn by Zedler from a study of the commentary on the De Anima and the Tahafut al-Tahafut in Latin translation that Averroes, having recognized two distinct entities, soul and intellect, was unable to unite them. He "found himself trapped in his own dilemma. Should he save knowledge or should he save man?" The result is that Averroes sacrifices man to save knowledge, unlike Aquinas who was able to unite both notions.[49] Zedler further suggests that Averroes wanted to prove the natural immortality of the soul but could "give no good philosophical reason why the soul must exist after death, but only an indication that it may exist after death." He was able to "provide only a 'Persuasive proof' which suggests that the soul could be maintained in existence." But the lack of a proof did not prevent him from assenting to the doctrine.[50]

The Problem of the Immortality of the Soul in Averroes

From our review of the principal studies of the twentieth century related to the question of the personal immortality of the soul in Averroes, it seems clear that some understanding of Averroes' Muslim consciousness may be helpful in order to decipher his doctrine of immortality. It has been pointed out that the notions of soul and revelation are different in Christianity and in Islam. Yet even those who argue that Averroes was a believing Muslim seem to agree with those who consider him a rationalist that there is a problem of soul and intellect in his philosophy. The conflict between reason and revelation remains unresolved. If some scholars have emphasized his allegiance to Aristotle, others have emphasized his acceptance of the religion of the Qur'an. That is, those who consider Averroes a fideist seem to imply that he, faced with a conflict between reason and revelation, opted for revelation over and against the teachings of Aristotle. And those who consider Averroes a rationalist seem to imply that he accepted Aristotle in the final analysis. Yet if Christian scholars' unfamiliarity with the Qur'an is a problem in their study of Averroes, their interpretation of Aristotle may also be a problem, for Aristotle's own doctrine of the soul is far from clear. Moreover, if Averroes does in fact distinguish between soul and intellect, as some claim, does he still concur with Aristotle that the life of reason is man's highest activity, and explain how this is so? Perhaps there is a difficulty in understanding not only his doctrine of the soul, but also in understanding his theory of the intellect. It may be that Averroes' doctrines of soul and intellect, even if they are distinct, are in harmony. And perhaps a proper understanding of soul and intellect in the thought of Averroes may do away with the apparent inconsistencies found in his writings. After all, those who consider Averroes a rationalist are right in pointing out that it is not enough to claim that Averroes accepted the personal immortality promised in the Qur'an; it must also be shown how Averroes' acceptance of this belief is compatible with the philosophy of Aristotle on the soul; otherwise one must conclude that philosophic truth was different from the truth of revelation even in the context of Averroes' Muslim consciousness. To sum up: twentieth-century scholarship has contributed a number of novel considerations, each one of which is important toward a coherent interpretation of Averroes and of the medieval constructions put upon him. But the synthesis of these contributions into such an interpretation remains to be accomplished.

Yet the considerations adduced here so far suggest a hypothesis which, as a preliminary step toward achieving the foregoing coherent interpretation of Averroes and of his role in the history of Christian thought, the present study will seek to develop and substantiate. It may be that Averroes' treatment of the personal immortality of the soul exemplifies the ideal of the harmony of faith and reason so stoutly defended by Aquinas. But Averroes' treatment of the soul, including the doctrine of its immortality, harmonizes philosophical reason with the Islamic faith and the doctrine of the Qur'an. Aquinas' emphasis on the importance of reason in understanding divine revelation has its counterpart in Averroes. And, like Aquinas,[51] Averroes admits that the truth arrived at by reason cannot be opposed to the truth of revelation. But Averroes' beliefs concerning the nature of divine revelation and its teaching about the nature of man are not the same as Aquinas'. Thus, it may be that Averroes was not a proponent of that kind of rationalism known as Averroism, even in what pertains to the question of the personal immortality of the soul. Even in this respect, it may be that what is true of Aquinas is equally true of Averroes: the doctrine of the personal immortality of the soul is what "faith proposes and reason investigates."[52] If this hypothesis is correct, the challenge that faces Averroes is to account for the personal immortality of the soul in such a way as to remain faithful to Aristotle's doctrines of soul and intellect and, at the same time, to the Qur'anic -- rather than to the Christian -- doctrine of human destiny.

Moreover, if Averroes is to be completely successful, he must meet the further challenge of conceiving a system of reward and punishment in the afterlife in a manner compatible with Aristotle and the Qur'an.

This study will attempt to establish that Averroes was successful to that very end, and, thus, that even when read in Latin translation Averroes can be more coherently and adequately interpreted than he has traditionally been. But what of the claim of such scholars as Mandonnet[53] that Averroes' views known to the West through his commentaries on Aristotle are different from his views expressed in his other works? The study hopes to show that there is no such contradiction. More particularly, the study will try to show that the doctrine of the soul found in Averroes' commentary on the De Anima is the same as that found in the Tahafut al-Tahafut, available in Latin translation as the Destructio Destructionum since 1527. As for the objection that the Latin translation was made from a Hebrew version of the original Arabic, and so can give no true representation of the mind of Averroes, Steinschneider has shown that it "rests faithfully on the Hebrew and the Hebrew rests faithfully on the Arabic except for minor deviations ... especially with proper names."[54] Rahilly also found the three texts to be in "perfect agreement," even though the Latin text sometimes "misses a word (especially a proper name)."[55] Consequently, the problem of understanding Averroes' doctrine of the immortality of the soul does not arise from a difference between the Latin and Arabic texts. This study will use the Latin text in an attempt to clear up the source of the misunderstanding from which the Western interpretation of Averroes has traditionally suffered, because it is the text known to the West; and it hopes to show the reorientation that should be given to the historical interpretation of Averroes before modern Western scholarship can proceed to understand definitively his role in the history of Christian thought.

Given its specific and limited purpose, this study shall not be concerned with establishing a coherent and adequate interpretation of the thought of Averroes as expounded in the full range of his works and in their original linguistic and cultural context. To do so would be, of course, a legitimate and most important task. But it would, of itself, explain little about the history of the interpretations of Averroes' doctrine in the West. The concern of this study is rather to establish the validity of the hypothesis under the stipulated conditions: the problems encountered by Christian interpreters of Averroes since the Middle Ages can be avoided, even when he is read in translation, if he is not ascribed purposes that he did not pursue, or premises that he did not assume.

This study shall, therefore, be centred upon a re-examination of Averroes' commentary on the De Anima, though in the light of his treatises on reason and revelation, which are now readily available. As the work that sparked the controversy on reason and revelation in the Latin West, Averroes' commentary on the De Anima is, of course, the key text for consideration. Indeed, Western scholars concede that the controversy on the immortality of the soul in the Middle Ages had its origin in, and was focussed on, Averroes' interpretation of Aristotle's De Anima, notably book III, chapter 5, where the Philosopher makes a distinction between an active and passive power of intellect, but leaves it unclear how either power is related to the human soul.[56] In his great commentary on the De Anima, Averroes interprets Aristotle to mean that both the active and passive powers of intellect are not powers of the soul. For Aquinas and the orthodox theologians, the total separation of the intellect from the soul meant, among other things, that death is total.

They considered this view irreconcilable with the Christian Faith. In an effort to harmonize the ambiguity of Aristotle with their own understanding of life after death, they therefore tried to show that Averroes' exposition of the soul is at variance with the thought of Aristotle. Aquinas, for example, states his reason and method for refuting Averroes as follows: "We intend to show that the aforesaid position is no less contrary to the principles of philosophy than against the teachings of the

Faith."[57] That is, "we shall show that the above-mentioned position is entirely opposed to his [Aristotle's] words and meaning."[58] Moreover, he candidly admits that the great commentary on the De Anima is the source of his knowledge of Averroes' theory.[59]

In short, it is because the great commentary on the De Anima has been at the centre of the controversy of the Commentator's view of man and his destiny since its entry into the Latin West that its reinterpretation in the light of his treatises on reason and revelation is in order. For the same reasons, evidently, the studies of Zedler and Nogales have been predicated on the same method.

More particularly: Averroes' works on reason and revelation are of special interest to us because they are brilliant discourses on the legitimacy of philosophic thought in Islam and anticipate the battle that Aquinas was to fight in the same cause in medieval Christianity. The Fasl al-maqal is a legal defense of the study of philosophy. In it Averroes not only accepts but also defends a unitary view of truth, and he explains how his doctrines of the three classes of men and the allegorical interpretation of Scripture permit him to effect a harmony between the Qur'anic doctrine of the soul and that of Aristotle within the juridical context of Islam. In the Kashf al-manahidj, a theological work, he discusses how the Qur'anic anthropology and eschatology are related to the Aristotelian notion of the soul as the form of the body, and in his commentary on Plato's Republic he makes clear the function of the philosopher in the Islamic state in securing the happiness of all men in this life and the next. In the Tahafut al-Tahafut, Averroes speaks not as the Commentator of Aristotle, but as a philosopher of Islam in his own name. He defends the study of philosophy against the theologian Algazali who wished to preserve the integrity of the Qur'anic doctrine of the resurrection against the philosophers of the Islamic East, who had taught a doctrine of the immortality of the soul. In order to show that the truth of his philosophy is in harmony with that of revelation, Averroes explains how his theories of soul and intellect are related and compatible with the Qur'anic doctrine of man and his destiny. This explanation is central to a coherent understanding of the commentary on the De Anima.

In accordance with the foregoing considerations, perhaps this investigation should most adequately begin with a brief outline of the Qur'anic anthropology, to be followed by a comparison of this anthropology with that of the Christian tradition as well as with that of Aristotle. Aristotle's De Anima will receive special attention because it contains the texts on soul and intellect which have given rise to the sharpest disagreements among scholars. Nevertheless, pertinent texts from the Ethica Nichomachea, Metaphysica, De Generatione Animalium will be consulted to help clarify his position on soul and intellect. Chapter one will be devoted to this task. Chapter two will discuss Averroes' views on reason and revelation, since these views are clearly part of the context in which the present work can attempt to suggest a reinterpretation of Averroes' doctrine of personal immortality. Against this background, chapter three will analyze Averroes' commentary on Aristotle's De Anima to determine how Averroes interpreted Aristotle's doctrine of the soul in relation to the intellect, and whether this interpretation is consistent with that offered in the Tahafut al-Tahafut, where he attempts to connect it with the revelation of the Qur'an, while still maintaining that the intellect is one for all men. Once this task is accomplished, chapter four will study Averroes' commentary on the De Anima to ascertain how he interpreted Aristotle's doctrine of man's beatitude in this life, in an effort to determine how it is related to the Qur'anic belief in reward and punishment in the next life.

At this point in the development of the study which occupies our attention, we should be in a position to reach a conclusion. Chapter five will sum up the discussion to that point and offer an interpretation of Averroes' understanding of personal immortality. If the hypothesis advanced here is borne out, the conclusion will be that the doctrine of the greatest Aristotelian of Islam concerning personal immortality can be most adequately understood when it is envisaged as a reasonable, and indeed viable, attempt to reconcile Aristotle and the Qur'an.

CHAPTER I

THE ANTHROPOLOGICAL BACKGROUND
OF THE AVERROISTIC CONTROVERSIES

The Qur'anic Anthropology

According to the Qur'an, death is the inescapable end of all men (S. 4:78),[1] for God has decreed that all men must die (S. 56:60). Life on earth is for "an appointed term" and conformable to God's will (S. 3:145). During his brief life span, man is tested "with evil and with good," and at death his soul is returned to God, the giver of all life (S. 21:35). However, though death is certain, life after death is equally certain, and there is a connection between this life and life after death. For all men are accountable to God "on the day of resurrection" (S. 19:95), after which they shall live forever in states of happiness or unhappiness depending on their submission to God's will in this life. The good will receive the gift of immortality in peace (S. 50:34), and their supreme reward will be to live in God's favour for all eternity (S. 54:54-55). In sum, if a subtle distinction between fate and destiny may be permitted, though death is man's fate, it is not his destiny.

There is, therefore, a world-to-come, both for the blessed (S. 76:11-22) and for the damned (S. 22:19-22). Yet, though immortality will come to all men on the day of resurrection, and happiness is offered to all, all men will not be equally happy in the world-to-come. This is so because the degree of man's happiness is contingent upon the degree to which he develops his soul in this life (S. 91:9), and it is for the progress of the soul toward God that he will be rewarded on the day of resurrection: He who does right in this life "does so only for the good of his own soul, and he who errs, errs only against it" (S. 17:13-15).

When the Prophet Muhammad taught the foregoing doctrine of the resurrection of the dead, it was the common belief of his countrymen that there was no afterlife. The Qur'an represents them as having scornfully said that there is only the present life: "we die and we live, and we shall not be raised. He is only a man who has invented a lie about Allah. We are not going to put our faith in him" (S. 23:37-38). The resurrection of the dead through a new creation was incomprehensible to reason, and the possibility seemed to be farfetched; for example, many asked: "When we are dead and have become dust, shall we be brought back again? That would be a far return!" (S. 50:3).

With reference to this sort of objection, the Qur'an teaches that life after death is a second creation. Birth and rebirth are gifts from God: From the earth "We have created you and into it We send you back, and from it We bring you back a second time" (S. 20:55). Man's hope to transcend death is not the hope to escape death, but the hope of the resurrection. At the resurrection man will not have the same body, for the present body is corruptible. Consequently, man will be given a new body to participate in the new creation. This is possible since God knows every type of creation. He has only to say: "'Be!' and it is so" (S. 36:76-81).

This overview of the Qur'anic picture of man and his destiny illustrates the structure of God's plan for man in which salvation is centred on the soul (nafs). However, the Qur'an also tells us that man is not only a unity of body and soul, but also that there is another element in man other than the soul which is different from the body. For example, S. 32:7-9 tell us that at the creation of man God breathed into him the divine spirit (rūh): "He began the creation of man from clay; Then He made his seed from a draught of despised fluid; Then He fashioned him and breathed into him of His spirit." The Qur'an, however, does not explain here, or elsewhere, what is the relationship between body, soul (nafs), and spirit (rūh). This fact has rendered its anthropology rather complex, and we must now examine how scholars have explained this relationship to try to ascertain what survives the corruption of the body and awaits the day of resurrection.

The Anthropological Background

By way of background, we note that, in the Qur'an, nafs (soul), and its plural anfus and nufūs, refers both to the individual self in a reflexive sense and to the human soul. Rūh, originally used for breath, with its plural arwāh used for winds, is used in the Qur'an, for the first time in Arabic, in the theological sense of spirit. Moreover, "no plural of ruh occurs in the Kur'an," and it never occurs with the meaning of soul.[2]

Despite the distinct usages of nafs and rūh in the Qur'an, however, the terms have been used interchangeably since early Islam. In fact rūh, first used for the human soul in the Umayyad period,[3] came to mean soul as opposed to body, and relatively little distinction was made between soul and spirit. This was the common practice of the Mutakallims or doctors of theology. Even today some contemporary writers distinguish only between the material and non- (or less-) material aspects of man. Characteristic of this practice are those influenced by modern spiritualism, among whom Tantawi Jawhari is most prominent. These spiritualists, like the Mutakallims, tend to use rūh rather than nafs in making the distinction between body and soul/spirit. However, many modern non-spiritualist writers in exegeting anfus (souls) use anfus and arwāh (spirits) interchangeably, with no effort to clarify their terminology. Thus M. Mahmud Hijazi writes:

> God it is who takes unto Himself the anfus and seizes them from their bodies at death ... and He takes the anfus that do not die in their sleep. And the meaning is that He takes these anfus during their sleep for God cuts off the connection of the arwāh with the bodies ... then after sleep the rūh returns to the body as it was.[4]

Other modern writers maintain that there is no difference between nafs and rūh. They are to be seen as two different terms for one element. Mahmud Ibrahim says, for example, that "The rūh is the name of the human essence ... before its connection with the body and after its separation from it ... and when it is connected to the body ... it is called nafs."[5]

But is the soul/spirit material? In the history of Islam there are those who have considered both the body and

the soul/spirit to be of a material nature, the difference
between them being more quantitative than qualitative. The
soul/spirit was thought to be diffused in the material body
as its animating or controlling principle. Thus, in the
fourteenth century, Ibn Qayyim al-Jawziya identified rūh
with nafs and said that it "is itself a body, different in
quiddity (al-māhīya) from the sensible body, of the nature
of light ... interpenetrating the bodily members as water
in a rose."[6] Moreover, the understanding of the soul/spirit as of a material nature influenced many to claim that at
the resurrection the soul will be part of the revivified
body, and not a separate spiritual substance joined to it.
The emphasis on the material nature of the soul/spirit was
also related to efforts of Muslim thinkers to avoid the
association of any other thing with God by affirming that
only God was non-material.

    Others, such as those influenced by Greek philosophy, denied that the spirit (or soul) was in any way material. They held that it was a purely spiritual substance
and so immortal by nature. For example, in the ninth century Al-Kindi, influenced by Neoplatonic philosophy, held
that man is essentially a spirit associated with a body,
and "salvation consists in the soul freeing itself from the
corporeal stains of the sensible world and returning to the
world of spiritual substances" from which it came.[7] This
view underlies much of later Muslim mysticism. Nor must we
forget that Aristotle's principle of the non-material character of spirit found a permanent place in Islam through
the influence of Algazali (1058-1111), whose interpretation
of man was held by the theistic philosophers in general and
by some of the Mu'tazilites and Shi'ites. In any event,
the notion of the soul/spirit as a spiritual substance had
some influence on classical Islamic theology, for while the
understanding of body, soul, and spirit as being of a material nature was never fully abandoned, it came to accept
the idea that some aspect of the human person will survive
man in death, and will be reunited with the body on the day
of resurrection.

    The challenge of how to distinguish between nafs

The Anthropological Background 33

and rūh is so great that even today many thinkers are hesitant to do so. Thus 'Abd al-Wadud Shalabi thinks that "it is among the affairs ... which God alone knows."[8] Others show their reluctance to deal with the issue by citing S. 17:85: "They will ask thee of the spirit. Say, 'The spirit comes at the bidding of my Lord, and ye are given a little knowledge thereof.'"

In the history of Islam, however, many scholars have recognized a distinction between nafs and rūh in their discussion of sleep and death. We shall now examine this distinction as it applies to that aspect of the human person which survives death with specific reference to S. 39: 42:

> God takes to Himself souls [al-anfus] at the time of their death; and those who do not die (He takes) in their sleep; and He holds back those on whom He has decreed death, and sends others back till their appointed time; -- verily, in that are signs unto a people who reflect.

In exegeting this verse, al-Zamakhshari (1075-1144) discusses the prevalent opinions on the state of the soul during sleep and in death and clarifies a distinction that has been accepted by many later commentators: "the soul taken at death is that which has life [al-hayāt] and the soul taken during sleep is that which has the power of distinguishing [al-tamyīz]." He goes on to say that the "difference between them is breathing [nafas], which continues with the sleeper and departs at death." While citing these views in terms of nafs alone, he quotes Ibn 'Abbas who made the same distinction, but who designated that which has breath and movement as the rūh:

> Between nafs and rūh is [that which is] like the rays of the sun, for the nafs is that which has intelligence ['aql] and the ability to distinguish [tamyīz] and the rūh is that which has breath and movement. And when the servant sleeps God seizes his nafs and does not seize his rūh.

In spite of these distinctions, al-Zamakhshari equates sleep with death and maintains that on both occasions man is deprived of his soul "which has life" (nafs al-hayāt wa'l-haraka) and of his soul "which has the power of distinguishing" (nafs al-'aql-tamyīz).[9] Few of his successors

have shared this belief, but the terminology he employs in
distinguishing between the soul of the sleeper and the soul
of the deceased can be found in their work. For example,
al-Tabarsi consistently uses nafs in explaining this verse,
"categorizing the soul of the sleeper as nafs al-'aql wa'l-
tamyīz and the soul of the deceased as nafs al-hayāt." And
though he does not specify the relation between nafs and
rūh, "he does indicate that during sleep the rūh stays with
the body and at death it departs."[10]

Al-Razi (1149-1209) offers another perspective on
the analogy of sleep and death. He uses nafs when exegeting this verse, "but describes the nafs as a shining
spiritual substance ... infusing all the members of the body and giving them life." According to him, the nature of
sleep and death is determined "by the degree to which this
light of the soul ... is connected to the body": at death
"the connection is severed both internally and externally;"
during sleep "it is severed externally only;" and in the
waking state "the light of the nafs occurs in all parts of
the body externally and internally." For him, then, though
sleep and death are alike, there is some distinction between them, since "death is a complete and absolute severing and sleep is an incomplete severing" of the light of
the soul.[11]

Contemporary commentators on this verse maintain
this distinction between nafs and rūh in their discussion
of sleep and death. For example, al-Maraghi says that God
takes the souls both at death and in sleep, "while in the
sleep state the spirits remain connected to the bodies,"[12]
and in saying so, he implies without specifying that the
spirits are cut off at death. Al-Jammal claims that "God
completely severs the connection of the arwāh with their
bodies at death," but "during sleep the rūh remains connected to the body and the souls are taken only partially
or externally."[13] Al-Tabataba'i states the distinction
clearly when he says:

> ... the intention of the souls [in the first part
> of the āya] is spirits connected to the bodies, not
> the totality of the spirits and bodies, for the to-
> tality is not seized at death. That which is

> seized [at death] is the spirit from the body ....
> And His saying (those who do not die, in sleep)
> refers to the <u>anfus</u> .... He takes unto Himself the
> <u>anfus</u> who do not die, at the time of their sleep.[14]

From our examination of the relationship of body, soul, and spirit, it is evident that, despite the common tendency to interchange the terms <u>nafs</u> and <u>rūh</u>, and to make a distinction only between the corporeal and non-corporeal aspects of the human person, many exegetes, both classical and modern, when pressed to define the nature of sleep and death, do make a distinction between them. And from the conflation of the views of al-Zamakhshari, Ibn 'Abbas, and al-Razi, a clarification of the two terms does emerge: The <u>rūh</u>, that by which life is bestowed on the individual and which remains attached to the body during sleep, is that which is taken by God at death; and the <u>nafs</u>, that by which the individual has the rational faculties of intelligence and discrimination, is that which is taken temporarily or partially in sleep, and completely in death.

Death in the Qur'an, therefore, does not consist in the separation of the soul from the body after which the soul continues to live a natural existence apart from it. This statement is reduplicative: it means the same as the statement, "At death man is shattered," because man is essentially an integral whole. The totality of death means therefore that the soul does not experience a disembodied state of happiness or unhappiness apart from the body between death and the resurrection. Between death and the raising of the dead there is an interval or "a barrier until the day when they are raised" (S. 23:100; also 18: 20).[15] That is to say, in the Qur'an the interval between death and the resurrection is a "sleep of souls."[16] There is no particular judgment before the resurrection. At the resurrection "the dead will have no knowledge of the time which has elapsed since dying; in fact, they will think that they have just awakened from a deep sleep."[17] And since the interim state of the dead "is a dreamless sleep without consciousness, it will seem to man that the judgment follows immediately upon death."[18]

We may conclude, thus, that the Qur'an has a conception of man which might reasonably be called unitary or monistic: although the Qur'an acknowledges that man has a soul for the moral status or quality of which he is required to account at death, this soul is not only neither an existent nor a substance, but it is not even a principle of subsistence which is able to think, will, or act without a body. That is why when God "takes" the soul at death man enters into a state of complete unconsciousness. But the Qur'an does not suggest where the soul may be once God has "taken" it, nor whether it perishes with the body or whether it is kept in a dormant condition of God's supernatural power. The Qur'an does not teach the natural immortality of the soul -- though, on the other hand, it does not explicitly deny it either. The important point, so far as the Qur'an is concerned, is that each man's existence is dependent on the will of God. Birth and rebirth are two distinct graces of a first and second creation. And it is clear that the resurrection of the body is not in any way conditioned upon the immortality of the soul. Both body and soul are dependent on the creative will of God.

In its early years Islam accepted this view. However, in its later manuals on eschatology we do find an elaborate mythology describing an interim state for the dead. There we can read, for example, that after death God resuscitates the body of the deceased to allow two angels to interrogate him about the faith, and after the questioning, to subject him to torments. The angels are identified as Munkar and Nakir, names which are non-Qur'anic. Scholars explain the mythology as the survival of conceptions of death from pre-Islamic Arabia. Others say that such notions also came into Islam as it expanded through the centuries. At any rate, there was a reaction to these ideas.

The Mu'tazilites generally refuted the idea of punishment in the grave on empirical grounds. For them any one could see from looking at a corpse that it neither revives nor survives. For the majority of philosophers, many Shi'ites, and others, the idea of punishment in the tomb was unthinkable, for it is predicated on the notion that the soul/spirit can be reunited to the body and the total individual suffer or be rewarded before the resurrection. In arguing their case, they maintained, as contemporary scholars do, that the passages in the Qur'an which seem to suggest a preparatory punishment for the dead before the resurrection (S. 75:26 ff.; 56:82 ff.; 6:93 ff.) do not mean that there is an intermediate state for the dead, for in the Qur'an death and judgment are "fused into a single event."[19]

The totality of death in the Qur'an is well established by Western scholars. Thus, Watt writes: "The Qur'an ... does not assert a natural immortality of the human soul, since man's existence is dependent on the will of God." When God wills, "he causes man to die, and when he wills he raises him to life again."[20] Sweetman finds that this "parallel between the first creation into the world and the second creation after death is well sustained throughout the Qur'an," and concludes that "the orthodox doctrine is most clearly a doctrine of the resurrection of the body and not a theory of the survival of the soul."[21] Sourdel judges that the Qur'anic eschatology is different from the Christian, since Muhammad has no "notion of the immortality of the soul."[22] If by Christian eschatology Sourdel means the eschatology of the New Testament, his judgment is, for reasons that will appear below, controvertible. On the other hand, if he means the eschatology ultimately developed by medieval Christian theology, possibly under the impression at times that this coincided at all points with the eschatology of the New Testament, then Sourdel's opinion would be more in keeping with modern Christian Scriptural scholarship. However, it is clear that Sourdel's comparison is intended to highlight the doctrine of the Qur'an. In this respect, Sourdel's interpretation is beyond dispute.

Finally, the Qur'an has no doctrine of the immortality of the soul because it upholds the conception of man common among Semitic peoples, a conception which we have, for reasons explained above, agreed to characterize as unitary or monistic. This is why "eternal life," the mode of existence after death, does not proceed from the indestructibility of the soul, but is given by God. And because God does not simply have the soul in mind, but man himself in his reality, man's hope to triumph over death is not the raising of the body, but the second creation of man. Resurrection is man's total hope. The raising of bodies from the dead is at best a partial fulfilment of that hope. The conquest of death offered by the Qur'an is, therefore, essentially a hope in God, Who at some future date will bring about the second creation in which all men are invited to participate. Despite the prospect of death, somehow man's life is meaningful and worthwhile, for God's love will prevail over death. The Muslim is certain that death will be undone. Death may take away life, but God will give back to man what death has taken away. Though a man dies, he shall rise again and live once more.

Moreover, some scholars claim that the difference between the Qur'an's monistic conception of man and the dualistic conception commonly found in Christian theology is not due to a difference in the revelation of the two religions, but "partly as a result of Greek influence." Elaborating on this point, Watt observes that while the monistic view "may recognize some distinction between body and soul or body and spirit, the body is an essential part of the man." On the other hand, according to the dualistic conception "man consists of two things, soul and body, of which the former is more important," and "in extreme forms of the view the soul is the true man and the body an unfortunate temporary addition."[23]

Possibly this statement by Watt should be qualified. For the dualism that he opposes to monism is only one possible form of dualism, and, indeed, one of the most extreme and least sophisticated forms of it. The duality of body and soul which defines a dualistic conception of man need not mean that body and soul are themselves substances. This would be true of the dualism found, for instance, in Plato when he speaks of the body as the tomb of the soul. For Watt's purposes the distinction between dualisms may not be relevant, but for present purposes it is very important: for even if body and soul are defined only as substantial principles, and even if the body is deemed to be necessary for the complete perfection of the soul, nevertheless such a conception of body and soul would have in some way to be considered dualistic. For in this view the soul would be recognized as a reality distinct from the body, and indeed be able to subsist and be saved by itself, even though the body may be united to it before death, and even though it may eventually participate in the salvation of the soul. Be it noted that the point at stake here is not whether such a dualistic account of man is correct or not: it may well be that the only true anthropology is that which describes man as composed of a body and a soul which is the form of the body, but which is subsistent in itself and which, when informing the body, communicates its subsistence to the whole. The point is rather that such an anthropology could not be said to be monistic or unitary in the same sense or with the full justification in which the term can be applied to the anthropology of the Qur'an. In relation to the latter's monism, such a doctrine would constitute some sort, however mitigated, of dualism.

On the other hand, we must also note that, for all its unmitigated monism, the anthropology of the Qur'an appears to imply a distinction between the essential requirement of human nature for a body and the contingency of the particular body which the soul animates. After death, man has, if not a new, at least a different, body, that is -- echoing the doctrine of St. Paul -- God gives him "a body as he has chosen" (1 Cor. 15:38),[24] suitable to the new creation. Thus the monism of the Qur'an does not imply materialism. What it seems to imply above all is that body and soul are inseparable. Like Sourdel, however, Watt may be correct when he states that the monistic conception of man found in the Qur'an is in harmony with the view of man found both in the Old and New Testaments. This is an important question that will be further explored below. For if the Christian belief in the immortality of the soul common in the Middle Ages is not aboriginal to Christianity, but is the result of the influence of Greek philosophy, and if it is the Qur'an rather than medieval Christianity whose anthropology remained closely bound with the Scriptural tradition, we may have found one of the fundamental reasons for the failure of Western scholars to appreciate what Averroes was trying to achieve in his attempt to reconcile revelation with philosophy with respect to the soul.

The Christian Anthropologies

Since Plato was the dominant Greek philosopher in Christian thought prior to the entrance of Aristotle in the thirteenth century, it may be helpful to recall briefly how Plato regarded the soul before we compare the Christian and the Qur'anic conception of man and his destiny. In the <u>Phaedo</u> Plato records Socrates' discourse on death as he lived the last day of his life. When a person dies, Socrates remarks, it is natural for his corpse, the visible part of him, to decay. But his soul, "the invisible part ... goes away to a place that is, like itself, glorious, pure, and invisible ... into the presence of the good and wise God." In this remark Socrates assumes that the soul is an entity separate from the body and can exist independently of it. Elsewhere he states specifically that death "is simply the release of the soul from the body." This dualism of body and soul is vital to Socrates' conception that the body is a hindrance to the soul in its pursuit of knowledge. Consequently, "if we are to have pure knowledge of anything, we must get rid of the body and contemplate things by themselves with the soul itself." Socrates denied the suggestion of some philosophers that the soul may "be dissipated like breath or smoke, and vanish away" at death by arguing, on epistemological grounds, "that what we call learning is really recollection."[25] His answer implies that the soul is an intelligence encaged in the body which recalls truths from a previous existence, and whose quality of existence after death depends on the acquisition of knowledge attained in the present life. The important point is that Socrates attributes intelligence to the soul to prove that it is imperishable and immortal.[26]

When we turn to the Biblical tradition, it is gene-

The Anthropological Background

rally held by scholars that "no hope of individual survival is expressed in the OT before some of its latest passages,"[27] probably written in the second century before Christ. For the most part, the people of the Old Testament had no hope of a future life for themselves, except through a continuation in their descendents. Their religion was thus "marked by an urgent seriousness about life on this earth."[28] That is, concerned with the destiny of a People, they were almost silent about man's personal destiny after death. In fact, the Hebrew mind never developed the notion of a soul which is separable from historical man.[29]

In the Old Testament, man is "a unity of flesh, soul, and spirit, not a trichotomy, nor a dichotomy of body and soul,"[30] for flesh (bashar), soul (nephesh), and spirit (ruach) are not three substances, but three images under which the Hebrews viewed man in his relationship to the world, to mankind, and to God: The image of man as body tells us that man is radically bound up with this earth. The image of man as soul tells us that man is bound up with his fellow humans. And the image of man as spirit tells us that man is just as radically bound up with and oriented toward God. The spirit in man is simply the spirit of God in man. It is not an anthropological reality.

The second account of creation found in Genesis tells us not only how God formed man, but also is a classic statement of the Hebrew view of man: "then the Lord God formed man of the dust of the ground, and breathed into his nostrils the breath of life; and man became a living being" (Gen. 2:7). We are not to conclude from the vitalizing breath given to man by God that man is a compound of body and soul, as in Plato, for "the Hebrew conceived of man as an animated body, not as an incarnated soul."[31] That is to say, the Old Testament knows "of no philosophical definition of the essence of man and of his constituent elements."[32] Consequently, the question as to whether man is made up of body and soul is irrelevant. Here man is seen as "a psychophysical organism made up of many parts forming a unity."[33] Indeed, it is not Biblical "to speak of a purely disembodied soul of man."[34]

Man's natural condition in the Old Testament is basically one of mortality: "In the sweat of your face you shall eat bread till you return to the ground, for out of it you were taken; you are dust and unto dust you shall return" (Gen. 3:19). Man shall go to his grave "as a shock of grain comes up to the threshing floor in its season" (Job 5:26). Reaching the end of his life, man is gathered to his people: "you shall go to your fathers in peace; you shall be buried in a good old age" (Gen. 15:15). Moreover, death was not regarded as a blessing. General opinion held that "a living dog is better than a dead lion." (Eccl. 9:4).

In a general way, throughout the Old Testament the People remained both the locus of continuity and of the ultimate meaning of life. Only in its later writings, after the fall of the Israelite kingdoms and the period of the exiles, is any mention made of the possibility of personal survival or of resurrection after death. With the oppression of the Hebrews, the individual ceased to regard himself as merely a constituent member of a chosen People. Finding himself adrift in the cosmos, he "became conscious of his personal value."[35] New forms of writing emerged to meet his sense of isolation. Wisdom literature counseled resignation in the face of death, as in Job. Apocalyptic literature considered the possibility of the restoration of the nation, as in Ezekiel 37, and Daniel foresaw this resurrection in conjunction with reward and punishment for the dead, when "many of those who sleep in the dust of the earth shall awake, some to everlasting life, and some to shame and everlasting contempt" (Dan. 12:2). The apocalyptic hope, however, was not based on the nature of man, but on the power of goodness of God. For man's hope was expressed, "not in terms of individual destiny, but rather in terms of God's dealing with the nation." It was not concerned with personal immortality, "but with the establishment on earth of an everlasting kingdom in whose untold blessings righteous Israel would share."[36]

The Anthropological Background 43

In the New Testament, likewise, death was accepted as the natural destiny of man. God alone is immortal. Everything else is subject to mortality (1 Tim. 6:16). Indeed, Jesus' eschatological teaching, as that of the Old Testament, is infused with an Israelite sense of history. And since man's existence is historical, it has a beginning and an end. Man's only hope of victory over death is the proclamation of the Kingdom of God, based on a faith that "he who will bring in the Kingdom of God in the future has appeared"[37] in the person of Jesus himself. Human life is again regarded as a unitary phenomenon. The conception of death as the liberation of the soul from the body in the Greek sense of immortality seems to have been as alien and incomprehensible to the writers of the New Testament as to those of the Old.

Because man does not live on as an immortal soul but dies in body and soul, he lives in the fear of death, an inevitability that is never glorified, not even by Christ and his apostles. Moreover, Jesus acknowledged the mortality of man not only in his teaching but also in his dying. In fact, he died in the totality of his manhood without possessing in his soul a guarantee of immortality. As Cullman has observed, it is for this reason that "the evangelists, who nonetheless intended to present Jesus as the Son of God, have not tried to soften the terribleness of his thoroughly human death."[38] Hence, in the New Testament, man's hope is not that from his mortal nature something immortal will survive, but that through the resurrection of the dead "the mortal puts on immortality" (1 Cor. 15:42-57) and robs death of its sting. In the words of González-Ruiz, in the Old and New Testament "there is no such thing as the 'soul' in the sense in which it is found in Greek thought. The biblical man is one unit." But it is even more important to emphasize that in the Bible, "there is no divine element in man which guarantees the survival of human personality after death."[39] Thus the Bible teaches not only that Christ was "the first born to rise from the dead" (Acts 26:23), "the beginning, the first-born from the dead" (Col. 1:18), but also that man "shall certainly be united in a resurrection like his" (Rom. 6:5) that "might walk in newness of life" (Rom. 6:4). Paul puts it aptly when he says, "God raised the Lord and will also raise us up by his power" (1 Cor. 6:14).

In the Biblical view, "the resurrection of the body is necessary for sharing in the eschatological salvation"[40] since there is no true life without the body. This in part explains why man's hope in the resurrection is a hope in a new creation, not only for himself, but also for the entire creation. According to Paul, "the whole creation has been groaning in travail until now; and not only the creation, but we ourselves" (Rom. 8:23-24). Deliverance will come not when God destroys matter, but when he sets it free from corruptibility. "Not eternal ideas, but concrete objects will then rise anew."[41] The incompatibility of the Christian belief in the resurrection with the Greek idea of the immortality of the soul is even apparent in Paul's own missionary activity: when he preached for the first time in Athens, laughter erupted when he spoke of the resurrection (Heb. 17:32).

In the Biblical view, we repeat, salvation is not only for the soul, but also for the body. Nothing is exempt from fundamental change. Paul labours to emphasize this point in 1 Corinthians 15:42-44 when he elaborates the contrast between the present and the resurrection body. "What is sown is perishable, what is raised is imperishable." "It is sown in dishonour, it is raised in glory." "It is sown a physical body, it is raised a spiritual body." "This mortal nature must put on immortality" (1 Cor. 15:53). In other words, Paul's use of antithesis -- perishable-imperishable, dishonour-glory, physical-spiritual, mortal-immortal -- is a conception of the afterlife that involves the whole man, not only his soul. It is an affirmation of the totality of human existence. The body is not the prison of the soul. It "is a temple of the holy spirit" (1 Cor. 6:19), in this life and the next.[42]

Significantly, Paul did not conjecture about the condition of the dead after death and before the resurrection since Jesus was not specific about it. When asked

about those who had already died, he did not comfort his
questioners with the idea of a disembodied existence for
the soul -- and the Greek doctrine of the immortality of
the soul was surely known to Paul -- rather, he insisted
that both the living and the dead are in the same position:
"We shall not all sleep, but we shall all be changed" (1
Cor. 15:51). That is to say, man's destiny lies not in the
nature of his soul, but with the returning Lord, since
"those who are alive, who are left until the coming of the
Lord, shall not precede those who have fallen asleep" (1
Thes. 4:15).[43] For Paul the dead are "those who have fallen asleep" (1 Cor. 15:20), and this view is found elsewhere in the New Testament (Luke 8:52; 2 Peter 3:4). More
importantly, this Biblical conception of death is compatible with that found in the Qur'an that the dead will
sleep until judgment day, when they will all be raised.

  If for the Christian death is total and resurrection man's only hope of triumph over death, however, the
question naturally arises as to what happens to the dead
between death and the resurrection. In the history of
Christianity there have been three possible answers: one,
"that they remain, awaiting revivification, in the virtual
non-existence of Shoel -- as it were 'asleep;'" two, "that
they are in some intermediate state -- as it were of incomplete blessedness;" and three, "that they are already
enjoying the blessing of the Heavenly Kingdom, having been
admitted to it immediately after death." However, the
traditional orthodox teaching, both Catholic and Protestant, is "that until the last day the souls both of the
blessed and the damned remain <u>disembodied</u>, though already
dwelling in what is to be their final place of abode;" yet
"on the Last Day there will be a General Resurrection
whereby the souls of both are reunited to their old bodies."[44]

  Indeed, there are passages in the New Testament
which would seem to indicate that there is an interim state
for the dead. For instance, when Jesus told the parable of
the rich man and Lazarus, he mentioned that Lazarus was
"carried to Abraham's bosom," and that the rich man was "in

Hades" (Luke 16:22-23). We recall also Jesus' promise to the thief on the cross, "Today you will be with me in Paradise" (Luke 23:43), and Paul's desire "to depart and be with Christ" (Phil. 1:23). John, moreover, states that he "saw under the altar the souls of those who had been slain for the word of God" (Rev. 6:9). However, a growing number of modern scholars now claim that the images "in Abraham's bosom," "in Hades," "in Paradise," "with Christ," and "under the altar" merely intimate the proximity of God to those who died before the last day because there is no speculation on the interim state of the dead in the New Testament.[45]

How, then, did the Biblical conception of death become eclipsed by the Greek doctrine of the immortality of the soul? Not surprisingly, the doctrine of the resurrection posed a problem for early Christianity. With the lapse of time, it became obvious that the coming Kingdom of God was not at hand, and Jesus' message of hope had to be taught to the Gentiles. The problem of cross-cultural interpretation between the Semitic and Greek mind had to be faced. That is, a new language was needed to express an uniquely Judaic concept "in a society for which the terminology of the followers of Plato was more readily comprehensible."[46] On the one hand, metaphysically speaking, the immortality of the soul was a necessary logical deduction for Plato. On the other hand, it was an inconceivable construct for the Semitic mind. Yet the Christian intellectual heritage is the result of the efforts of the church fathers to blend the Platonic tradition as it had descended to Hellenistic culture with the Semitic as mediated by the early Christians.

Any effort made in retrospect to separate these two traditions is difficult, and recent studies bear out this observation. In fact, while the writings of the church fathers are heavily weighted toward accepting that the soul is the real man, and Wolfson and others[47] think that the immortality of the soul is necessary, or at least implicit in Judeo-Christian thought, there is a growing consensus among scholars, as we have seen, that the New Testament is unaware of the doctrine of the immortality of the soul, and consequently the adoption of the Greek position by the early Christians is a radical adjustment of questionable validity. Perhaps Pelikan is right in suggesting that the conflict between immortality and resurrection is more apparent than real at this point in Christian thought, since the church fathers adapted the Greek conception of immortality in such a way as to appropriate the Biblical belief in the resurrection.[48] That is, the doctrine of the immortality of the soul is not a truth which the church fathers sought to establish for its own sake; it is an interesting truth which is only methodologically important in their attempt to establish the plausibility of the resurrection. In other words, if the soul is linked to the body, and the soul survives, for them the body ought also to come to life again. Pelikan is supported by Tresmontant[49] and those scholars who claim that the church fathers considered the Platonic dualism of body and soul contrary to a Christian anthropology.

At any rate, by the end of the patristic period, though the notion of the resurrection as a restoration of a People continued to be prominent, "the idea of the disembodied afterlife for the soul was also current."[50] From the picture of death as a sleep which would last until the day of resurrection, this latter view led to a conception of death in which there was an active life for the individual soul during the interim between death and the resurrection.

And so the tension between the Platonic and Semitic conceptions of man continued into the early Middle Ages. This was facilitated by the fact that, as Leclercq has pointed out, the theology of the early medieval period was a "theology of admiration."[51] More particularly, since the emphasis in education at this time was literary rather than philosophical, the method of theologians was essentially to transmit the achievements of the Fathers. Indeed, in the earlier Middle Ages, "logic ... was the only philosophical discipline of Greek origin that occupied a place in the scheme of the seven liberal arts."[52] And, even then, the study of logic was rather rudimentary, based as it was on the <u>logica vetus</u> of Aristotle. To put it another way, because the theologians of the early Middle Ages did not possess an adequate knowledge of logic to advance the theological method, they based the authority of a view on the reputed sanctity of its author. When they found "little about the post-mortem condition of the soul in the authorities of tradition,"[53] they had no tools with which to solve the problem of immortality and resurrection that Greek philosophy had posed to Christian thought.

However, with the translation of Aristotle's works into Latin in the middle of the twelfth century, his <u>logica nova</u> came to the fore in the schools, and, as Knowles has stated, "the change from rhetoric to logic as the <u>pièce de resistance</u> of the curriculum is the index of a cultural revolution."[54] With the aid of the <u>logica nova</u>, medieval thinkers made another attempt to integrate the Greek and Christian notions of death in a metaphysically satisfying manner, yet this effort did not reach its peak before the high Middle Ages. While it is true that the introduction of the <u>logica nova</u> to the Latin West was revolutionary because of its content, it is also true that Aristotle's <u>De Anima</u>, which was the centre of the medieval controversy on the soul, had few readers at the time of its translation into Latin in the twelfth century. In fact, as has been stated before,[55] it was the translation into Latin of Averroes' great commentary on it in the thirteenth century which triggered the controversy that established the basic cast of Christian eschatology for centuries to come.

The medieval Christian reaction to Averroes was inevitable, for by this time there seems to have been some ossification of the idea that the soul is immortal, a view perhaps intensified by the prestigious teaching of Augustine, which reflects that of Plato, that man is a soul using a body. Moreover, the orthodox theologians had come to hold "that the soul is judged at the hour of its separation from the body and enters immediately into its reward and punishment."[56] The greatest of the orthodox theologians was, of course, Aquinas. And so, when he was confronted by Averroes' much celebrated commentary on Aristotle's <u>De Anima</u>, which insisted that body and soul are co-equal constituents of man, he "did his best to accommodate Greek philosophical reasoning to what he believed were the exigencies of the Christian faith."[57]

More concretely, the Thomistic notion of man, as stated by Pegis, "is intended by its author to be an answer to the classic Aristotelian dilemma voiced in the twelfth century by the great Averroes."[58] Pegis further specifies that the dilemma which Aquinas faced was a choice between the Platonic and Aristotelian views of the soul.[59] "According to the Platonic view, the soul is joined to the body as one complete being to another." The Aristotelian opinion, as Aquinas reports it, is "that the soul is not by itself of a certain nature; it is part of human nature."[60] As we shall see, Aquinas' understanding on this point is the same as that of Averroes; nevertheless, Aquinas calls Averroes "a corrupter of Peripatetic philosophy."[61] In any event, Aquinas argues that while other forms are dependent on matter for their being and operation, the human soul is independent of the human composite for its being "because the dignity of such a form transcends the capacity of matter." For him, this explains "why nothing prevents the soul from having an operation or a power beyond the reach of matter."[62] In fact, he says that in as much as "it transcends the being of corporeal matter, having of itself the power to subsist and to act, the human soul is a spiritual substance"[63] in its own right. Man is a substance and the human soul is a substance, for "nothing prevents the soul from being an intellectual substance and the form of the body."[64] In other words, since the same soul is a substance and a form, the soul is a substance as a form.[65] In sum, Aquinas emphatically refuses to grant Averroes that the soul, as the form of the body, shares in the totality of death, but insists that it is an intellectual, immaterial substance.

Why does Aquinas feel constrained to do so? Kreyche suggests that it was because he needed "a philosophical argument for the immortality of the soul," whereas Averroes placed all intellectual operations outside the soul to leave "no room for an argument showing the soul is a spiritual substance and immortal." Moreover, even though it must be admitted that the doctrine of Aquinas is in some sense Aristotelian, Kreyche goes as far as to raise the question as to whether Aquinas' epistemology is not Platonist, and in answer replies that, if it is, "it is because he felt drawn into this by the presupposition of his theology that the soul of man is immortal." And immortality is more compatible with Platonic than with Aristotelian philosophy.[66]

It is interesting to note that, despite the fact that Aquinas argued philosophically that the soul is an immaterial substance capable of happiness or unhappiness in the interim state between death and the resurrection, the conflict between immortality and resurrection continued into the fourteenth century. In 1336, for example, Benedict XII had to censure "a respectable army of supporters, among them the most famous names of tradition, Latin as well as Greek,"[67] including his predecessor Pope John XXII, who taught that death is a kind of sleep which had to be undergone by every soul until the end of time. And, in the fifteenth century, at the Council of Florence in 1439, the papacy found it necessary to try to impose the Western understanding of the afterlife on the Greeks, who, in general, did not accept the view of death represented by Aquinas. Nevertheless, the debate between immortality and resurrection lasted into the sixteenth century, until immortality became the recognized Christian position at the Fifth Lateran Council in 1513, when the Averroists and Alexandrists were condemned.

In fact, even the Reformers, for all their emphasis on the priority of Scripture, retained the structural concept of the soul of the philosophical tradition that had won the day in the Middle Ages. As Gatch has stated, "Luther's criticism of Aristotle's De Anima for teaching that 'the soul dies with the body'" shows clearly "that Luther regards immortality as an essential part of good philosophy."[68] Calvin, too, considered the state of souls before the resurrection to be an active one. In fact, he was so convinced of this that he regarded Pope John XXII's doctrine of the sleep of souls "as proof of the fallibility of the papacy."[69] In short, both in Catholic and Protestant Christianity, immortality triumphed over resurrection until the twentieth century.

Indeed, today, long after the Averroistic controversy in the Middle Ages, both Catholic and Protestant scholars recognize that the Christian hope, like the Qur'anic, is a hope based on the resurrection of the dead, rather than a belief in the immortality of the soul. Thus Cullman says that "The teaching of the great philosophers Socrates and Plato" on the immortality of the soul "can in no way be brought into consonance" with the New Testament teaching on the resurrection of the dead.[70] And Gleason writes that historically "the two concepts belong to two contrasting and religious worlds."[71]

Ratzinger asserts that immortality and resurrection are "two complete answers to the problem of the future of man." By way of explanation, he specifies that in contrast to the dualistic conception of man which characterizes the Greek doctrine of the immortality of the soul, the Christian doctrine of the resurrection "presupposes the indivisible unity of man," since in the Bible body and soul are inseparable. The raising of the dead, not of bodies, is thus not "a partial aspect of the hope of man, but concerns the salvation of man as <u>one</u> and indivisible."[72]

In the Christian framework then, as in the Qur'anic, man's destiny is human. It is not the destiny of the soul, but of man, both body and soul. Rahner recognizes this when he says that when we affirm that man is transformed into a new manner of existence in death "we are not speaking of a rectilinear continuation of man's empirical reality beyond death.... No, in this regard death puts an end to the <u>whole</u> man."[73]

Marcel considers the survival of the doctrine of the immortality of the soul in Christian thought to be "an idealistic attempt to rescue immortality by asserting that the thinking subject, of its very nature, cannot die." He prefers "to leave such imaginings to the antiquated philosophy which originated them," since "to begin with, such a subject cannot even live."[74] Kunneth also observes that the resurrection of Jesus testifies to the totality of death. "From this standpoint the idea of the immortality of the soul appears to be an attempt to escape the fatal destiny of the world." It is "a piece of philosophical self-deception regarding the situation of mortal man."[75]

The same author goes as far as to point out four major respects in which the Biblical doctrine of the future of man differs from the Greek. Firstly, the Greek idea of the immortality of the soul is the "philosophic expression of man's being made for unbroken living." It is a conception through which man, by his own nature, can achieve ever-lasting life and "is ultimately indifferent towards faith in God." Secondly, and in contrast, the doctrine of the resurrection of the dead has "its ground in an unconditional revelation of God." Consequently, it stands in a relationship of fundamental antithesis to the idea of the immortality of the soul centred on the nature of man. Thirdly, the Biblical teaching is not a doctrine of the active existence of an immaterial soul-substance, because the promise of the resurrection itself renders questionable "every philosophical optimism which imagines that it can command life and immortality." Fourthly, since the presupposition of the doctrine of the resurrection is "the destruction of the whole psychophysical existence of man in death," it is preposterous for man to think that he can build a bridge between this life and the next anchored in his own soul.

In sum, it would seem that Watt has good reason for thinking that the dualistic conception of man that came to dominate Christian thought is partly the result of Greek influence, since the monistic conception of man found in the Qur'an is continuous with the Biblical tradition. More fundamentally, in the light of recent scholarship it may be asserted that both the New Testament and the Qur'an seem to teach that faith in the resurrection is precisely the same as faith in God. In fact, "God alone, through his saving power, can offer man the opportunity to overcome his innate mortality."[76] Expressed differently, according to the revelation accepted as final in both Christianity and Islam, the future life is, presumably, the condition man enjoys once he has been raised to "eternal life" by God after death. But "eternal life" is not a survival over death; "it is a new creation of bodily life."[77] This observation brings us to the point where we are ready to examine the Aristotelian anthropology before proceeding to reconsider the problem of reason and revelation in the thought of Averroes.

The Aristotelian Anthropology

It is well known that in his earlier writings Aristotle accepted the dualism of his teacher Plato. In his Eudemos, Aristotle not only argued for the immortality of the soul, but also for its pre-existence and migration from body to body, and for the survival of individual consciousness after death. In his Protrepticos, he also speaks of the body as the prison of the soul. By the time he wrote his Physics, "he conceived of the soul as the energy of life that resides at a certain point in the body."[78] Thus one can still distinguish between that which moves (body) and that which causes it to move (soul). Ultimately, however, in his De Anima, Aristotle abandoned the dualism of body and soul as separate substances and advocated a monistic view of man in which body and soul form one complete substance. Because the interpretation of this treatise was the centre of controversy in the Middle Ages, we shall now examine it to determine what was the problem.

The De Anima is organized into three books. In book I, Aristotle acknowledges the difficulty of the subject, enumerates the views of earlier philosophers about the soul, and discusses these in some detail. In book II he begins an exposition of his own theory, which he concludes in book III. Let us now consider the highlights of the treatise.

In book I, Aristotle states that his aim is to grasp the essential nature and accidents of the soul, which is the principle of animal life. He then mentions some pertinent questions which need to be examined before a general definition of the soul can be reached:[79] Is soul a substance? If not, to what category does it belong? Is it divisible into parts? Is it homogeneous in all animals? If not, are the differences between souls generic or specific? He observes that if the soul is without parts then there are many kinds of soul, but if the soul is homogeneous, the homogeneous soul must be made up of parts. However, at this point Aristotle admits that if the soul is made up of parts, it "is also a difficult problem to decide which of these parts are in nature distinct from one another."[80] He notes that Democritus identifies soul and mind,[81] whereas Anaxagoras seems to think that mind is "simple, unmixed, and pure."[82]

In criticizing the theory that the soul is self-moving, Aristotle remarks that "if the old man could recover the proper kind of eye, he would see just as well as the young man."[83] That is to say, he explains, when the body decays, the soul is clearly deprived of its activity, even though its existence continues. He then observes that what is true of the soul in this respect is also true of the intellect, since the mind "seems to be an independent substance within the soul."[84]

At the end of book I, Aristotle favours the view that the soul is a unity in spite of the fact that the body is divisible into parts.[85] He goes on to point out that if the soul is divisible into parts, each part of the soul should keep a part of the body together, but "this seems an impossibility; it is difficult even to imagine what sort of bodily part mind will hold together, or how it will do this."[86]

It is interesting to note that in book I, even before Aristotle formulates his own theory of the soul, he is already concerned with the relation of soul and body, and of soul and intellect.

In book II, Aristotle, speaking in his own name, claims that "the soul must be a substance in the sense of the form of a natural body."[87] He also asserts that "the soul is the first grade of actuality of a natural body having life potentially in it."[88] Moreover, he offers a general definition of the soul "as the first grade of actuality of a natural organized body."[89] The definition depends on the fundamental distinction between matter and form, or the potential and the actual. Indeed, these are the two aspects of every being. Body and soul are two correlative terms by which we explain the characteristic mode of existence of a natural body. The soul is something relative to a body. It resides in a definite body[90] and is to be regarded as one with that body.[91] We should not identify the living being with the body, for the natural body has only the potentiality of life. The soul is the actualization of that potentiality. The body is to be looked at simply as the material for the expression of the soul. The soul is, therefore, as defined by Aristotle, the entelechy, the realization or actualization of that life which a body possesses in potentiality. Body and soul are not two complete entities. Each soul belongs to a particular body, and each body is the seed-plot of a particular soul. The idea that man continues his existence as a disembodied or disincarnate soul after death seems, for Aristotle, to be a contradiction in terms. Form and matter are simply two aspects of one concrete being -- man, in our study -- that alone really exists.[92]

But having defined the soul as the form or actuality of a body, Aristotle ceases to be consistent. While maintaining the essential correlativity of body and soul, he now suggests that there may be parts of the soul which are separable from the body "because they are not the actualities of the body at all." He then goes on to say that "we have no light on the problem whether the soul may not be the actuality of its body in the sense in which the sailor is the actuality of the ship."[93] Moreover, this last statement, if taken seriously, subverts the whole position he has laid down, reintroducing the idea, ostensibly previously discarded, of the soul as the inhabitant of the body.

In addition, Aristotle also tells us that there is no clear evidence to show whether the soul is only logically divisible into parts or actually divisible with the body.[94] Finally, he says that the intellect does not seem to be part of the soul, but "a widely different kind of soul, differing as what is eternal from what is perishable," and "capable of existing in isolation from other psychic powers."[95]

In book II, then, there are two lines of thought in conflict. On the one hand, the soul is defined as the form of a natural body. On the other hand, we are asked to entertain the possibility of a soul, or part of a soul, which is not the entelechy of a body. Moreover, we observe that it is Aristotle's concern with the intellect which occasions the conflict. Understandably, the relation of the soul to the intellect is one of the major problems which Averroes has to resolve.

Yet, in book III, the task is further complicated by the fact that Aristotle's treatment of the intellect is also unclear. Here he establishes its three attributes in a comparison with sense perception. In the first place, according to him, the intellect is "impassible," even though it receives intelligible forms in a manner analagous to the reception of sensible forms by the faculty of sense.[96] Hence, in the second instance, the intellect must be devoid of all sensible forms; that is, it must be "unmixed." In fact, the intellect is a mere aptitude or capacity to think. Until it actually thinks, it is nothing at all.[97]

Aristotle goes on to describe the intellect as "the place of forms,"[98] a description Platonic in its conception.[99] If scholars, like Raymond Martin,[100] find Averroes' doctrine of the intellect Platonic, it is therefore helpful for us to keep in mind that it is Aristotle's own doing. Finally, Aristotle gives his explanation of why the intellect is "unmixed" in contrast to sense perception: "the reason is that while the faculty of sensation is dependent upon the body, mind is separable from it."[101] In sum, for Aristotle the intellect is "separable, impassible, and unmixed."

So far, the intellect has been treated as one, and Aristotle's delineation of it is obscure. Yet he adds to the confusion when, in the celebrated passage which sparked the Averroistic controversy on the soul, he makes a dis-

The Anthropological Background 57

tinction between an intellect that becomes all things and
an intellect that makes all things:

> Since in every class of things, as in nature
> as a whole, we find two factors involved, (1) a
> matter which is potentially all the particulars
> included in the class, (2) a class which is pro-
> ductive in the sense that it makes them all (the
> latter standing to the former, as e.g. an art to
> its material), these distinct elements must like-
> wise be found within the soul.
> And in fact mind as we have described it is
> what it is by virtue of becoming all things, while
> there is another which is what it is by virtue of
> making all things....
> Mind in this sense of it is separable, impas-
> sible, unmixed, since it is in its essential nature
> activity.[102]

Aristotle seems to mean that the human soul is potentially
intelligent, but in order that its potentiality be made actual, it needs the co-operation of an active principle that
is "separable, impassible, and unmixed." In other words,
Aristotle seems to make a distinction between an active intellect that makes things actually intelligible and a passive intellect that receives these intelligibles. Beyond
this point his meaning is ambiguous. For example, are the
attributes of the intellect "separable, impassible, unmixed" equally applicable to the active and passive intellect?

To make matters worse, Aristotle amplifies his account with the following observation, which has ever been
an occasion of speculation and controversy among his interpreters:

> Actual knowledge is identical with its ob-
> ject: in the individual, potential knowledge is in
> time prior to actual knowledge, but in the universe
> as a whole it is not prior even in time. Mind is
> not at one time knowing and at another not. When
> mind is set free from its present conditions it ap-
> pears as just what it is and nothing more: this
> alone is immortal and eternal (we do not, however,
> remember its former activity because, while mind in
> this sense is impassible, mind as passive is des-
> tructible), and without it nothing thinks.[103]

What is the significance of the word "destructible" in the
last sentence of the quotation? Does it suggest that the
intellect which becomes all things is a sense power or
something dependent on sense? Moreover, what does Aristo-

tle mean when he says that the intellect is "alone immortal and eternal"? When he says that at death the mind is "set free from its present conditions," we are reminded of Plato's conception of death as the liberation of the soul from the body. But does he mean that individual consciousness continues after death or that it is reabsorbed into an external reason?

Aristotle does say elsewhere in the De Anima that no living thing, and so, no man, can participate in what is eternal by uninterrupted continuance, since "nothing perishable can forever remain one and the same."[104] For him, therefore, man's triumph over death is possible only in an existence in "something like itself -- not numerically but specifically one."[105] Important also is his acknowledgement that man is the only animal in which there is thinking[106] and that the soul cannot think without a phantasm.[107]

In addition, it is appropriate to mention, from his other treatises, a few statements that are related to the subject of soul and intellect in the context of man and his destiny. More particularly, Aristotle states in the De Generatione Animalium that reason comes to man "from the outside."[108] And in the Metaphysica he considers mind, thought, and the object of thought to be identical.[109] Finally, Aristotle observes in the Ethica Nicomachea that, although man is mortal and intellect is eternal, the life of reason is man's highest activity.[110]

The difficulty of understanding Aristotle's exposition of the intellect[111] and of the relation of the intellect to the soul is notorious.[112] Among the better-known Greek commentators, Theophrastus[113] and Themistius[114] believed that Aristotle intended both the active and the passive intellect to be powers of each human soul. However, Alexander of Aphrodisias, as has been mentioned before,[115] maintained that the active intellect was a separately existing substance, though he placed the passive intellect within the individual human soul. The controversy came to a head with Aquinas and Averroes.

In defense of the view that, while man is a substance, the human soul is a substance in its own right,

Aquinas concurred with Theophrastus and Themistius that each soul has its own active and passive intellect. On the other hand, Averroes went beyond Alexander of Aphrodisias in insisting that the passive intellect -- that is, the intellect he termed possible or material -- as well as the active intellect are not powers of the soul. Granted that Aquinas' interpretation allows him to remain faithful to his medieval Christian belief that the soul, apart from the body, is capable of experiencing states of happiness or unhappiness between death and the resurrection, in an Islamic context, is Averroes' position contrary to revelation? Before this question can be answered, the problem of reason and revelation must first be considered.

In closing the discussion of the anthropological background of the Averroistic controversy, it may be appropriate to observe that, for Aristotle and the Qur'an, and presumably also for the New Testament, body is an integral part of man, and soul is dependent on it for its activity. However, in contrast to the Qur'an and the New Testament, Aristotle is concerned with man's life in this world, not in the next. Consequently, scholars who use elements of his thought in arguments favouring a future life must admit that his De Anima does not include an exposition of the personal destiny of man after death. They may certainly use aspects of his psychology for this purpose, but not for an end that is his.

CHAPTER II

AVERROES ON REASON AND REVELATION

Reason and Revelation in Islam Before Averroes

If the sixth century witnessed a waning in the vigour of Christian thought, the seventh century witnessed the birth of one of the world's great religions, Islam. Like Judaism and Christianity, it is a religion of a book, though it is closer to Judaism, since it is primarily a religion of law. The central teaching of the Qur'an is its uncompromising doctrine of the unity and transcendence of God and the dependence of man on his Creator.

After the death of the Prophet Muhammad, it did not take long for his followers to realize that the Qur'an, like the Bible, abounds in anthropomorphisms, inconsistencies, and incongruities. Fortunately for them, though they regarded the Qur'an as a special revelation from God, the Qur'an itself, like the Psalms, recognizes that man progresses toward its truth through the exercise of reason:[1] "In the creation of the heavens and the earth and (in) the alternation of night and day are signs (of His sovereignty) for men of understanding" (S. 3:190).[2] In fact, scholars have claimed that the Qur'an itself recognizes that there are three degrees of knowledge in ascending order of certitude.[3] The first is knowledge acquired through logic and inference, as in the study of history: "Is it not a guidance for them (to know) how many a generation We destroyed before them, amid whose dwellings they walk? Surely in this are signs for men of judgment" (S. 20:128). The second is knowledge gained through observation and perception, as in the objective reflection on nature: in the alternation of night and day, in the rain that revives the dead earth, in the movements of the winds and the clouds "are signs (of Allah's sovereignty) for people who have sense" (S. 2:164; also 30:23-25). Finally, there is also knowledge given by God through his messengers, the prophets: "And messengers We have mentioned unto thee before ... in order that mankind might have no argument against Allah after their coming" (S. 4:164-166).[4] The unambiguous acceptance of reason by the Qur'an opened the way to a rational discussion of its truth. Moreover, the Qur'an itself makes use of reason to buttress the doctrine of the future life as a second creation (S. 50:2-11).

According to Qur'anic scholars three classes of men, corresponding to the three ways God's message is to be thought, are also recognized by the Qur'an:[5] "Call unto the way of thy Lord with wisdom, and fair exhortation, and reason with them in the better way" (S. 16:125). Controversialists were soon to defend their own method of interpretation on the basis of this text. Soon the term "wisdom" became synonymous with philosophy, and philosophers cited this verse in defense of the study of philosophy against literalist theologians. "Exhortation" was recognized as the method of preachers, and "reason" became identified with the reasoned debate of theologians. Furthermore, as Arberry has stated, scholars took this verse "to confirm Aristotle's threefold differentiation of proof into demonstrative, rhetorical and dialectical."[6]

It is fitting to mention also that, while the Qur'an describes itself as a "Scripture that maketh plain" (S. 12:1; 26:1; 28:1), it openly admits to ambiguous allegorical passages which would cause dissension among men. No one knows their explanation save Allah. "Those who are of sound instruction say: We believe therein; the whole is from our Lord; but only men of understanding really heed" (S. 3:7). Understandably, it became a source of controversy as to whom "those who are of sound instruction" were.[7] In fact, the interpretation of this text led to bitter quarrels between theologians and philosophers; naturally, both the philosophers and the theologians claimed that the reference was to themselves.

More specifically, the dialectical theologians were the first thinkers in Islam to concern themselves with the harmony of reason and revelation. On the one hand, the Mu'tazilites, who had their origin in the eighth century, made use of Greek philosophical ideas in their exposition of the attributes of God and man, and resorted to allegorical interpretation to resolve the ambiguities and inconsistencies of the Qur'an.[8] In order to allay any doubts that might linger in wavering minds, they maintained that the Qur'an confirms the findings of reason; and in support of their position they wrote commentaries on the Holy Book to demonstrate its rational teachings. They also held that man was the independent agent of his own actions and defended their view by appealing to those verses of the Qur'an which seem to ascribe responsibility for human action to man himself, such as: "Every soul is a pledge for its own deed" (S. 74:38); "man hath only that for which he maketh effort" (S. 53:39); "Whoso doeth right it is for his soul, and whoso doeth wrong it is against it. And the Lord is not at all a tyrant to His slaves" (S. 41:46). For them the soul was the true essence of man and an immaterial substance. Thus they "made man's ultimate destiny depend on himself" rather than on God.[9]

On the other hand, literalist theologians, skeptical of philosophy, accepted the materialistic pictures of God found in the Qur'an and tried to understand them in human terms. For example, there was much debate whether Allah's throne was carried by eight angels or eight types of angels. The followers of Ibn Karram (d. 869) were unsure "whether Allah is as big as his throne, whether it is equal to his breadth."[10] Malik ben Anas (d. 795) is said to have concluded that with respect to Allah's sitting on His throne, the "sitting is known, whereas its mode is unknown. Belief in its truth is a duty."[11]

More importantly, the followers of the great al-Ash'ari (893-935) challenged the Mu'tazilite conception of man as contrary to revelation. In vindication of God's unity and omnipotence, they denied that man was the complete agent or "creator of his deeds."[12] In the Ash'arite view, to make man fully free would be blasphemous, for it would be tantamount to a curtailment of God's absolute power and unity, and a tacit admission of polytheism. The Ash'arites insisted on the contingent nature of creatures and cited the Qur'an in rebuttal of the Mu'tazilite doctrine of man: "Allah doeth what He will" (S. 22:18); "He hath no partner" (S. 25:2); "Allah is the Creator of all things, and He is the One, the Almighty" (S. 13:16). The Mu'tazilite conception of the soul as an incorporeal substance was also objectionable on the ground that, as de Boer puts it, it "would not harmonize properly with the Muslim doctrine of the transcendent nature of God, who has no associate. The soul belongs to the world of body."[13] Besides God, there is room only for corporeal substances. Indeed, it is because of the Qur'an's conception of God that it is emphatic in maintaining the totality of death, including that of man:[14] "Everything will perish save His countenance" (S. 28:88; also 55:26-27).

Though the Mu'tazilites were champions of a reasonable creed against anthropomorphism and literalism, Islamic thought became more strictly philosophical through those religious thinkers, known as <u>falasifa</u>, who tried to harmonize the revealed law of the Qur'an with the Neoplatonic and Aristotelian traditions.[15] These thinkers recognized that revelation was superior to Greek philosophy. That is, they thought of themselves as Muslims first, and as philosophers second. Nevertheless, they made their syntheses "as philosophers rather than as theologians,"[16] while not considering themselves to be independently speculating philosophers, as were their Greek masters.

These religious philosophers of Islam understood the problem of philosophy and revelation as resulting from the difference between divine and human law. As Muslims, their identity was based on a revelation centred on God; Greek philosophy was the product of reason and centred on rational man. In order to effect a harmony of faith and reason, they therefore conceived of happiness as the consequence of rational activity directed toward God, and its consummation as consisting in coming to be like Him. Thus, by giving the highest good admitted by philosophy a religious content, they transformed the entirely metaphysical concept of their teachers, Plato or Aristotle, into a religious value. For them, then, life had a two-fold aim:

happiness in this world and eternal happiness hereafter, which is the joy of contemplating and being with God.

In other words, just as the problem of St. Augustine was how "to express the God of Christianity in terms borrowed from the philosophy of Plotinus,"[17] so the problem of the philosophers of Islam was how to clothe their religious beliefs in the language of Plato or Aristotle. Like the Jews of Alexandria, they regarded their revelation as containing absolute truth, although they maintained that reason can arrive at no different truth, because truth is one and indivisible. And, while maintaining that reason is not opposed to revelation, they acknowledged that man has need of God, especially in matters beyond reason, which are made known to him through the revealed law of Islam. Their attitude may be compared to that of the Prophet Muhammad himself, "who considered the new religion as the final revelation of religious truth but by no means the first."[18] Philosophy is the best means of explaining by demonstrative argument what is within man's faculty to grasp, though it falls short of God's purpose, which is to lead man to a life with Him in a world-to-come. Hence, though the falasifa maintained that rational activity is man's highest activity, they were obliged to recognize that the perfection of reason was not attainable by philosophy alone, for it depends also on right beliefs made known to man through the Qur'an.

The first of the falasifa is generally held to be Al-Kindi. In the ninth century he defended the study of philosophy against the theologians by identifying it as one of the three avenues to truth recognized by the Qur'an. He considered the philosophers "those who were of sound instruction,"[19] and philosophy the most noble of human crafts, defining it as "the knowledge of things in their realities to the limit of human power."[20] Al-Kindi paid eloquent tribute to the philosophers of Greece and went on to say that "We should not be ashamed to acknowledge the truth and to assimilate it from whatever source it comes to us, even if it is brought to us by former generations and foreign peoples."[21] He was the first philosopher of Islam to start the practice of restating accurately what Aristotle and the ancients had said, and then commenting on it in the light of revelation, "and this according to the usage of [the] Arabic language."[22] He had full confidence that the revelation of the Qur'an was compatible with the truth "ascertainable by intellectual processes,"[23] that is, with the findings of philosophy.

Al-Kindi considered the inconsistency between philosophy and revelation a linguistic problem, and invoking "the authority of the Koran, ... interpreted allegorically its abstruse statements."[24] He was the first philosophical thinker in Islam to state that the agent intellect was not a power of the human soul, and, indeed, he and all medieval Islamic philosophers admitted that there was only one agent intellect for all men.[25] Though considered Aristotelian, the Aristotelianism of the Islamic East was intermingled with Neoplatonic teachings, as mentioned before. It is no surprise, therefore, that the reconciliation of philosophy with revelation achieved by Al-Kindi shows signs of Neoplatonism. His God was the One of Plotinus, and he understood the soul to be a separate substance like Plato. He recognized the limitations of his philosophical conclusions and accepted the resurrection promised by the Qur'an.[26]

In the tenth century, Alfarabi's synthesis of reason and revelation was essentially his effort to interpret the teachings of Plato and Aristotle in such a way that they formed a harmony, and to interpret this harmony in the light of the Qur'an. His task was rendered considerably easier by the presence of Neoplatonic elements in what he considered to be the writing of Aristotle -- the _Theology of Aristotle_. Alfarabi accepted Aristotle's view that rational activity was the supreme aim of human life, and not only believed that philosophers were superior to theologians, as Al-Kindi did before him, but also endorsed the method of allegory and the withholding of knowledge from the uninitiated. As for the afterlife, he considered the physical description of the world to come given in the Qur'an to be an accommodation to the masses, and his conception of what happens to the soul after death is unclear:

on the one hand, it seems to have been his view that only a chosen few will achieve personal immortality; on the other hand, his conception of life after death leaves no room for the resurrection of the body.[27]

In the eleventh century, Avicenna's Aristotelianism, like that of his predecessors in the Islamic East, was characterized by a reliance on Neoplatonic ideas. Although he accepted the Aristotelian notion that the soul is the form of the body, he, like Plato, regarded it as a rational substance capable of existing apart from the body after death. For Avicenna, man's hope was bound up with the personal immortality of the soul, and to reconcile this view with revelation he interpreted the Qur'anic doctrine of a physical resurrection allegorically, considering it a mere accommodation to the masses, since "true happiness and spiritual pleasure are not comprehended by them at all and have no place whatever in their understandings." In Avicenna's opinion, the Prophet Muhammad did not teach a purely spiritual survival because he was concerned with the salvation of all men, and the masses can be motivated to practice virtue only through their love of physical pleasure and their fear of physical pain. After death the soul alone, "stripped from the body and of physical impressions," is destined to contemplate "the Essence of Him to whom belongs the kingdom most mighty" as its eternal reward. "Misery in the world to come is the opposite of this."[28]

Though Avicenna denied the doctrine of the resurrection and offered the boldest argument for the personal immortality of the soul to be found in Arabic literature, he exerted the decisive philosophic influence on Christian thought in the thirteenth century to yield an "Avicennizing Augustinianism."[29] However, even in the eleventh century the theologian Algazali had branded both his and Alfarabi's conception of life after death incompatible with revelation, and, in so doing, had dealt a fatal blow to the Neoplatonic Aristotelianism of the Islamic East.

Finding the spiritual immortality of Alfarabi and Avicenna objectionable, Algazali emphasized that "eternal life" required a belief in the physical resurrection of the body. In his view their denial of a concrete heaven and hell, together with their assertion that these are "mere parables coined for the common people and intended to connote a spiritual reward and retribution ... is contrary to the belief of all Muslims."[30] The world-to-come is a second creation. With unwavering faith Algazali called upon the philosophers of Islam to place their trust in God and His promise given in the Holy Book.

Algazali insisted, like the Ash'arites before him, that the Muslim hope of triumphing over death was a hope centred on the nature of God, not on the nature of the soul as a rational substance. Challenging the philosophers to accept the faith as revealed, he championed the view that the theologians, rather than the philosophers, were "those who were of sound instruction." However, even Algazali recognized the allegorical method for interpreting the Qur'an, since there are differences among men which should be kept in mind when teaching the faith. As he puts it, the door of understanding is "only open to those who know and are 'established in knowledge.' Moreover, not every mystery is to be revealed or divulged."[31]

Reason and Revelation According to Averroes

The withering attack of Algazali on the study of philosophy had to be repulsed, and so the task fell to the Islamic West to show that the thought of Aristotle, purged of Neoplatonism, was compatible with the Qur'anic revelation. The thrust of this effort reached its climax in Spain in the twelfth century with Averroes,[32] as was mentioned in the Introduction.[33]

In order to appreciate Averroes' synthesis of Aristotelian philosophy and revelation with respect to man and his destiny, it may be helpful to view through Christian eyes the problem which Aristotle posed to revealed religion. Gilson, speaking for the medieval scholastics, thinks that the first difficulty which Aristotle presented was his notion of God as self-thinking Thought. The challenge which a religious philosopher faced, therefore, was how to clothe his belief in the personal God of revelation in the language of Aristotle so that Aristotle's self-thinking Thought became one with the personal God of revelation. The second problem which a medieval philosopher had, according to Gilson, was how to reconcile Aristotle's conception of the soul as the form of a physical body with his belief in the nature of life after death.[34]

Averroes, like the Christian scholastics, accepted the challenge of giving expression to his faith within the Aristotelian framework. The task before him involved purifying the Aristotelianism of his predecessors in the Islamic East by ridding it of its principal Neoplatonic accretions, namely, the notions of God as the One and of the soul as a rational spiritual substance capable of functioning without a body. This was imperative since, as we have just seen, for Aristotle God is self-thinking Thought and the soul is dependent on a body for its operation. In its simplest terms, then, the situation before us is as follows: for Aristotle the contemplation of God is man's highest good,[35] and the exercise of reason is man's highest activity. This means that Averroes must demonstrate that it is through reason that man achieves his highest perfection. We have also been taught by revelation that man grows in perfection as he grows in the knowledge of God. In other words, it is clear that to fulfill his objective Averroes must show this: that through growth in the knowledge of God, both for Aristotle and the Qur'an, man progresses in the fulfillment of his destiny.

However, Averroes' synthesis of Aristotle and the Qur'an must also acknowledge, with the Ash'arites, that God is the supreme ruler of the world: indeed he is the principal agent in the world, to which every other agent is somehow subordinated. And he must concur also with the Ash'arites and Algazali that the soul belongs to the world of body. Consequently, Averroes must show that man's only hope of being victorious over death is in the resurrection of the dead, and not in the doctrine of the personal immortality of the soul. Put another way, to defend the study of philosophy against the theologians, Averroes must recognize that the existence of souls as spiritual substances capable of happiness or unhappiness apart from the body after death is contrary to the Qur'anic revelation which, as we have seen, conceives of the afterlife as a second creation, and he must do so within the framework of Aristotle's psychology. Averroes' exposition of the future life will be given in the next two chapters. In this chapter we shall confine the discussion to his views on the relation of philosophy to revelation and examine his thesis that philosophers are superior to theologians as interpreters of the Qur'an.

As we have seen, for the theologians of Islam the consistency of Scripture with scientific truth about the world was secondary compared to the correct interpretation of the Qur'an in the light of their own system of theology in an Arabic context. On the other hand, the philosophers tried to satisfy the natural urge of the mind for internal coherence by accommodating the meaning of Scripture to the observed truth about the world and to Greek philosophy. They rested their case on the concept of the unity of truth. However, the difference in method between the theologians and the philosophers led to differences in the interpretation of the Qur'an. Like Tatian, Tertullian, and the Fathers of Antioch, the theologians became suspicious of philosophy and, favouring literalism, questioned the study of philosophy. It is in this context that Averroes wrote his Fasl al-maqal in defence of the philosophers.[36]

At the very beginning of the Fasl al-maqal, Averroes states the purpose of the treatise. It is to examine "whether the study of philosophy and logic is allowed by the Law, or prohibited or commanded -- either by way of recommendation or as obligatory."[37] Thus Averroes, from the start, makes his defence of the study of philosophy depend on what revelation itself, understood in the Islamic sense of law,[38] has to say on the subject. The Fasl al-maqal, then, does not attempt to defend the truths of philosophy philosophically. It confines itself to offering a legal defence of the study of philosophy within the juridical context of Islam.

After making this point clear, Averroes goes on to say that if philosophy is truth arrived at through observation and reflection on the world, and "the Law has rendered obligatory the study of beings by the intellect and reflection on them,"[39] it is evident that the Qur'an calls men to the study of philosophy. And such indeed is the case, for the Qur'an unambiguously acknowledges that men can recognize the truth of its revelation through reflection and observation, as we have seen.[40] It is appropriate to recall here that Irenaeus,[41] and the Psalmist before him,[42] had admitted that men can know God through reason alone.

It is important to stress that in mediaeval Islam philosophy was not conceived of as a speculative science in the modern sense, but rather as a demonstrative science in the Greek tradition. That is, the *falasifa* thought of philosophy as "yielding a knowledge of reality which is demonstrative according to the Aristotelian conditions: conclusions drawn by flawless logic from indubitable premises." It is this characterization of philosophy as the systematic application to the world of "the most perfect kind of reasoning, ... the kind called 'demonstration,'" which provides the key to understanding Averroes' defence of philosophy in the *Fasl al-maqal*.[43]

Moreover, in his defence of philosophy as demonstrative reasoning, Averroes echoes the thought of Al-Kindi when he says that we should examine the truth discovered by the ancients before the birth of Islam, "and if it is all correct we should accept from them, while if there is anything incorrect in it, we should draw attention to that."[44]

Having established the meaning of philosophy, Averroes now states that men assent to the truth through demonstrative, dialectical, and rhetorical argumentation, for "the natures of men are on different levels with respect to their paths to assent."[45] He goes on to assert that these three types of assent are recognized by the law and cites the text of the Qur'an on the basis of which, as we have already mentioned, Islamic philosophers and theologians defended their right to interpret Scripture: "Summon the way of your Lord by wisdom and good preaching, and debate with them in the most effective manner."[46] That is, by equating "wisdom" with the demonstrative argumentation of philosophy, "good preaching" with the rhetoric or persuasion suitable for teaching the vast number of the laity, and "debate" with the dialectical reasoning of theologians, Averroes not only establishes that philosophy is one of the three legal methods of interpreting revelation, but also that Aristotle's threefold differentiation of proof into demonstrative, rhetorical, and dialectical are compatible with the Qur'an's own teaching.

The Qur'an regards philosophy as licit, meritorious, and even obligatory for some -- the men of demonstration. Averroes now answers the familiar objection of the theologians that philosophy teaches doctrines contrary to Scripture, as we have seen in the case of the accusation of Algazali. Because Western scholars have taught that Averroes championed a doctrine of double truth, we should pay special attention to his answer:

> Now since this religion is true and summons to the study which leads to knowledge of the Truth, we the Muslim community know definitely that demonstrative study does not lead to [conclusions] conflicting with what Scripture has given us: <u>for truth does not oppose truth but accords with it and bears witness to it</u>.47

Philosophy and revelation cannot be opposed to each other, since truth is one. It is evident that there would have been no problem if Averroes had advocated a theory of double truth, in which two propositions, one of which is the contradictory of the other, can simultaneously be true. It is, on the contrary, because Averroes holds a unitary view of truth that a problem arose for Western interpreters of his doctrine of man. For him Scripture makes statements about the same world as that of philosophy. Hence a conflict between revelation and philosophy is conceivable only if philosophy contradicts revelation. Averroes' answer is inevitable once it is granted that the Qur'an and philosophy are both reliable sources of the same kind of truth: factual descriptive knowledge about the world.

However, though revelation and philosophy are not opposed to each other, it is the Qur'an, not philosophy, that carries supreme authority. This is understandable since, for Muslims, it is the speech of God communicated to

the Prophet Muhammad by the angel Gabriel. But the Prophet
Muhammad is dead, and Scripture not only contains ambiguous
passages, but also abounds in incongruities and anthropomorphisms which only "those of sound instruction" are qualified to interpret. Consequently, Islam recognizes a con-
tinuing human element in the interpretation of the law:
collective, through the doctrine of consensus (ijma), and
when this is impossible to achieve, personal, by "those who
are of sound instruction." That is, orthodoxy is defined
in terms of acceptance by the Muslim community.[48] But
since even among the learned there is a wide divergence of
interpretation on some matters of doctrine, consensus on
these matters is unattainable. Hence qualified scholars
are permitted within the recognized limits of the law to
interpret them. It is important for Western scholars to
know that orthodoxy has never been defined by ecclesiasti-
cal councils in Islam, as in Christianity. Even the existing text of the Qur'an was determined by consensus.

It is against this background that Averroes must
explain how apparent contradictions of philosophy and revelation are to be reconciled. We must accept the fact that
Averroes was a Muslim and accept his defence of the study
of philosophy from its Islamic standpoint.

Remaining faithful to the law, Averroes says that
Scripture and philosophy are reconcilable through allegorical interpretation, which he defines as:

> [the] extension of the significance of an expres-
> sion from real to metaphorical significance, with-
> out forsaking therein the standard metaphorical
> practices of Arabic, such as calling a thing by the
> name of something resembling it or a cause or con-
> sequence or accompaniment of it, or other things
> such as are enumerated in accounts of the kinds of
> metaphorical speech.

Indeed, all Muslims accept the principle that some expressions of Scripture can be interpreted allegorically. They
disagree only "over which of them should and which should
not be so interpreted." The criterion used for deciding
the issue in Islam is to permit the allegorical interpretation of a passage only if a more literal meaning is shown
to be impossible: "But when it happens ... that we know

the thing itself by the three methods, we do not need to coin images of it, and it remains true in its apparent meaning, not admitting allegorical interpretation."[49]

Averroes concurs with Algazali and the theologians that this rule does provide a check on the arbitrary interpretation of the Qur'an, but he points out that a further criterion is needed to decide which allegorical interpretation is precise when several are possible. According to Averroes, such certainty can only be achieved through demonstration, which gives factual information about the world. In other words, Averroes interprets "those who are of sound instruction" as a reference to the philosophers rather than to the theologians:

> God has described them as those who believe in Him, and this can only be taken to refer to the belief which is based on demonstration; and this belief only occurs together with the science of allegorical interpretation. For the unlearned believers are those whose belief in Him is not based on demonstration; and if this belief which God has attributed to the scholars is peculiar to them, it must come through demonstration, and if it comes through demonstration it only occurs together with the science of allegorical interpretation.[50]

Such an idea was unlikely to endear Averroes to theologians, but again we must acknowledge that the Fasl al-maqal is a legal defence of philosophy, and the conclusion is inevitable once we grant that philosophy is a demonstrative science that gives certain knowledge of the world.

But, should a philosopher err, would he be forgiven by God? Averroes thinks so. He bases his judgment on the Aristotelian theory of the relations of will and intellect, namely, that when we arrive at a conclusion after thorough rational inquiry, our only choice is to accept it:[51] "And since free choice is a condition of obligation, a man who assents to an error as a result of a consideration that has occurred to him is excused, if he is a scholar." More importantly, he defends his opinion by citing the words of the Prophet himself: "If the judge after exerting his mind makes a right decision, he will have a double reward; and if he makes a wrong decision he will have a single reward."[52]

Averroes now narrows down the issue to the future life. There is consensus on two classes of texts in the Qur'an: those which all Muslims agree should be taken in their literal meaning, and those which all Muslims agree must be interpreted allegorically. However, there is a third class of texts: those about which there is no consensus. The texts about the future life fall into this category, since theologians think that it is possible "to take these passages in their apparent meaning," while men of demonstration "interpret these passages allegorically and ... give the most diverse interpretations of them."[53]

Since there is no consensus on the nature of eternal life, "a scholar who commits an error in this matter is excused, ... provided that the interpretation given does not lead to a denial of its existence."[54] That is, while Averroes is most insistent that it is unbelief to deny the existence of life after death, with impartiality he admits that it is legal to permit alternative allegorical interpretations of it. We have here a remarkable instance of Averroes' objectivity, since he himself accepts the theologians' interpretation of man's hope of victory over death as that of the resurrection of the dead, and not a theory of the immortality of the soul as did his predecessors in the Islamic East, as we shall see in the next chapter.

Averroes concludes the treatise with a view voiced by Christian[55] and Muslim thinkers before him, namely, that Scripture should be taught to people according to their ability, since to teach interpretations of the Qur'an to people which are beyond their ability is tantamount to "summoning people to unbelief" and "contrary to the summons of the Legislator." He adds, perhaps with Algazali in mind, that it was not the philosophers but the theologians who erred in this regard, for it was the indiscretion of the Mu'tazilites and Ash'arites which "threw people into hatred" and dissension in Islam.[56]

In sum, the <u>Fasl al-maqal</u> is a defence of the study of philosophy against the theologians of Islam. From the very beginning Averroes bases his defence on the revealed law. Once the identity of purpose between philosophy and revelation is established, he makes philosophers the best qualified interpreters of the law. That is, the Qur'an teaches the same truth as that which the philosophers seek to demonstrate, since there is only one truth for all men. In the absence of any recognized authority in Islam to settle the dispute between the philosophers and the theologians, Averroes' conclusion that "philosophy," not theology, "is the friend and milk-sister of religion"[57] is as defensible as any.

It is perhaps evident by now that one reason why Christian scholars have had difficulty in understanding Averroes' views on reason and revelation may be their apparent unawareness of the fact that there is a difference in the Christian and Islamic conception of revelation. For this reason it may be helpful to elaborate the point that whereas for Christians revelation has the connotation of belief, for Muslims it has the character of law. Revelation for Muslims, as Rosenthal puts it, is

> not simply a direct communication between God and man, not only a transmission of right beliefs and convictions, a dialogue between a personal love of God, of justice and of mercy and man whom he has created in his image; it is also and above all a valid and binding code for man, who must live in a state in order to fulfil his destiny. In short, it is the law of the ideal state.[58]

To put it another way, Islam, in comparison with Christianity, is a lay theocracy. Like Judaism, it is a religion wedded to a political community which functions according to a law delivered to it by a prophetic lawgiver. Muslims regard their religiously determined state as the best social setting for attaining happiness, not only in this life, but also in the next. The distinction in the gospel of Mark between what is God's and what is Caesar's (Mark 12:17), which is fundamental to Christian thought as evidenced by the separate development of canon and civil law, has no parallel in Islam.[59]

Accordingly, what is uppermost in the mind of Averroes is not a creed or a set of dogmas, but an all-comprehensive social order founded on the revealed law of God to the Prophet Muhammad. This is so in his Fasl al-maqal as in his commentary on Plato's Republic, where he again establishes that philosophy is not opposed to religion, but has the same purpose:

> The only way to know what it is that God wills ... is through prophecy. If you investigate the laws, this knowledge is divided into abstract knowledge alone -- such as our religious law commands regarding the perception of God -- and into practice, such as the ethical virtues it enjoins. Its intention as regards this purpose is identically the same as that of philosophy in respect of class and purpose.[60]

In the commentary on Plato's Republic, Averroes defends the view that the Islamic state is the ideal polity. For him it is the highest expression of Islamic civilization, just as the republic, the Greek polity, is the political ideal of Greek civilization. Although both are based on law, the Islamic state, based on revealed law, is superior to the Greek polity based on nomos, as revelation is superior to myth. Averroes recognizes the sovereignty of the revealed law by adapting to the requirements of Islam Plato's demand that the philosopher must have the right beliefs and convictions. That is, he makes the revealed law the Islamic equivalent to Plato's constitution of the ideal state. He then assigns to the philosopher the most important political function in Islam by making him the best qualified to interpret this law, on the ground that he alone can penetrate its meaning through demonstrative reasoning.[61]

Yet while Averroes, like Plato,[62] thinks that the majority of men are amenable to persuasion only, he insists, as he does in the Fasl al-maqal, that the revealed law "contains the whole truth in a way that is accessible to all three classes of men." The law of Plato, "though laid down for the whole state, was designed to enable only the philosophers to reach the highest perfection."[63] For Averroes, philosophers in the Islamic state must accept the same truth as other men to reach the goal of happiness in this world and the next.

In his commentary on Plato's Republic, Averroes acknowledges, in effect, the superiority of revelation to philosophy, since he never questions the truth of the former, whereas he does point out the inadequacy of the latter.

To give another example, Averroes never questions the
Qur'anic conception of death as a sleep from which a man
awakes to a new creation, but he does criticize Plato's
theory of the separated soul. More particularly, Averroes
does reject Plato's theories of the natural immortality of
the soul and of its reward and punishment apart from the
body, arguing that they are the product of "rhetorical or
dialectical argument" based on myths and fables, which "are
of no consequence;" he is very skeptical as to whether
these theories can be proved by demonstrative reasoning.
But another and better reason for rejecting these tales, he
adds in contrast, is the excellence of the revealed law,
which, as we have seen, teaches a monistic conception of
man and exhorts all men to place their total hope in triumphing
over death, not in the nature of the soul, but in the
resurrection of the dead: "However, we see here many men
who hold fast to their statutes and religious laws and at
the same time lack these tales, yet are not inferior to
those who possess these tales."[64] Needless to say, Averroes'
attitude to Plato's theory of immortality is evocative
of Algazali's refutation of the theories of spiritual
immortality propounded by the philosophers in the Islamic
East, as we have seen.

In the Tahafut al-Tahafut, which has existed in
complete Latin translation since 1527, we also have a succinct
expression of Averroes' views on the relation of philosophy
to revelation. In this work, Averroes clearly
states that the philosophers of the revealed religions must
accept the precepts and principles of their particular religion
since they came to man through the prophets. However,
because the revealed law of Islam is the third and
final testament of God to mankind, the philosophers of Islam
accept a more perfect law than their Jewish and Christian
counterparts. We need not be surprised at Averroes'
acknowledgement that truth can be found among Jews and
Christians. It is the teaching of the Qur'an itself[65] and
recalls Paul's noble tribute to the shrines of Athens (Acts
17:23). Indeed, the common tendency of Christians to re-

gard the truth of the Bible as an absolute opposition to the truth of other religions is non-Islamic:

> Further, he is under obligation to choose the best religion of his period, even when they are all equally true for him, and he must believe that the best will be abrogated by the introduction of a still better. Therefore the learned who were instructing the people of Alexandria became Mohammedans when Islam reached them, and the learned in the Roman Empire became Christians when the religion of Jesus was introduced there. And nobody doubts that among the Israelites there were many learned men, and this is apparent from the books which are found among the Israelites and which are attributed to Solomon.[66]

Moreover, since revelation comes from God, the "learned among the philosophers do not permit discussion or disputation about the principles of religion," for the laws of religion are the necessary knowledge of man's conduct before God. Indeed, so important are these principles of law in Islam that Averroes states that he who denies them, even a philosopher, denies his dependence on God, and so strikes at the central doctrine of the Qur'an:

> For whereas every science has its principles, and every student of this science must concede its principles and may not interfere with them by denying them, this is still more obligatory in the practical science of religion, for to walk on the path of the religious virtues is necessary for man's existence, according to them, not in so far as he is a man, but in so far as he has knowledge; and therefore it is necessary for every man to concede the principles of religion and invest with authority the man who lays them down. The denial and discussion of these principles denies human existence, and therefore heretics must be killed.[67]

As in the Fasl al-maqal and the commentary on Plato's Republic, Averroes, like the theologians, once more stresses the teaching of the Qur'an (S. 4:164-166) that the revealed law is superior to philosophy as the final arbiter of truth, since "the knowledge which results from revelation comes only as a perfection of the knowledge of the intellect." Besides, it is through revelation that God gives to man "any knowledge which the weakness of the human mind is unable to grasp."[68]

That is to say, revelation is a mercy bestowed on all men for their salvation, since the inability of man to acquire the knowledge of what he ought to do to fulfill his life is either absolute, that is beyond the abilities of all men, or relative, that is beyond the abilities of some men.[69] For this reason, Averroes says, it is necessary for philosophers to consult the revealed law on every subject on which they philosophize. If their conclusion agrees with revelation, "we arrive at a more perfect knowledge; if, however, reason does not perceive its truth," then philosophers must concede "that human reason cannot attain it, and that only the Holy Law perceives it."[70] There is only one truth.

We have seen Averroes, like Al-Kindi, pay tribute to the philosophers of Greece and admit his indebtedness to them. We now see him explain why the philosophers of Islam are in a superior position to the ancients: they have that knowledge made known to them by God through revelation which surpasses human understanding. Without the benefit of revelation, the ancient philosophers, and so Aristotle, were unable to penetrate any issue which goes beyond reason, such as miracles; "nor did they discuss any of the things which are said to happen after death."[71] Though aware that there are more things in heaven and earth than are expressed in their philosophy, the ancient philosophers confined themselves to what is knowable to reason alone. But the unknowable has been made known, and so ancient philosophy must be brought into harmony with revelation, as is the case with the existence of God, "or beatitude or the the virtues. For the existence of all these cannot be doubted, and the mode of their existence is something divine which human apprehension cannot attain."[72]

There is no denying that Averroes has a high regard for philosophy and for Aristotle, but Averroes does admit the limitations of philosophy in comparison with revelation. As has been stated before,[73] for him philosophy is a demonstrative science which follows the principles of reason alone. Religion, however, takes its origin not in reason alone, but "in inspiration and reason." In fact, Averroes tells us explicitly that "a natural religion based on reason alone must admit that this religion must be less perfect than those which spring from reason and revelation," and that a faith philosophically understood is superior to a blind faith.[74] When he says so, he merely voices the teaching of the Qur'an, as we saw at the beginning of the chapter.

Averroes then states what is by now a familiar theme: philosophers, theologians and the masses have no choice but to acquiesce in matters on which God has legislated. Yet, whereas revelation, concerned with the felicity of all, makes use of demonstrative, dialectical, and rhetorical argumentation, philosophy, concerned with the needs of a few, relies solely on demonstrative reasoning. However, the results arrived at through demonstration are not different in substance from those achieved through dialectical or rhetorical methods, since there is only one truth:

> In short, the religions are, according to the philosophers, obligatory, since they lead towards wisdom in a universal way to all human beings, for philosophy only leads a certain number of intelligent people to the knowledge of happiness, and they therefore have to learn wisdom, whereas religions seek the instruction of the masses generally.[75]

Averroes makes the same point again as we saw him make in his commentary on Plato's *Republic*: what distinguishes a philosopher of Islam from a philosopher of the Greek polity is his acceptance of the identical truth as others within the state:[76] "Since the existence of the learned class is only perfected and its full happiness attained by participation with the class of the masses, the general doctrine is also obligatory for ... this special class."[77] We also know that this is so because the Islamic state is a lay theocracy. That is, it is a political community wedded to a revealed law. Moreover, there was no separation of "Church" and state in medieval Islam as there was in Christianity.

In sum, it is because of the importance of religion for the life of the state that Averroes assigns to the philosopher the responsibility for interpreting the revealed law, since, as a man of demonstration, he is best qualified to do so. In other words, for Averroes the place of the philosopher in the state is most important because his function is most sacred. For this reason, a philosopher's religious formation is not only crucial, but should he despise the law, he would be guilty of committing a heinous act of sacrilege, punishable by the law:

> For it belongs to the necessary excellence of a man of learning that he should not despise the doctrines in which he has been brought up, and that he should explain them in the fairest way, and that he should understand that the aim of these doctrines lies in their universal character, not in their particularity, and that, if he expresses a doubt concerning the religious principles in which he has been brought up, or explains them in a way contradictory to the prophets and turns away from their path, he merits more than any one else that the term unbeliever should be applied to him, and he is liable to the penalty for unbelief in the religion in which he has been brought up.[78]

It is God's promise of a future life which distinguishes divine from human law. Consequently, the Islamic state exists in recognition of the fact that man is created not only to be a citizen of this world, but also is destined to be a citizen in a world-to-come. That is to say, philosophy and revelation are not mutually exclusive in medieval Islam, but are centred on one aim: man and his destiny. It is on this note that Averroes concludes his Tahafut al-Tahafut, as we have seen him do on his Fasl al-maqal and commentary on Plato's Republic:

> In short, the philosophers believe that religious laws are necessary practical arts, the principles of which are taken from natural reason and inspiration.... The philosophers further hold that one must not object ... to any of the general religious principles, ... for instance bliss in the beyond and its possibility; for all religions believe in the acceptance of another existence after death, although they differ in the description of this existence.[79]

The foregoing study of Averroes on reason and revelation now allows us to reach a conclusion concerning a comparison of his views with the prevalent medieval ideas on the subject, more particularly, with those of Aquinas. More importantly, the conclusion that the preceding analysis shows confirms the thesis of Asín y Palacios that the principles of Aquinas for reconciling philosophy with revelation are the same as those of Averroes,[80] in spite of the difference in the meaning of revelation in Christianity and Islam.

Reason and Revelation According to Aquinas

To begin with, Aquinas' attitude to Greek philosophy is identical to that of Averroes,[81] since he too claimed that we should "take account of the opinions of the ancients no matter who they were," and for the same reasons: "First, we shall profit from what is sound in their views. Secondly, we shall be put on our guard against their errors."[82] That is to say, while Aquinas, like Averroes, grants the superiority of revelation to philosophy, he does not think that they are mutually exclusive, but have the same purpose, the happiness and salvation of man. In reply to the objection that it is not permissible to investigate rationally the truths of revelation, he answers that "since the perfection of man consists in his union with God, it is right that man ... strive to attain to divine truths, so that his intellect may delight in contemplation and his intellect in the investigation of things of God."[83] Moreover, Aquinas, like Averroes,[84] openly affirms "that with which the human reason is naturally endowed is clearly most true," and "since only the false is opposed to the true, ... it is impossible that the truth of faith should be opposed to those principles that the human reason knows naturally."[85]

In maintaining the sovereignty of revelation, both Aquinas and Averroes[86] agree that God has revealed to men truths which natural reason can attain not only because the masses are not philosophers, but also because even philosophers need an infallible guide against error to know the truths attainable by reason with a higher degree of certitude.[87] And interestingly enough, Aquinas not only holds with Averroes that revelation is a mercy bestowed on all men for their salvation, but also is of one mind with him that only "those men who cannot see its truth in the light of reason are held in conscience to accept it by simple faith,"[88] and supports the allegorical interpretation of

Scripture.[89] Aquinas even concurs with Averroes[90] that the truth of revelation should be explained to people according to their ability lest the faith of the majority be destroyed by the interpretation of the learned few.[91] Furthermore, as Gilson concedes,[92] both Aquinas and Averroes equate the achievement of human reason alone with the philosophy of Aristotle,[93] and consider his method of demonstrative reasoning a superior criterion of truth than the dialectical arguments of theologians, which are designed to produce opinion and faith, but not certainty.[94] That is, for Aquinas, as for Averroes, philosophers are the best qualified interpreters of revelation.

Though Aquinas and Averroes are thus in agreement on the principles for reconciling reason and revelation, there is, however, one fundamental difference between them, namely, their view on what was the revealed truth concerning man which had to be reconciled with Aristotle. For, on the one hand, as we have seen, though Aquinas accepts the biblical view that man is a unity of body and soul, he maintains that the soul is a substance in its own right, which enters immediately into its reward and punishment apart from the body after death. For Averroes, on the other hand, the soul, as an integral part of man, cannot experience states of happiness or unhappiness apart from the body. Consequently, reward and punishment must wait until the resurrection of the dead. Averroes' reconciliation of Aristotle with the Qur'anic doctrine of man and his destiny will be given in the following two chapters.

CHAPTER III

THE IMMORTALITY OF THE SOUL

Soul and Intellect in the Commentary on the De Anima

In book I of his commentary on the De Anima, Averroes agrees with Aristotle[1] that, if one seeks a general principle of animal life, the question whether there are different kinds of soul or a plurality of parts of one soul must be considered. However, Averroes specifies that if the soul is made up of parts it is difficult to distinguish the intellect from the other parts of the soul:

> And also when he declared that souls are not many according to their subject, but according to their parts, yet the same in subject, it is proper to examine whether we ought to posit a principle for consideration first of the entire soul and then afterwards of its parts, or whether we ought first to consider the parts of the soul, and afterwards the soul as a whole in so far as it is soul. Then he said, and which is very difficult, etc. That is and when we posit it to be many according to its parts, it is difficult for us to distinguish these parts, and to allot differences by which they differ from one another. For in some parts the differences are discernible, and in other parts they are obscure; for example, as between the intellect and the imagination, and between the imagination and sense.[2]

Therefore, when he encounters the view attributed to Anaxagoras[3] that the intellect is distinct from the soul, Averroes, wishing to emphasize the unity of the soul, stresses that the intellect is alone aloof from matter:

> And he said, Anaxagoras, etc. That is, but Anaxagoras seems to say, in so far as it is apparent, that the soul is other than the intellect. But although this is apparent from his discussion, nevertheless he himself asserts that they are of the same nature, that is of the same genus; and by so doing he asserts that the intellect is more worthy to be the foundation of all things and he places it before all things. For he says the intellect is alone simple, unmixed, and pure, that is, free from matter and not mixed with it.[4]

Averroes also gives his support to this latter view, that the intellect is "simple, unmixed, and pure," in his discussion of Aristotle's remark that an old man would see with the clarity of a young man if he had a young man's eyes.[5] For when Averroes observes that it is the activity, not the existence of the soul, which is affected by the decay of the body, just as it is the activity, not the skill, of the artisan which is lost by the deterioration of his tools, he asserts: "since this account is ample with respect to the senses, how much more [cogent] is it in the case of the intellect."[6]

Again, when Aristotle considers whether the soul is divisible because the body is divisible,[7] Averroes says that the soul is one and gives unity to the distinct parts of the body:

> [But] if we assert that the soul is divided essentially through the division of the members in which it exists, and it is self-evident that the soul which is in separate organs is one, what therefore unites the parts of the soul so that it can be said to be one? For no one is able to say that it is the body, since it is more correct to say that the body is one since the soul is one, and not the opposite. And he intended this when he said: <u>for it must be considered to be contrary</u>, etc. That is, for the opinion we hold naturally is contrary to his opinion in this respect, namely that the soul is more worthy to be the cause of the conjoining of the body, and of the unity in number than that the body be the cause of the conjoining of the soul. For everything which exists is not one or continuous through its matter, but through its form.[8]

And having said so, Averroes returns to agree with Aristotle[9] that the intellect is apparently not an attribute of the body. Yet he takes the same opportunity to explain that plurality of parts of the soul results from the distinct powers which complete it, and to emphasize that the principle of unity or continuity of man must be found within the soul:

> [To] assert that some part of it unites with any part of the body and exists in it seems almost impossible, for it seems impossible that the intellect is attributed to any organ of the body. And you ought to know that this doubt does not follow here, except that it is not determined whether the soul is one in so far as it is a subject and many as to its powers (so that the division of the soul into parts would be like that of a fruit into smell, colour and taste), or it is one according to

one common nature and many because that nature has diverse powers (so that the division of the soul into its parts would be like that of the division of a genus into its species). Because the previously mentioned doubt happens according to this analysis; for when we assert that it is one according to subject alone, this does not happen; for the subject of its parts will be one only, and certain of these parts will be the subject of certain other parts.[10]

To sum up: Averroes' commentary on book I of the De Anima reflects the matter treated in Aristotle's review of the opinions of his predecessors. Yet already we notice that, while Averroes is concerned with affirming that a very close relationship exists between body and soul, he is equally concerned with isolating the intellect from the soul. Does this not indicate that Averroes is conscious of the problem of reason and revelation? His insistence that the soul properly belongs to a body is, of course, in accordance with the Qur'an's monistic conception of man. When he continually favours the view that the intellect is not a part of the soul, does he not show his concern with safeguarding the belief that the future of man lies not in the nature of his soul, but totally in the resurrection of the dead?

We have seen that it is not until book II of the De Anima that Aristotle tries to formulate his own definition of the soul. We must therefore follow Averroes as he in turn tries to clarify the ambiguity of Aristotle concerning soul and intellect with the aid of revelation.

Commenting on Aristotle's statement that "the soul must be a substance in the sense of the form of a natural body,"[11] Averroes claims that the soul is not a body, nor an accident of a body, but exists in a body as the form of a composite substance:

> But that it is not a substance in the sense of a body is stated in the second figure [of a syllogism] through those two aforesaid propositions, namely that the soul is in a subject, and the body is not in a subject. Indeed since it is a substance in the sense of a form, it is clear from this that it is a substance in a subject. For a form is properly this, namely, a substance in a subject. And it differs from an accident, since an accident is not part of the composite substance under consideration, but

form is part of this composite substance. And also we say equivocally that form is in a subject, and accident is in a subject. For the subject of an accident is a body composed of matter and form; and it is something existing in act and has no need of an accident to exist in it; but the subject of a form does not have actual existence, in so far as it is a subject, except through the form, and has need of the form to exist in act; and this applies especially to the ultimate subject which is not stripped of form completely.[12]

And when Aristotle says that "the soul is the first grade of actuality of a natural body,"[13] Averroes again insists on the essential correlativity of body and soul:

When he declared that the soul is a substance according to form, and forms are perfections of things having forms, and that they are in two ways, he began to demonstrate that perfection is in the definition of the soul as a genus. And he said: <u>And this substance is perfection</u>, etc. That is, substance in so far as it is a form is the perfection of a body having a form, and as it has already been declared that the soul is a form, it is necessary that the soul should be the perfection of such a body, that is the perfection of a natural body having life in potency in so far as it is perfected through the soul.[14]

On this foundation, Averroes reopens the question of the relationship of the intellect to the soul when Aristotle offers his general definition of the soul. Aristotle's definition is: "If, then, we have to give a general formula applicable to all kinds of soul, we must describe it as the first grade of actuality of a natural organized body."[15] On which Averroes remarks:

He expresses this opinion in the form of a doubt, when he says: <u>If therefore it must be said</u>, by excusing himself from any question which may arise from parts of this definition. For we speak of the perfection of the rational soul and of other powers of the soul in an almost purely equivocal way, as we shall see afterwards. One could therefore hesitate and say that the soul does not have a universal definition. And for that reason he says: <u>If therefore</u>, etc., as if to say, if therefore the possibility of finding a universal definition embracing all parts of the soul should be given to us, this would be it.[16]

Here, attentive to the conditional clause which prefaces the definition, Averroes notes that Aristotle leaves the question as to whether or not the intellect is a power of the soul unanswered. Therefore, speaking in his own name, he asserts that since the soul is the first perfection of the body, to speak of the perfection of the rational power and of the other powers of the soul involves some equivocation. And this observation again shows that Averroes is aware that there is a disparity between soul and intellect. Moreover, he immediately goes on to repeat once more that body and soul are two aspects of one reality:

> And since it was stated that the soul is the first perfection of a natural body, and that an animated body has the being it has because of the fact that it has a soul, without a doubt body and soul, although they are two, become the same reality, just as this fact cannot be doubted in the case of wax and iron with a figure that exists in them, and generally, in matter of any kind, and in the thing that exists in that matter. For although the terms <u>one</u> and <u>being</u> are used in very many ways, nevertheless, they are more appropriately applied to the form, the first perfection in all these things, than to that which is the composite of matter and form.[17]

Averroes now discusses Aristotle's suggestion that a part of the soul may not be the actuality of the body.[18] Does Aristotle's suggestion imply that he is using the word "soul" equivocally, or is he contradicting his own definition that the soul is the form of a body? As far as is known, Aristotle does not clarify the point elsewhere in the <u>De Anima</u>, and so it remains a matter for interpretation by scholars, both Christian and Muslim. It may be helpful to remind ourselves here once again that according to the Qur'an the soul can have no operation apart from the body after death. If, therefore, Averroes is to succeed in harmonizing philosophy with revelation, this much is certain: he cannot compromise the Qur'anic view of death by granting to the soul operations after death.

Averroes understands the problem as follows:

> Having accepted in the universal definition of the soul that it is the perfection of a natural body, he begins to consider the question of separatedness by asking to what extent it is included in the definition. And he says: <u>now since the soul</u>, ctc. That is, since it is obvious from this that what is said in the definition of the soul is unclear, he begins to consider the possibility as to whether the soul is separated from the body either according to

The Immortality of the Soul

> all its parts or through some part of it, if it is innately divisible. For it is clear that some powers of the soul are perfections of parts of the body in so far as they are natural forms perfected by matter. But such a power cannot be separated from that through which it is perfected.[19]

That is to say: Averroes recognizes that there is a question of separatedness to be considered in the light of Aristotle's general definition of the soul. For Aristotle, on the one hand, all parts of the soul -- if it has parts -- cannot be separated from the body. On the other hand, if some part of the soul is separated from the body, the other parts cannot be separated from the body, since they are dependent on matter for their perfection.

Averroes gives two reasons why "it is possible for some one to say" that a part of the soul can be separated from the body:

> That is, but this is not clear in all parts of the soul, since it is possible for some one to say that a certain part of it is not a perfection of any organ of the body, or to say, granting that it is a perfection, nevertheless, certain perfections can be separated, like the perfection of a ship through the pilot. For these two reasons, therefore, it does not seem clear from this definition that all parts of the soul cannot be separated.[20]

It is important to note here that Averroes does not admit either that a certain part of the soul is not the perfection of a body, or that a part of the soul can be the perfection of a body like a sailor in a ship. He merely observes that "it is possible for some one to say" so. In other words, within the perspective of the Qur'an's monistic conception of man, his observation may be interpreted to be the systematic clarification of his own position as an Aristotelian philosopher of Islam. At any rate, he notes that "Alexander says from this definition, it is clear that all parts of the soul are not separated."[21] However, he postpones discussing Alexander's own theory according to which, as we know,[22] the material intellect is a part of the soul. As he puts it, "we shall speak of this when we consider the rational power."[23]

In deciding to do so, Averroes is following Aristotle's next suggestion that the intellect does not seem to be a part of the soul, but a distinct species of soul.[24] And once again Averroes clearly states his own understanding of the word "soul":

> After he says that an investigation must be made with respect to each of these principles to see whether it is a soul or not, and he begins to establish the identity of the power which does not seem to be a soul, but concerning it, it is rather obvious that it is not a soul. And he says: <u>But the intellect and the speculative power</u>, etc. That is, so far it has not been stated whether the intellect in act and the power which is perfected by the intellect in act is a soul or not, as has been declared in the case of the other principles, since that power does not seem to use a corporeal instrument in its activity as the other powers of the soul do.[25]

Averroes is here quite explicit in affirming that since the intellect is not dependent on a body for its activity, "it is rather obvious that it is not a soul." This clarification of the meaning of soul and intellect is consonant with the teaching of the Qur'an that a reciprocal relation always exists between body and soul. In fact, it is because it is the view of the Qur'an that Averroes can state categorically that the use of a corporeal instrument is the decisive factor in determining whether a particular power should be called "soul" or not. However, his comment also reveals that he is willing to use the word "soul" equivocally as a vague term for the intellect.

Having declared his position, Averroes now elucidates Aristotle's doubt as to whether the intellect is a power of the soul:

> And therefore it is not clear from the aforesaid definition whether [the intellect] is a perfection or not. For in every instance in which it is revealed or will be revealed that a power is perfected in the way that forms are perfected by their matter, it is by necessity a soul. And when he declares that this point is obscure in the case of the intellect, he begins to show which opinion of two contradictory opinions under investigation is clearer in the judgment of men and according to what is evident, until this issue is resolved demonstratively later on.[26]

Averroes attributes Aristotle's failure to give an unqualified definition of the soul to his reluctance to say that the intellect is not a "soul" strictly speaking:

The Immortality of the Soul

> But, however, it is better to say, and it seems to be more evident after investigation, that [the intellect] is another kind of soul, and if it is designated soul, it is so by way of equivocation. And if such is the nature of the intellect, then it is necessary that it alone, of all the powers of the soul, can be separated from the body, just as the eternal is separated, and is not tainted through the corruption [of the body]. And this will be whenever it is not conjoined with it and whenever it is conjoined with it.[27]

When Averroes refers in this passage to the intellect as a power of the soul, saying, "if such is the nature of the intellect, then it is necessary that it alone, of all the powers of the soul, can be separated from the body," we must therefore understand that he is not using the word "soul" according to strict definition, but equivocally. This is made evident by the fact that in the very quotation he acknowledges that body and soul are reciprocally related. Furthermore, when Averroes here emphasizes Aristotle's distinction between an intellect that is eternal and man who is mortal, does he not in effect deny that man is in complete control of his actions and affirm that he is dependent on God for his activity? Indeed, one may say that it is Averroes' concern with the Qur'an's conception of man and his relationship to God which in part furnishes the reason why the intellect is "conjoined" (<u>copulatur</u>) to man. Moreover, the theory of conjunction is of great importance for understanding how man's beatitude in this life is related to a system of reward and punishment in the next, as we shall see in the next chapter.

In sum: In book II of the <u>De Anima</u>, Aristotle has two lines of thought in conflict. After defining the soul as the form of a natural body, Aristotle asks us to entertain the possibility that a part of the soul may not be the perfection of a body. We have seen that it is Aristotle's concern with the intellect which prompts this suggestion, a suggestion which creates an ambiguity as to whether or not the intellect is a part of the soul. Averroes solves the problem in harmony with revelation by insisting that any power of the soul must be perfected by matter. That is, he interprets the intellect to be a power <u>sui generis</u> which is, strictly speaking, not a part of the soul. Thus, Averroes' solution is consistent with the monistic conception of man found in Aristotle's own philosophy and in the Qur'an. Furthermore, by making soul and intellect distinct, Averroes is in accord with Aristotle's suggestion that the intellect is external to man and comes to him "from the outside,"[28] and with the Qur'anic doctrine of the creaturehood of man.

But if the intellect is distinct from the soul, what are its characteristics? In book III of the De Anima, as we recall, Aristotle establishes the attributes of the intellect as "separable, impassible, and unmixed" in a comparison with sense perception.[29] We must, therefore, continue to follow Averroes to determine how he interprets these attributes. Our examination will show that Averroes is consistent in his position that the intellect is not a part of the soul.

Averroes begins his exposition of the distinctive character of the intellect as follows: "[We] must first investigate the intellectual activity to determine whether it is an action or a reception; for we first know the activities of the soul before we know its substance."[30] He proceeds, like Aristotle, to fix the characteristics of the intellect by contrasting it with sense.

First, he considers the alternative ways in which the intellect may be said to be passive:

> [And] if it is passive, whether it is passive on account of the fact that it is material in some way and mixed with the body, that is, a power in a body, just as sense is passive, or whether it is in no way passive, since it is in no way material or mixed with the body, but it has only that notion of passive which is receptivity.[31]

Averroes now states that though intellection is like sensation the passivity of the intellect is not the same as the passivity of sense:

> [It] must be one of the two alternatives: either it undergoes some change and modification from the object of knowledge like the change a sense undergoes from the object of sense, since the perfection of a sense is [to be] a power in a body, or it does not undergo change similar to the change and modification of the senses from the object of sense, because the first perfection of the intellect is not

[to be] a power in a body; indeed, it is in no way affected by such change. And he intended this when he said: or something similar. That is, it does not suffer a modification identical to the modification of a sense; that is to say, it does not undergo a change a sense undergoes, but it is only similar to sense with respect to the notion of receptivity, since it is not a power in a body.³²

In other words, Averroes says that a sense undergoes change appropriate to a power in a body. But since the intellect is not the perfection of a body, it cannot undergo this type of change. Consequently, the only similarity between intellect and sense with respect to passivity is the notion of reception.

Averroes explains further why the intellect is not passive in the same way as sense is passive:

And after he says that it is necessary to investigate this activity of formation through the intellect to see whether it is passive or active, he begins to say what he wishes to make known, namely that it is a passive power in some sense, and that it is not changeable, since it is neither a body nor a power in a body. And he says: It is proper to say that it is not passive, etc. That is, after close investigation, it will become clear that that part of the soul through which formation comes about is a power unchangeable by the form which it comprehends, but it does not participate in the notion of passion, except in this respect only, that it receives the form which it comprehends, and because it is in potency that which it comprehends, like a sentient being, not because it is actually some individual thing, either a body or a power in a body, like a sentient being.³³

Evidently, it is because Averroes has already clarified the ambiguity between soul and intellect with the help of revelation that he is able to insist on the difference between the passivity of the intellect and sense: though the intellect is a passive power in some sense, since it is not a power in a body, it is "not changeable." That is to say, the intellect is passive only because, like sense, it is receptive of forms. Yet it has no nature of its own but the capacity to become that which it understands. Indeed, it is none of its objects until it knows them. To state it another way, though the intellect receives intelligible forms in a manner analogous to the reception of sensible forms by the faculty of sense, since the intellect is not a part of the soul, it is rightly described by Aristotle as "impassible."

Averroes now comments on Aristotle's second attribute of the intellect, "unmixed":

> That is, it is necessary that it be not mixed, in order that it may understand all things and receive them. For if it were mixed, then it would be either a body or a power within a body, and if it were one of these, it would have a form proper to itself, which form would prevent it from receiving some foreign form.³⁴

Here Averroes explains that since every thing is a possible object of thought, it is necessary that the intellect be free from all sensible forms in order to know.

For Averroes, any discussion of the passivity of the intellect must acknowledge that it is free from matter and unalterable. It is by insisting on this point that he remains in harmony with the Qur'anic conception of man and his relationship to God, and with the Aristotelian view that the intellect is not a human power. So important is the distinction between soul and intellect to Averroes that he again explains why the intellect which receives forms is "impassible" and "unmixed":

> That the substance which receives these forms can not be a body or a power in a body, becomes clear from the propositions of which Aristotle makes use in this discussion. One of these is that this substance [the material intellect] receives all material forms, and this is [something well] known about this intellect. The other is that everything which receives something else must necessarily be devoid of the nature of that which it receives and that its essence (<u>substantiam</u>) is not the same in species as the essence (<u>substantiam</u>) of that which it receives. For, if that which receives is of the same nature as that which is received, then something would receive itself and that which moves would be the same as that which is moved.³⁵

For the same reason, he stresses the consequences of the distinction:

> From these two propositions it follows that the substance which is called the material intellect does not have any of the material forms in its nature. And since the material forms are either a body or forms in a body, it is evident that the substance which is called the material intellect is not a body or a form in a body. For this reason it is not mixed with matter in any way at all.³⁶

Averroes now concludes that since the intellect is a substance which is "impassible" and "unmixed," it is also "separable" from the body:

> And you should know that what he states is necessarily [so], [namely] that, since it [the material intellect] is a substance, and since it receives the forms of material things or material [forms], it does not have in itself a material form, that is [it is not] composed of matter and form. Nor is it one of the material forms, for the material forms are not separable [from bodies].[37]

Averroes even explains that though the passive power of intellect is called material in analogy with prime matter, it is not in any way material:

> Since this is the definition of the material intellect, it is clear that it differs in respect to itself from prime matter in that it is in potentiality all the concepts (_intentiones_) of the universal material forms, while _prime matter_ is in potentiality all these sensible forms, not [as] knowing and comprehending. And the reason why this nature, that is, the material intellect, distinguishes and knows, while prime matter does not distinguish or know, is that prime matter receives differentiated, that is, individual and particular forms, while [the material intellect] receives universal forms. And from this it is clear that this nature, [that is, the material intellect] is not some individual thing, either a body or a power in a body.[38]

To underscore his interpretation of the intellect as "separable, impassible, and unmixed" in comparison with the powers of sense, Averroes repeats the decisive criterion for determining whether or not the intellect is a power of the human soul: whether it has a corporeal instrument. Since there cannot be a corporeal instrument for the intellect, the conclusion is clearly that the intellect is not a power of the human soul:

> Then he gave a second reason over and above this. And he says: <u>For if it were mixed</u>, etc. That is, for if it were a power in a body, then it would be some disposition and some corporeal quality; and if it should have a quality, then that quality would be attributed to what is hot or cold (namely to an aggregate in that which is an aggregate), or that quality would exist in an aggregate in so far as it is added to an aggregate, just as in the case of a sensible soul and [things] similar to it, and so it would have a corporeal organ.[39]

So far we have seen that Averroes is in harmony with

the Qur'an's monistic view of man, according to which there is an essential reciprocal relation between soul and body. Moreover, by making soul and intellect distinct, Averroes ensures that the future life is consistent with revelation, since it cannot be interpreted as the spiritual survival of the soul as an intellectual substance, as taught by Plato and his followers. If man is to triumph over death, his only hope is in God and His promise of the resurrection. In other words, by excluding the intellect from the soul, Averroes in fact affirms that man's activity is dependent on the will of God, which is the principal doctrine of the Qur'an.

With the distinction between soul and intellect clearly established in harmony with revelation, Averroes now returns to consider Alexander's theory that the material intellect is a power of the soul. He does so in connection with his exposition of the following statement of Aristotle: "What it thinks must be in it just as characters may be said to be on a writing-tablet on which as yet nothing actually stands written: this is exactly what happens with mind."[40] Averroes' comment is:

> That is, and this is to be understood when we speak of this universal concept; namely, concerning passivity which is in the intellect, because it is merely reception without change, just as the reception of a picture in a tablet. For just as the tablet is not affected by the picture, neither does change occur in it from this, but the only thing found in it belonging to the notion of passivity is that it is perfected by the picture after it was painted potentially; this is the disposition of the material intellect.[41]

That is to say, the material intellect is like the aptitude of a tablet-without-a-picture which is potentially able to receive all pictures. But it is not like the tablet itself, since the tablet is material. In other words, the material intellect is the aptitude-of-the-intellect for receiving universal intelligibles. And since it is potentially all things but nothing in act, the material intellect is "separable, impassible, and unmixed."

As is to be expected, Averroes emphatically rejects Alexander's theory of the soul:

> Moreover, Alexander takes a stand on this last statement and says that it is more befitting natural

things, namely the concluding statement that the material intellect is a generated power, and so we judge from it that he is of the opinion that it is among the powers of the soul, that preparations are made in the body through themselves by commingling and combination. And he says that this is not unthinkable, namely that from a commingling of the elements should come such a noble and wonderful thing, although it is removed from the substance of the elements on account of the greatest mixture.[42]

In Averroes' judgment, Alexander's view makes the material intellect a preparedness or aptitude of the body. But the material intellect cannot be a power of the body. This is the nature of the soul.

Since, for Averroes, there can be a harmony between reason and revelation only if the immateriality of the intellect is sharply distinguished from the materiality of the soul, he now argues with great subtlety that, even on philosophical grounds, Alexander's interpretation of Aristotle is unsound. His argumentation is as follows: To discuss a preparedness or aptitude without reference to a subject is nonsensical. The aptitude of the material intellect is not a mere aptitude or preparedness, but the aptitude-of-the-intellect. Therefore, "to say that the material intellect is similar to the preparedness which is in the tablet, not to the tablet in so far as it is prepared ... is false." The reason is that "preparedness is a mere privation and does not have any nature of its own but the nature of its subject." Furthermore, if Aristotle intended to speak of the nature of preparedness only, then his remarks do not apply to the intellect, which is incredible, since every preparedness must have reference to the thing to be prepared. In fact, in order to understand the nature of preparedness, it is necessary to know the nature of the thing to be prepared. Yet Alexander thinks that he can describe the preparedness proper to the intellect without knowing the nature of the intellect, which is impossible. With great rancour Averroes thunders against Alexander: "O Alexander! do you think that Aristotle intended to present us with the nature of a preparedness only, not the nature of the thing prepared ...? I am ashamed of this discourse and this strange exposition.[43]

Averroes is evidently so determined to achieve a harmony of reason and revelation that he again emphasizes that since the material intellect is not a body, nor a power in a body, neither can it be the forms of the imagination. So confident is he that the nature of the soul is different from the nature of the intellect that, in spite of his great admiration for his master, he says: "Even if this were not the opinion of Aristotle, we would still have to accept it as the true opinion."[44]

It is very important for us to recognize that Averroes is uncompromising in his adherence to the Qur'anic doctrine that the soul is an integral part of man; but in the absence of an elaborate doctrine of the intellect in the Qur'an, he feels free to accommodate himself to any reasonable hypothesis. This is quite clear from his own admission that his treatment of the intellect may be incomplete. In fact, he even begs other philosophers to offer their suggestions for its improvement:

> All these things being as they are, it seems to me proper to write down what appears to me [to be correct] concerning this subject. And if that which appears to me [to be correct] will not be complete, let it be the starting point for something which can be completed. Now, I beg those brethren who see what has been written, that they may write down their questions and perhaps in this way that which is true about this subject will be discovered, if I should not have discovered it. But should I have discovered [what is true], as I think I have, then [this truth] will become clear through these questions. For truth, as Aristotle says, agrees with itself and bears witness to itself in every way.[45]

When, therefore, Averroes shows emotion in defending his interpretation of the soul against Alexander, this acknowledgment surely indicates that it is because he has certain knowledge of it from a source other than philosophy, that is, from revelation. For indeed, this passage shows Averroes to be as unshaken in his belief in the unity of truth in the commentary on the <u>De Anima</u> as in his works on reason and revelation which we have already examined.[46] Not surprisingly, elsewhere in the commentary he again humbly admits that his theory of the intellect is subject to correction: "Now this appeared to me in this sought-for manner. And if later on more appears to us, we will write."[47]

The Immortality of the Soul 99

Thus, Averroes is adamant in his assertion that soul and body are two aspects of one reality. And fastidiously supporting this Qur'anic doctrine, he remains faithful to the conception that the intellect is not a power of the soul, a conception, as we have repeatedly seen, compatible with Aristotle and revelation. But the problem then emerges: if there is unity of knowledge and the intellect is not a power of the soul, it would seem to follow that man has no knowledge. Yet, it is obvious that man has knowledge, and that the knowledge of every man is different. Let us now consider how Averroes meets this challenge and finds it possible to explain how knowledge exists in man and in the intellect.

The intellect must be one or many. This much is clear. In finding a solution, Averroes ponders the problem of the first alternative:

> And there happen to be many other impossibilities to this position. Since if the first perfection were the same in all men and was not numbered according to their enumeration, it would happen that when I acquire something intelligible, you, too, would acquire the same [intelligible], and when I forget something intelligible, you also would [forget it]. And many other impossible things follow from this position.[48]

The unicity of the intellect shows that there is a unity of knowledge, but it does not account for the diversity of knowledge among men.

Averroes now considers the second alternative, knowing full well that according to the common Islamic opinion it is contrary to revelation, since granting to every man his own agent intellect would make him co-creator with God, a conception incompatible with the Qur'an's insistence on the creaturehood of man. However, he finds that the proposition that each man has his own intellect is even philosophically indefensible:

> And if we were to assert that the intellect is many, it would follow that something known by me and by you is one in respect to species and two in respect to individual, and thus something known would possess something else known and this would go on to infinity. Thus it would be impossible that a student learns from a teacher if the knowledge which exists in the teacher is not a force genera-

ting and producing the knowledge which is in the student, in the same manner as one fire produces another fire alike to it in species, which is absurd.⁴⁹

Averroes then tries another approach to the problem. There is unity of knowledge because the intellect is one. There is diversity of knowledge among men because men are many. It cannot be denied that knowledge exists in the intellect or in men. But why is each man's knowledge different? Since truth is one, philosophy and revelation cannot be in conflict. On what point are Aristotle and the Qur'an in agreement? Matter is, of course, the principle of individuation. Averroes has found his solution: there are two subjects in knowledge:

> But if we assert that something known by me and by you is many in respect to that object (in subiecto) according to which it is true, that is in respect to the imaginative forms, and one in respect to the subject through which it is an existing intellect (and this is the material intellect), these questions are resolved completely.⁵⁰

Each man's knowledge is different because intelligibles are true in respect to the imaginative forms of his soul which are individuated by matter; but nevertheless knowledge is one because intelligibles exist in the material intellect. Soul and intellect are distinct. Reason and revelation are in harmony.

We still ask: Is man a mere animal or is he rational? Averroes assures us that, although soul and intellect are distinct, soul is in some sense rational. Whereas the intellect is "unmixed" and can judge infinite things not acquired from sense, the powers of the soul are "mixed individual powers" capable of judging only individual finite intentions:

> We can know that the material intellect must not be mixed from judgment and from our understanding of it. For because through it we judge things infinite in number in a universal proposition, and it is manifest that the judging powers of the soul, that is, its mixed individual powers, judge only finite intentions, it happens contrariwise that that which does not judge finite intentions must necessarily not be a mixed power of the soul. And when we have joined to this that the material intellect judges infinite things and not things ac-

quired from sense, and that it does not judge finite intentions, it will come about that it is not a mixed power.⁵¹

Averroes now specifies three powers of man's rational soul recognized by Aristotle and describes their function:

> There are three powers [in man], whose being was declared in the De Sensu et Sensato, that is, the imaginative, and the cogitative, and the memorative. For these three powers are in man to present the form of an imagined thing, when sensation is lacking. And so it was said there, that when these three powers help each other, they will represent an individual thing as it is in its own being, even though we do not sense it.⁵²

These powers can represent an absent sense object to the intellect:

> Now, the imaginative and the cogitative and the memorative powers are only in the place of sensation, and so they are necessary only in the absence of the sensible object, and they will all help each other to represent the image of a sensible thing, so that the separated rational power may look at it, and extract from it the universal intention and then receive it, that is, comprehend it.⁵³

The cogitative power is the most important of these powers, since it is "a kind of reason." It is so important that, together with imagination, Aristotle refers to it as an intellect. However, Averroes insists that, as the reason proper to man, it is merely a "passible intellect" and must be distinguished from intellect strictly speaking, which is immaterial and "impassible," as we have seen:

> And he [Aristotle] means here by the term "passible intellect" the forms of the imagination in so far as the cogitative power proper to man acts on them. For this power is a kind of reason, and its action is nothing more than to put the intention of a form of imagination together with its individual which is in the memorative power, or to distinguish the one from the other in the formative power and in the imagination. And it is evident that the intellect which is called "material" receives the imagined intentions after such distinction.⁵⁴

In its rational activity, the cogitative power is able to be creative: "It is possible that a man can cogitate about something to such an extent that from this he discovers some individual which he has not sensed before; but he did sense a similar one, yet not this one."⁵⁵

It is through the cogitative power that man is different from other animals, "for other animals do not have cogitation, but in place of cogitation they have imagination."[56] Indeed, it is because man alone of all animals has a cogitative power that he can make choices and form opinions:

> [Aristotle says] that "imagination is in other animals, but cogitation in rational ones." For to choose to perform this imagined thing and not that, belongs to the action of cogitation and not to the action of imagination. For that which judges that this imagined object is more lovable than that must necessarily be the same power which numbers [individualizes] the images and in the case of some judges they are more pleasing.... Likewise, cogitation numbers images, and compares them with each other, until it can be affected by the imagination of one of them. And this is the reason why the rational animal has opinion; for opinion is a consent which rises from cogitation.[57]

Nevertheless, the cogitative power, as a power of sense, cannot know things in their universality, but is restricted to knowing the individual forms of the imagination:

> [Aristotle] did not intend that the senses comprehend the essence of things, as some have thought, for this is the work of another power which is called intellect. He intended to say that the senses, together with the comprehension of their proper sensibles, comprehend the individual intentions divided into genera and species.... This individual intention is the one which the cogitative power distinguishes from the imagined form, and strips it from all these common and proper sensibles which are joined to it, and places it in the memorative. And this is the same form that the imaginative comprehends, but the imaginative comprehends it joined to the sensibles, though its comprehension is more spiritual.[58]

The attribution of the powers of man's rational soul to different parts of the brain by Aristotle and others is in keeping with the view that the reason proper to man is distinct from that of the intellect:

> It is said that the imaginative power is in the front of the brain, and the cogitative in the middle, and the memorative in the rear. And this was not only said by the physicians, but also in <u>De Sensu et Sensato</u>.... For the cogitative power is of the genus of powers existing in the body. And Aristotle openly said this in that book, when he

posited the individual distinct powers in four
orders. In the first place the common sense, then
the imaginative power, then the cogitative, and
then the memorative.... Although therefore man
properly has a cogitative power, that does not
make this power to be the rational distinctive
power; a rational power deals with universal representations, not singulars.[59]

The intellect has need of the rational powers of the soul, for "without the cogitative power and the power of the imagination, the material intellect would understand nothing."[60] Yet the intellect differs from man's rational soul as the "impassible" from the "passible":

And so we must not object to the argument [about
the separation of the intellect] that there is a
change in the intellect on account of the change
in the imaginative and cogitative power particularly; for this latter is the way in which we think
that weariness is found in the intellect. It is
there only accidentally. For the cogitative power
is of the genus of sensible powers.[61]

The cogitative power is dependent on the body for its operation. Obviously, it can have no activity after death:

The cogitative power is not the material intellect
... but it is a particular material power.... One
must not say that it composes singular intelligibles.... For there is no cogitation, except in
distinguishing the individuals of those intelligibles, and presenting them in act, as if they were
present to sense. And so, when such individuals
are present to sense, then cogitation ceases, and
the action of the intellect in them remains. And
from this it is clear that the action of the intellect is different from that of the cogitative power
which Aristotle calls the "passible intellect," and
which he said was generable and corruptible ...
since it has a limited instrument, that is, the
middle ventricle of the brain; and man is not generable and corruptible except through this power.[62]

It is time to recall here that though Aristotle says that the soul is the form of man's mortal body and that the intellect is external to man he regards the life of reason as man's highest activity.[63] When Averroes maintains that the cogitative power is in some sense rational, he does not go against Aristotle's position, since he insists that it is a bodily power in contrast to the intellect, which is immaterial. Moreover, through his insistence that the rational powers of the soul are dependent on the body for their activity, Averroes remains in accord with the Qur'an's monistic view of man and its teaching on the totality of death. Without the resurrection, man has no hope of "eternal life." Soul and intellect are distinct. Reason and revelation are in harmony. Is there any connection between man's unique rational soul and a system of reward and punishment? This question will be answered in the next chapter, after we have a better understanding of Averroes' thought on the future life.

Soul and Intellect in the Tahafut al-Tahafut

In the Tahafut al-Tahafut, Averroes speaks not as the Commentator of Aristotle, but in his own name as a philosopher of Islam. Let us therefore leave the commentary on the De Anima and turn to this work, in which we shall show that Averroes' exposition of soul and intellect is consistent with that found in his commentary. Moreover, we shall find here his explicit explanation of how the Aristotelian doctrine of man is to be harmonized with the Qur'anic conception of the afterlife.

In the Tahafut al-Tahafut, Averroes reiterates that the intellect is not a rational power of the soul like the imaginative, cogitative, and memorative powers. And again he uses the same criterion as in the commentary on the De Anima for making this judgment -- "there is no particular organ for the intellect":

> When it is conceded that the intellect is not related to one of man's organs -- and this has already been proved, since it is not self-evident -- it follows that its substratum is not a body, and that our assertion that man knows is not analogous to our assertion that he sees. For since it is self-evident that he sees through a particular organ, it is clear that when we refer sight to man absolutely, the expression is allowed according to the custom of the Arabs and other people. And since there is no particular organ for the intellect, it is clear that when we say of him that he knows, this does not mean that a part of him knows. However, how he knows is not clear by itself, for it does not appear that there is an organ or a special place in an organ which possesses this special faculty, as in the case with the imaginative faculty and the cogitative and the memorative faculties,

The Immortality of the Soul

the localization of which in parts of the brain is known.⁶⁴

Moreover, the unity of knowledge demands that the intellect be one and eternal. The intellect is therefore "conjoined" to man and distinct from the soul:

> The meaning of the philosophical theory he relates is that the intellect apprehends, in relation to the individuals which have a common species, a single entity, in which they participate and which is the quiddity of this species without this entity's being divided into the things in which the individuals qua individuals are divided, like space and position and the matters through which they receive their plurality. This entity must be ingenerable and incorruptible and is not destroyed by the disappearance of one of the individuals in which it exists, and the sciences therefore are eternal and not corruptible except by accident, that is to say by their connexion with Zaid and Amr; that is, only through this connexion are they corruptible, and not in themselves, since if they were transitory in themselves this connexion would exist in their essence and they could not constitute an identity.⁶⁵

To express it another way, the intellect cannot be a rational power of the soul, since there is only one intellect for all men, but as many souls as there are men:

> And the philosophers say that, if this is established for the intellect and the intellect is in the soul, it is necessary that the soul should not be divisible in the way in which individuals are divisible, and the soul in Amr and in Zaid should be one single entity. And this proof is strong in the case of the intellect, because in the intellect there is no individuality whatever; the soul, however, although it is free from the matters through which the individuals receive their plurality, is said by the most famous philosophers not to abandon the nature of the individual, although it is an apprehending entity.⁶⁶

In other words, there are two subjects in knowledge, man and intellect, but whereas there is a diversity of knowledge among men, there is a unity of knowledge in the intellect.

> As for Ghazali's objection, it amounts to saying that the intellect is something individual and that universality is an accident of it, and therefore Ghazali compares the way in which the intellect observes a common feature in individuals to the way in which the senses perceive the same thing many times, since for Ghazali the intelligible is a unity, but not something universal, and

> for him the animality of Zaid is numerically identical with the animality which he observes in Khalid. And this is false, and if it were true, there would be no difference between sense-perception and the apprehension of the intellect.[67]

With systematic thoroughness, Averroes continues to elaborate the distinction between soul and intellect. He now says that every attribute of a body is divisible in one of two ways. It may be divisible quantitatively, as in the case of colour:

> First it may be meant that the definition of every part of this attribute which inheres in the particular body is identical with the definition of the whole: for instance the white inhering in the white body, for every part of whiteness which inheres in the individual body has one and the same definition as the whole of whiteness in the body.[68]

Or, it may be divisible in respect to intensity, as in the case of vision:

> Secondly, it may be meant that the attribute is attached to the body without a specific shape, and this attribute again is divided through the division of the body not in such a way that the intension of the definition of the whole is identical with the intension of the definition of every part -- for instance, the faculty of sight which exists in one who sees -- but in such a way that it is subject to a difference in intensity to the greater and lesser receptivity of the substratum, and therefore the power of sight in stronger in the healthy and the young than in the sick and the old.[69]

That which is not divisible in either way is not an attribute of a body:

> When this premise is assumed in this way, namely by holding that everything which is divisible in either of these two classes has a body as its substratum, it is self-evident, and the converse, that everything which is in a body is divisible according to one of these two classes, is evident too; and when this is verified, the converse of its opposite is also true, namely that which is not divisible according to one of these two classes cannot be in a body.[70]

Universal intelligibles are not divisible in either way. Consequently, the intellect is not an attribute of a body:

> If to these premises there is added further what is evident in the case of the universal intelligibles, namely that they are not divisible in either of the

two ways, since they are not individual forms, it
is clear that there follows from this that neither
is the substratum of these intelligibles a body,
nor is the faculty which has the power to produce
them a faculty in a body; and it follows that their
substratum is a spiritual faculty which perceives
itself and other things.[71]

That is to say, the intellect is "separable, impassible, and unmixed" in comparison with the rational powers of the soul:

This proof can be completed by saying that
the intellect is not attached to any animal faculty
in the way the form is attached to its substratum,
for the denial of its being attached to the body
implies necessarily the denial of its being attached to any animal faculty which is attached to
the body. For, if the intellect were attached to
any of the animal faculties, it would as Aristotle
says be unable to act except through this faculty,
but then this faculty would not perceive the intellect. This is the argument on which Aristotle himself bases his proof that the intellect is separate.[72]

Thus far we have seen that Averroes' distinction between soul and intellect in the <u>Tahafut al-Tahafut</u> is consistent with that given in his commentary on Aristotle's <u>De Anima</u>. In both works Averroes insists that since there is no corporeal instrument for the intellect the intellect is not a power of the soul. Moreover, through this insistence, he defends the unicity of the intellect as well as the view that knowledge varies from man to man according to the degree of development of his soul. Is Averroes' exposition of the soul affected by the religious preoccupations of his predecessors, of which he was fully conscious?

Life After Death

Let us pay close attention to Averroes as he elaborates his discussion of the soul. He now claims that when a body decays the soul loses its activity, but surely not its existence. This is so because the soul is an attribute of a body in the second of the two ways in which this is possible, that is, it is related to a body as vision to the eye:

For of those things in the body which are divided in this second way, i.e. which are not by de-

finition divisible through the division of their
substratum it was sometimes doubted whether they
are separable from their substratum or not. For
we see it happen that most parts of the substratum
decay and still this kind of existence, i.e. the
individual perception, does not decay; and it was
thought that it might happen that, just as the
form does not disappear through the disappearance
of one or more parts of its substratum, in the
same way the form might not disappear when the
whole was destroyed, and that the decay of the act
of the form through its substratum was similar to
the decay of the act of the artisan through the
deterioration of his tools.[73]

Averroes himself then points out that his explanation of the survival of the soul is faithful to Aristotle's De Anima:[74]

And therefore Aristotle says that if an old man had
the eye of a young man, he would see as well as the
young man, meaning that it is thought that the decrepitude which occurs to the sight of the old man
does not happen because of the decay of the faculty
but because of the decay of the organs. And he
tries to prove this by the inactivity of the organ
or the greater part of it in sleep, drunkenness,
and the illnesses through which the perceptions of
the senses decay, whereas it is quite certain that
the faculties are not destroyed in these conditions.[75]

More importantly, Averroes clearly states that his
certainty for the inactivity of the surviving soul is the
image of death as sleep in the Qur'an:

But the discussion of the soul is very obscure, and therefore God has only given knowledge
of it to those who are deeply learned; and therefore God, answering the question of the masses
about this problem, says that this kind of question
is not their concern, saying, 'They will ask thee
of the spirit. Say: "The spirit comes at the bidding of my Lord, and ye are given but a little
knowledge thereof."'[76] And the comparison of death
with sleep in this question is an evident proof
that the soul survives, since the activity of the
soul ceases in sleep through the inactivity of its
organ, but the existence of the soul does not
cease, and therefore it is necessary that its condition in death should be like its condition in
sleep, for the parts follow the same rule. And
this is proof which all can understand and which is
suitable to be believed by the masses, and will
show the learned the way in which the survival of
the soul is ascertained. And this is evident from
the Divine Words: 'God takes to Himself souls at

the time of their death; and those who do not die in their sleep.'[77]

At any rate, for Averroes the soul cannot be equated with the individual, since body and soul are two aspects of one reality:

> As for the thesis of the numerical plurality of immaterial souls, this is not a theory acknowledged by the philosophers, for they regard matter as the cause of numerical plurality and form as the cause of congruity in numerical plurality. And that there should be a numerical plurality without matter, having one unique form, is impossible. For in its description one individual can only be distinguished from another accidentally, and there is often another individual who participates in this description, but only through their matter do individuals differ in reality.[78]

Having established his doctrine of the soul, Averroes turns his attention to Algazali who, we recall, had attacked philosophers for denying that man needs a body to triumph over death. He points out that he recognizes that man's only hope for a future life is the resurrection of the dead, and not the nature of his soul, and says that "the philosophers in particular, as is only natural, regard this doctrine as most important and believe in it the most."[79]

More particularly, he adverts to the fact that his doctrine of man and his destiny emphasizes that a body is an integral part of man, unlike Avicenna's, which is a theory of the personal immortality of the soul. Thus, he even explains how man will participate in eschatological salvation: his earthly body will be replaced by a resurrection body:

> But Avicenna's opponents may ask his partisans through what the individuation and numerical plurality of soul takes place, when they are separated from their matters, for the numerical plurality of individuals arises only through matter. He who claims the survival and the numerical plurality of souls should say that they are in a subtle matter, namely the animal warmth which emanates from the heavenly bodies.[80]

That is to say, when man awakes at the resurrection, he will be reconstituted with the same soul but a different body:

> [It] must be assumed that what arises from the dead
> is simulacra of these earthly bodies, not these bo-
> dies themselves, for that which has perished does
> not return individually and a thing can only return
> as an image of that which has perished, as Ghazali
> declares. Therefore the doctrine of the resurrec-
> tion of those theologians who believe that the soul
> is an accident and that the bodies which arise are
> identical with those that perished cannot be true.
> For what perished and became anew can only be spe-
> cifically, not numerically, one, and this argument
> is especially valid against those theologians who
> hold that an accident does not last two moments.[81]

Needless to say, Averroes' interpretation of the resurrection is faithful to the Qur'an, since it acknowledges that continuity between this life and the next is through the soul. Moreover, his interpretation of the resurrection body as a new creation is consistent with Aristotle's teaching that "nothing perishable can remain forever one and the same."[82] It can overcome death only in an existence in "something *like* itself -- not numerically but specifically one."[83]

Indeed, like St. Paul, Averroes maintains that deliverance will come not when God destroys matter, but when he sets it free from corruptibility. Consequently, nothing is exempt from fundamental change. At the resurrection the whole world will be created anew, for only the "names" of things, that is, their identity through their form, will be the same. As Averroes puts it:

> Thus to present the beyond in material images is
> more appropriate than purely spiritual representa-
> tion, as is said in the Divine Words: 'The like-
> ness of the Paradise which those who fear God are
> promised, beneath it rivers flow.' And the Prophet
> has said: 'In it there is what no eye has seen, no
> ear has heard, nor ever entered the eye of man.'
> And Ibn Abbas said: 'There is no relation in the
> other world to this world but the names.' And he
> meant by this that the beyond is another creation
> of a higher order than this world, and another
> phase superior to our earthly.[84]

Averroes' exposition of the future life in the *Tahafut al-Tahafut* must not be considered as at all inconsistent with his exposition of the same subject in his other works. For example, in his *Kashf al-manahidj*, in an account which parallels that examined in the *Tahafut al-Tahafut*, Averroes also affirms that it is the activity of

The Immortality of the Soul 111

the soul which ceases with death, not its existence. Furthermore, he again states that his exposition of the soul is based on the Qur'anic conception of death as sleep and the Aristotelian view that the soul is related to the body as vision to the eye:

> The whole of this [argument] is found on the immortality of the soul. If it is asked 'Does Scripture contain an indication of the immortality of the soul or at least a hint of it?', we reply: This is found in the precious Book in the words of the Exalted, 'God receives the souls at the time of their death, and those which have not died He receives in their sleep', [and so on to the end of] the verse. The significant aspect of this verse is that in it He has equated sleep and death with respect to the annihilation of the soul's activity. Thus if the cessation of the soul's activity in death were due to the soul's dissolution, not to a change in the soul's organ, the cessation of its activity in sleep [too] would have to be due to the dissolution of its essential being; but if that were the case, it would not return on waking to its normal condition. So when it does return to it, we know that this cessation does not happen to it through anything which attaches to it in its substantial nature, but is only something which attaches to it owing to a cessation of its organ; and [we know] that it does not follow that if the organ ceases the soul must cease. Death _is_ a cessation; it must therefore be of the organ, as is the case of sleep. As the Philosopher says, 'If the old man were to find an eye like the young man's eye, he would see as the young man sees.'[85]

He also asserts, as we have seen him do in the previous chapter, that, though all Muslims believe in a life after death, since there is no consensus in Islam as to its nature, alternative interpretations of it are permitted by the law:

> The truth in this question is that every man's duty is [to believe] whatever his study of it leads him to [conclude], provided that it is not such a study as would cause him to reject the principle altogether, by denying the existence [of the future life] altogether; for this manner of belief obliges us to call its holder an unbeliever, because the existence of this [future] state for man is made known to people through their Scriptures and their intellects.[86]

Consequently, some Muslims believe that creatures in the world-to-come will have the same bodies and the same souls:

> One sect holds that existence is identical with this existence here with respect to bliss and pleasure, i.e. they hold that it is of the same sort and that the two existences differ only in respect of permanence and limit of duration, i.e. the former is permanent and the latter of limited duration.[87]

Others think that the future life will be a purely spiritual existence:

> Another group holds that there is a difference in the kind of existence. This [group] is divided into two subdivisions. One [sub-] group holds that the existence symbolized by these sensible images is spiritual, and that it has been symbolized thus only for the purpose of exposition; these people are supported by many well-known arguments from Scripture, but there would be no point in enumerating them.[88]

Still others maintain that in the next world creatures will have the same soul but different bodies:

> Another [sub-] group thinks that it is corporeal, but believes that that corporeality existing in the life beyond differs from the corporeality of this life in that the latter is perishable while the former is immortal. They too are supported by arguments from Scripture, and it seems that Ibn 'Abbas was one of those who held this opinion, for he is reported to have said, 'There is nothing in this lower world like the next world except the names.'[89]

Averroes concedes that all three interpretations are permissible by the law. However, he chooses the third possibility, since it permits an understanding of the future life on terms compatible with reason and revelation. That is, it permits a harmony of the Qur'anic doctrine of the resurrection of the dead as a second creation with the Aristotelian doctrine that "nothing perishable can remain forever one and the same."[90] It can conquer death only in an existence in "something _like_ itself -- not numerically but specifically one":[91]

> It seems that this opinion is more suitable for the élite; for the admissibility of this opinion is founded on facts which are not discussed in front of everyone. One is that the soul is immortal. The second is that the return of the soul to other bodies does not involve the same absurdity as [its] return [to] those same [earthly] bodies. This is because it is apparent that the materials of the bodies that exist here are successively

transferred from one body to another: i.e. one and
the same material exists in many persons at different times. Bodies like these cannot possibly all
exist [at the same time], because their material is
one: for instance a man dies, his body is transformed into dust, that dust is transformed into a
plant, another man feeds on that plant; then semen
proceeds from him, from which another man is born.
But if other bodies are supposed, this state of affairs does not follow as a consequence.[92]

In sum, by maximizing the possibilities of thought permitted by Aristotle and the Qur'an, Averroes shows that reason and revelation are not mutually exclusive, but centred on one aim: man and his destiny. More specifically, Averroes first resolves Aristotle's doubt as to whether or not the intellect is a power of the soul by upholding the Qur'anic view that the soul can have no operation apart from the body after death. He is certain that the intellect is not a power of the soul because there is no corporeal instrument for the intellect. Averroes then harmonizes the Qur'anic conception of death as the unconsciousness of sleep from which a man awakes to a new creation with the Aristotelian statement that the soul is related to the body as vision to the eye. That is, Averroes acknowledges that continuity between this life and the next is through the soul, while maintaining that, as the perfection of an organic body, the soul can have no activity apart from a body. Man will enter into "eternal life" when the resurrection body takes the place of his earthly body at the new creation.

To view it another way, Averroes' exposition of the soul is an explanation of the future life guaranteed by the Qur'an in Aristotelian terms. It is a defence of the monistic conception of man found in Aristotle and the Qur'an. It is an affirmation that the truth of philosophy is not opposed to the truth of revelation, since truth is one. It is a vindication of the study of philosophy against the attack of the theologians. It is a rejection of the Platonic idea that man conquers death through the intrinsic nature of his soul. Indeed, for Averroes, as for the masses, man's death is total. That is to say, he concurs with revelation that man's existence in this life and the next is dependent on the will of God. Though death takes away life, God will give back to man what death has taken away. This is the Muslim hope. It is this hope which Averroes has defended. And in defending this hope, he does not deny a system of reward and punishment. What he says is that the soul cannot experience states of happiness or unhappiness apart from a body if the Qur'anic doctrine of the resurrection of the dead is to be meaningful.

Having established that Averroes' doctrine of the soul is not a denial of the future life, in the following chapter we shall examine his commentary on the De Anima to determine how his interpretation of Aristotle's doctrine of man's beatitude in this life is related to the Qur'anic teaching of reward and punishment after the resurrection.

CHAPTER IV

THE NATURE OF MAN'S BEATITUDE

Averroes' Theory of Intellection

In the previous chapter we saw Averroes maintain that the soul is rational in some sense, but that its knowledge is distinct from that of the material intellect.[1] This is so because the knowledge of the soul is individual, whereas the knowledge of the material intellect is universal. Moreover, we saw that the particular knowledge of the soul represents the rational development of each man. However, Averroes does note that though man is without intellect strictly speaking he is united to the material intellect through his soul.[2]

In greater detail, we saw that for Averroes the material intellect is "separable, impassible, and unmixed" in order to know.[3] It is "separable" because it is not a power of the body. It is "impassible" because it receives the forms of man's imagination after they have been abstracted from their individual conditions without undergoing any change in its nature. It is "unmixed" because it knows universals, an impossible act for a power of the body. Yet, while Averroes insists that the intellect is distinct from the soul, he does admit that the reason proper to man has a necessary function to play in intellectual knowledge. In other words, Averroes admits that the two subjects in knowledge are related. He does so when he says that the cogitative power prepares the individual forms of the imagination with the aid of memory for their reception by the material intellect.[4] He even admits that the material intellect can know nothing without the aid of man's reason.[5]

Granted that the material intellect is distinct from the soul, we must now investigate how the material intellect is related to the agent intellect. This is necessary because Aristotle, as we may recall, makes a distinction between an active principle of intellection, which makes all things, and a passive principle of intellection, which becomes all things.[6] Nor must we forget that according to the religious thinkers of Islam man does not have his own agent intellect; man's activity is dependent on the will of God.[7] Averroes must again harmonize reason with revelation.

In order to effect such a harmony, Averroes accepts Aristotle's distinction between the two principles of intellection. He points out that, since the forms which exist in the imagination are only intelligibles in potentiality, they have need of an active principle of intellection to make them intelligibles in actuality, before the passive principle of intellection can receive these intelligibles:

> Therefore, the rational soul must consider the forms (_intentiones_) which are in the imaginative faculty, just as the senses must inspect sensible things. And since it appears that the forms of external things move this power in such a way that the mind abstracts these forms from material things and thereby first makes them intelligibles in actuality, after they had been intelligibles in potentiality -- it appears from this that this soul [the intellect] is [also] active, not [only] passive. For in so far as the intelligibles move [the intellect], it is passive, but insofar as they are moved by it, it is active.[8]

The passive principle of intellection is what Averroes usually terms the material intellect. The active principle of intellection he identifies as the agent intellect:

> Thus one should hold the opinion which has already become clear to us from Aristotle's discussion, namely, that there are two kinds of intellect in the soul. One of these is the receiving intellect whose existence has been shown here, the other is the agent intellect and this is the one which causes the forms which are in the imaginative faculty to move the material intellect in actuality, after they had only moved it potentially.... And these two kinds of intellect are not generable or corruptible.[9]

Does Averroes regard the agent and material intellect as two intellects or one? The question is pertinent, in view of the fact that he refers to them as external substances:

> It was necessary to assign these two powers to the soul in us, namely, the power to receive knowledge

and the power to actuate it, although the agent and the receiving intellects are eternal substances.[10]

It is important to note Averroes' explicit statement that though the agent and material intellect may be considered two intellects from one point of view, they are essentially one intellect:

> When one considers the material intellect and the agent intellect, they will appear to be two in one way and one in another way. For they are two through the diversity of their action; for the action of the agent intellect is to generate, of the other to be informed. But they are one because the material intellect is perfected through the agent intellect and understands it. And from this we say that because the intellect is united to us, they appear to be two powers in us, one of which is active, the other of the genus of passive powers.[11]

Now, it is reasonable that Averroes should say that the material intellect is essentially and ontologically one with the agent intellect in the light of Aristotle's identification of mind, thought, and the object of thought. But why does he make the material intellect accidentally, or as it were psychologically, many (that is, multiplied in individual souls) by making it dependent on intelligibles from man's passible intellect in order to know? He does so to relate the two subjects in knowledge, man and the material intellect. Hence he explains that intelligibles are true with respect to the passible intellect in man, but they exist in actuality in the material intellect:

> But what has been said concerning the fact that these [speculative] intelligibles consist of two [principles], one of which is generated, the other of which is not generated is according to the course of nature. For since conception by the intellect, as Aristotle says, is like sense perception by the senses -- but perception by a sense is accomplished through two principles, one of which is that object through which sense perception becomes true (and this is the sensible outside the soul), and the other is that subject through which sense perception is an existing form (and this is the first actuality of the sense organ), it is likewise necessary that the intelligibles in actuality have two principles, one of which is the object (<u>subiectum</u>) through which they are true images, the other one of which is that subject (<u>subiectum</u>) through which the intelligibles are one of the things existing in the world, and this is the material intellect.[12]

Moreover, it is by relating the two subjects in knowledge that Averroes is able to explain how intelligibles are generable only with respect to man's possible intellect and not in relation to the material intellect. In other words, Averroes unites the material intellect with the possible intellect in the individual human soul in order to affirm both that the knowledge of mortal man ceases with his death and that the knowledge of the intellect is eternal:

> All these matters being as we have related, it is only necessary that the intelligibles in actuality, that is the speculative intelligibles, are generable according to the object through which they are true, that is according to the imaginative forms, but not according to that subject through which they are one of the existing things, that is, according to the material intellect.[13]

For the sake of clarity Averroes illustrates how the agent intellect is related to the two subjects in knowledge by means of a comparison between vision and intellection. In effect, he says that, just as in vision there are two subjects of one form, the subject in which colour is potentially visible and the medium in which colour is seen, so also in intellection there are two subjects, the passible intellect, in which the forms of the imagination are potentially intelligible, and the material intellect, in which these intelligibles exist in actuality. And just as colour can only be seen when illuminated by light, so too the intelligibles in the passible intellect can only activate the material intellect when activated by the agent intellect:

> Indeed, you should know that the relation of the agent intellect to the receiving intellect is as the relation of light to the transparent medium, and that the relation of the material forms to the receiving intellect is as the relation of colour to the transparent medium. For just as light is the perfection of the transparent medium, so is the agent intellect the perfection of the material [intellect]. And just as the transparent medium is only moved by colour and receives it when it is illuminated, so also the [material] intellect only receives the intelligibles which exist in it when the material intellect is perfected by the agent intellect and illuminated by it. And just as light makes colour in potentiality exist in actuality, as a result of which it [colour] can move the transparent medium, so also the agent intellect makes

the intelligible forms in potentiality exist in
actuality, as a result of which the material intellect receives them. In this manner one must understand about the material and agent intellect.[14]

Yet, how can the material intellect always know, since man's passible intellect is unable to generate intelligibles apart from a body after death? Does not Averroes say that the material intellect can know nothing unless it is united to the passible intellect? Averroes' answer to this question is that though man as an individual is mortal, man as a species is not. Consequently, there will always be intelligibles in the passible intellects of living men to enable the material intellect to know:

> For as we have said, it does befit the intellect
> which is called material, that at one time it should
> understand, and at another time only in respect to
> the forms of the imagination which exist in each
> individual, not in respect to the species; for in-
> stance, it does not befit it that at one time the
> intellect should understand the concept of a horse
> and at another time only in respect to Socrates and
> Plato. But simply and in respect to the species, it
> always understands this universal concept, unless
> the human species ceases to exist altogether, and
> this is impossible. And accordingly, this argument
> will be according to its evidence. And when he
> said: <u>but universally it is neither in time</u>, etc.,
> he meant that the intellect which is in potency,
> when it has not been received in respect to some
> individual, but has been received simply and in
> respect to any individual, then it will not be found
> at one time understanding and at another time not,
> but it will always be found understanding.[15]

The same point is made by Averroes through an analogy:

> For if knowledge belongs in some proper fashion to
> human beings, just as the obvious kinds of crafts
> belong in some proper fashions to human beings, one
> should think that it is impossible that philosophy
> should be without any abode, just as one must be of
> the opinion that it is impossible that all the nat-
> ural crafts should be without any abode. For if
> some part of the world lacks them, that is, these
> crafts, for example, the northern quarter of the
> earth, the other quarter will not lack them, since
> it is clear that they can have an abode in the
> southern part, just as in the northern.[16]

By way of summary, Averroes reiterates that his doctrine of the material intellect as ontologically one with the agent intellect and psychologically many with respect to the passible intellect in individual men must be understood in the context of the two subjects in knowledge:

> The manner in which we have described the essence of the material intellect answers all the questions arising about our statement that this intellect is one and many.... For if we assert that something known by me and by you is many in respect to that object (<u>in subiecto</u>) according to which it is true, that is <u>in respect</u> to the imaginative forms, and one in respect to the subject through which it is an existing intellect (and this is the material intellect), these questions are resolved completely.[17]

Let us pause briefly to consolidate our findings thus far: (1) By uniting the material intellect to the passible intellect in the individual soul, Averroes is able to maintain that the material intellect is not a power of the soul. (2) Through this union, Averroes is able to account for the universality of knowledge in the material intellect and for the diversity of knowledge among men. (3) Averroes acknowledges that the knowledge of the material intellect in contrast to mortal man's is eternal. He does so by distinguishing between man as an individual and man as a species. (4) By asserting that the material intellect is essentially or ontologically one with the agent intellect, though accidentally or psychologically many in respect to man, Averroes shows himself mindful of the Qur'anic doctrine of man's creaturely relationship to God and of Aristotle's suggestion that the intellect is not a human power.[18] (5) When he makes man's participation in the knowledge of the material intellect depend upon the activity of the agent intellect, Averroes recognizes the Qur'anic teaching that there is a transcendent agent in the universe on whom man as a creature is dependent for his happiness. (6) By maintaining that the agent and the material intellects are ontologically one, Averroes claims that the object of thought becomes the product of thought, and the intellect knows itself through itself. This claim is in harmony with Aristotle's identification of mind, thought, and the object of thought,[19] as well as with the Qur'anic view that soul is something relative to a body. In sum, Averroes' exposition of soul and intellect testifies to his belief in the totality of death, as that which Aristotle teaches and the Qur'an affirms.

Man's Perfection as Union with the Agent Intellect

After establishing his theory of intellection in concord with the Aristotelian and Qur'anic conception of man and his relationship to God, Averroes proceeds to examine whether man can be united psychologically as well as ontologically to the agent intellect. In other words, he considers whether man's final perfection is union with the agent intellect through knowledge. His reasoning follows naturally from the fact that man's passible intellect is indirectly one with the material intellect, (that is, through its multiplication in the individual soul) and the material intellect is ontologically one with the agent intellect:

> It is proper for us to investigate and consider finally whether that intellect which is in us can understand anything which is in itself intellect, and free from matter, just as it understands that which makes itself intellect in act after it was intellect in potency ... whether it is possible that the material intellect understands separate things or not; and if it understands them, whether it is possible that it understands them in so far as it is conjoined with us or not.... And that investigation which he undertakes is clearly difficult and ambiguous, and it is proper for us to investigate this according to our ability.[20]

Averroes begins his study with a discussion of habitual knowledge. According to him, habitual knowledge or intellect in habit is the knowledge possessed by man and the material intellect which they have the power to understand habitually. It may be compared to the memory of a scholar through which he functions:

> For this is the definition of habit, namely that having the habit it understands through itself that which is proper to itself from itself and when it wishes, without that which it may need in this anything from the outside.[21]

In fact, habitual knowledge results from the involvement of the passible intellect with the agent intellect in the process of intellection:

> And you must know that use and practice are its causes, because it appears from the potency of the agent intellect which is in us for the purpose of of abstracting, and the material intellect for the purpose of receiving; they are, I say, the causes

of the existing habit through use and practice in the passible and corruptible intellect, which Aristotle called passible.[22]

For this reason, "the intellect which is in habit (and is speculative) is other than the agent intellect."[23]

Averroes goes on to explain that man's habitual or speculative knowledge is of two kinds. First, there is speculative knowledge which he possesses naturally, that is, the knowledge of first propositions. Man does not know how or when these propositions come to him, but ultimately they exist in him through the agent intellect. Second, there is speculative knowledge which he acquires with the help of these first propositions. He does not possess this speculative knowledge naturally, but acquires it voluntarily and with effort. It is important to note that for Averroes the speculative knowledge which man acquires voluntarily is not acquired independently of first propositions, but is derived from them as conclusions from premises. That is, first propositions are not the only factor in man's acquired or habitual knowledge, since, as we have seen repeatedly, the agent intellect must perfect man's knowledge before the material intellect can receive it. Hence, man's acquired or habitual knowledge is a consequence of two factors, first propositions and the agent intellect. Averroes puts it this way:

> And when these two foundations have been posited, namely the intellect which is in us has these two actions, namely to understand intelligibles and to make them; but intelligibles come into existence in us in two ways; either naturally (and they are first propositions, which we do not know when they come into existence, both from where and how) or voluntarily (and they are intelligibles acquired from first propositions); and it was declared that the intelligibles held by us naturally are from something which is in itself intellect (and is the agent intellect); and when this is stated, it is necessary that the intelligibles held by us from first propositions are a composite product of propositions known and the agent intellect.[24]

Averroes now observes that when we understand how the agent intellect is related to the intellect in habit as quasi-form to quasi-matter, we shall understand how man finds his ultimate perfection in union with the agent intellect:

[It] seems to us that when we know the method according to which the intellect which is in habit is the quasi-matter and the subject of the agent [intellect]. And when that mode has been established by us, we can perhaps easily know the method according to which it is conjoined to separable intellects.[25]

But aware of the fact that the knowledge of the agent intellect is eternal as well as of the fact that the speculative knowledge of mortal man ceases with his death, before proceeding further Averroes inquires how the agent intellect can be eternally related to the intellect in habit: "What therefore is that relation, and how does it befall the agent intellect to have this relation with the intellect which is in habit, which is both one and eternal, and generable and corruptible?"[26] In reply to the question, he reminds us that there are two subjects in knowledge, man and the material intellect. That is to say, the agent intellect will always be able to know since speculative intelligibles will always exist in the material intellect: "But since we have established that the material intellect is eternal and speculative intelligibles are generable and corruptible in that way in which we have mentioned."[27]

With this question answered, Averroes makes use of two principles to explain how the relationship of the agent intellect to the intellect in habit is similar to that of form to matter or, to put it differently, of agent to instrument. He states the first principle as follows: "For of all things which have two perfections but one subject, and of the perfections one is more perfect than the other, it is necessary that the relation of the more perfect to the less perfect be just as the relation of form to matter."[28]

To illustrate this principle, Averroes points out that when a transparent medium is the common subject of light and colour the relationship between light and colour is akin to that of form to matter, since light is the cause of colour being received by the transparent medium: "And similar to this is the transparent medium, which receives colour and light simultaneously; and light is the efficient cause of colour."[29] Now, as we know, the material intellect is the common subject for the agent intellect and the intellect in habit, since the agent intellect perfects the material intellect to receive the speculative knowledge of man. It follows, therefore, that the agent intellect is related to the intellect in habit as quasi-form to quasi-matter: "[It] is clear that the subject of speculative intelligibles and of the agent intellect according to this analysis is one and the same, namely the material [intellect]."[30]

Averroes' second principle is that "in every action done through the combined activity of two diverse factors, it is necessary that one of the two of these [factors] be the quasi-matter and instrument, and the other be the quasi-form or agent."[31] Applying this principle to his previous statement that the agent intellect and first propositions are two factors in man's speculative knowledge, Averroes again establishes that the agent intellect is related to the intellect in habit as quasi-form to quasi-matter:

> Therefore the knowledge which is in us results from the intellect which is in habit and the agent intellect, either in such a way that the propositions are quasi-matter and the agent intellect is quasi-form, or in such a way that the propositions are quasi-instrument and the agent intellect is quasi-efficient [cause]; for the relation in this is exactly similar.[32]

Averroes stresses that the relationship between the agent intellect and the intellect in habit is analogous to that which exists between form and matter:

> Viewed in this way, it happens by necessity that the intellect which is in us in act is a composite of speculative intelligibles and the agent intellect, so that the agent intellect is the quasi-form of the speculative intelligibles and the speculative intelligibles are the quasi-matter.[33]

However, he is careful to point out that the relationship is not truly or directly one of form and matter:

> [The] discussion does not necessarily say that matter is matter and instrument is instrument, but that there is necessarily here a proportion or relation between the agent intellect and the propositions, and that they are similar to matter and instrument in some way, not because it is true matter or true instrument.[34]

The point that Averroes wishes to establish is that man is indirectly related to the agent intellect as to his intelligible form, since the agent intellect is the quasi-form of the intellect in habit, to which man is united in his act of knowing: "That through which something performs its own proper action is a form; therefore since we perform our proper action through the agent intellect, it is necessary that the agent intellect be a form in us."[35] Put another way, man is indirectly related to the agent intellect as to his form, since the agent and material intellects are (ontologically) united, and the material intellect is (psychologically) united to man through speculative knowledge:

> Moreover, since speculative intelligibles are conjoined to us through the forms of the imagination, and the agent intellect is conjoined to speculative intelligibles (for that which understands them is the same, namely the material intellect), it is necessary that the agent intellect be conjoined to us through the continuation of speculative intelligibles.[36]

On this foundation, Averroes proceeds to explain how man can know the agent intellect perfectly through growth in knowledge. In other words, he is ready to show that man's proper perfection is union with the agent intellect, in harmony with the Aristotelian conception that man's highest activity is rational and the Qur'anic doctrine that man's happiness is dependent upon the degree to which he develops his soul: "At last therefore we have found a way according to which it is possible for that intellect to be united to us finally, and the reason why it is not united to us from the beginning."[37]

Averroes therefore asserts that it is through the acquisition of knowledge that man progresses from potential, to partial, to perfect union with the agent intellect:

> And it is clear that when all speculative intelligibles exist in us in potency, then it is united to us in potency. And when all speculative intelligibles exist in us in act, then it will be united to us in act. And when some are in potency and some in act, then it is united to us partially and partially not; and we are said to be moved toward union.[38]

However, man's progressive union with the agent intellect is through the continuation of his intelligibles with the material intellect, since the function of the agent intellect, as we have seen, is to activate man's intelligibles for their reception by the material intellect and to perfect the material intellect to receive these intelligibles in actuality. When, therefore, man acquires all knowledge, the material intellect, on receiving this knowledge, is perfectly united to the agent intellect. But since the material intellect receives the agent intellect as its perfection only through its union with man, man in possession of all knowledge shares in the perfect union of the material intellect with the agent intellect, which is called <u>intellectus adeptus</u>: "When the material intellect is conjoined in so far as it is perfected through the agent intellect, then we are conjoined with the agent intellect. And this disposition is called acquisition and acquired intellect (<u>intellectus adeptus</u>)."[39]

In other words, man's final union with the agent intellect through the continuation of his intelligibles with the material intellect is similar to his final union with the agent intellect through the intellect in habit, since man's habitual knowledge is continuous with that of the material intellect: "And then it is clear that the relation of it to us in that disposition is just as the relation of the intellect which is in habit in us."[40] The point we must recognize, because of its importance for reason and revelation, is that the material intellect receives the agent intellect as its acquired form by being united to man's speculative intelligibles or intellect in habit. That is to say, man is not directly, but indirectly, united to the agent intellect through his acquired knowledge. The soul and the agent intellect are distinct, though interdependent entities, and reason and revelation are in harmony:

> [Since] the agent intellect will be just as the acquired form of the material intellect through the mediation of speculative intelligibles which are made and acquired from the material forms by the material intellect through the operation of the agent intellect, they make the intellect which is here called the intellect in habit, whose proper form is nevertheless the agent intellect when that very intellect in habit is perfected. And then the material intellect, through this very agent intel-

lect as its proper form, understands all things, and therefore forms entirely freed from matter.[41]

According to Averroes, then, the agent intellect is not only the efficient and formal cause of knowledge, but the final cause as well. Consequently, it is the agent intellect which attracts the human mind to find its proper perfection in union with it. For since man is united to the material intellect in his progress toward union with the agent intellect through intelligibles, he is also united through intelligibles to the agent intellect as to his intelligible form. That is, since man is necessarily united to the material intellect in the process of intellection, it is his destiny to share in the material intellect's act of understanding the agent intellect and to find in union with the agent intellect his ultimate perfection:

> The continuation of the agent intellect in us does not take place through a new act of understanding of separate substances or other substances, just as the continuation of the material intellect in act, according to Aristotle, does not take place through a new act of understanding of the imaginative intentions. But on the contrary, through the continuation of the agent intellect with the material intellect through the mediation of speculative intelligibles, it becomes an act of understanding in us of separate forms and other forms.[42]

Man's ultimate perfection is unique among creatures, and follows from the fact that the agent intellect is related to him ontologically as well as psychologically, since it is related to him not only as his agent, but also as his intelligible form:

> And when this continuation is not posited, there will be no difference between comparing it to man and to all beings, except through the difference of its action in its objects. And according to this mode of its relation to man, it will not be other than the relation of an agent to man, not the relation of a form, and the question of Alfarabi touches on what he said in his Nichomachean Ethics. For I am confident in the continuation of the intellect with us in declaring that its relation to man is a relation of form and agent, not a relation of agent alone.[43]

Averroes concludes his study with the explicit statement that man's final union with the agent intellect is his way of coming to be like God through his knowing:

> In this way, then, as Themistius says, man is assimilated to God, in that he is and knows, in some way, all things. For things are nothing other than his knowledge, and the cause of things is nothing other than his knowledge. How marvellous that order, and how extraordinary is that mode of existence![44]

Reward and Punishment

Having examined the nature of man's happiness in this life, we are now ready to determine how Averroes' theories of soul and intellect are related to a system of reward and punishment in the life-to-come. As we have seen, Averroes acknowledges six intellects. The agent intellect is a separate substance. The passible intellect is not strictly speaking an intellect, but the cogitative power of the soul which is inoperative without a body after death. The speculative intellect is the same as the intellect in habit. The intellect in habit is not an intellect distinct from the passible intellect and the material intellect. Rather, it refers to the intelligibles of the passible intellect actualized by the agent intellect and received by the material intellect which enable man and the material intellect to have habitual knowledge. Since it is dependent on the passible intellect for intelligibles, it is eternal only in respect to man as species, and not in respect to individual men. The *intellectus adeptus* is the material-intellect-in-act through which man is united to the agent intellect. We are left with the material intellect which is essentially or ontologically one with the agent intellect but accidentally or, as it were, psychologically many through its union with man. That is to say, for man to be happy, the passible intellect must be united through its habitual knowledge to the agent intellect through the material intellect. In other words, since matter is the principle of individuation for the soul and necessary for the union of the material intellect with man, there can be no happiness for the soul without a body.

When a man dies and his body decays he loses his union with the material intellect. But, as we have seen in the previous chapter, Averroes accepts the future life of man as a second creation guaranteed by the Qur'an. Consequently, though death is total, when a man is reconstituted whole and entire at the resurrection, his soul will have a body that is eternal. That is, his soul will again be individuated by matter, and he will once more be united to the material intellect. And just as man's happiness in this life comes to him through his participation in intellectual activity, so in the future life happiness will come to him in the same way. And just as the degree of a man's happiness in this life is dependent on his acquired knowledge, so will it be for all eternity. That is, according to a man's progress toward union with the agent intellect in this life, he will be happy or unhappy in the life beyond. The Aristotelian doctrine that man's highest activity is rational and the Qur'anic doctrine that the degree of man's happiness in the life-to-come is contingent upon the degree to which he develops his soul in this life are in harmony.

To sum up: it is through the distinction between, and continuation of, the two subjects in knowledge, man and the material intellect, that Averroes is able to harmonize Aristotle's doctrines of the eternity of the intellect and the nature of man's happiness in this life with his belief in a system of reward and punishment in a future life as taught by the Qur'an. As for the relation of the intellect to man, perhaps we can best understand it by means of a simile.[45] The intellect resembles sunlight mirrored in a kaleidoscope of manifold reflecting bodies, in which men are like dewdrops, varying in size and shape. The quantitative differences in the glassy surfaces, observable in the dewdrops, may be compared to the passible intellect, that is, to their individual different dispositions. When the sun, the agent intellect, sends out its rays on the dewdrops, the smooth glassiness of these drops of dew becomes luminous, capable of mirroring external objects, and this luminosity, a common character in every dewdrop, may be compared to the material intellect. The material intellect, in our comparison the sunny luminosity, is not an emergence from the dewdrops. Water can never turn into sunshine. Rather, the material intellect is to be conceived as analogous to the sun which radiates actively and is reflected passively, although its luminosity can come into existence only in the presence of dewdrops. The radiance of the sun -- the agent intellect -- in conjunction with the luminosity of the sun -- the material intellect -- results in a refraction, different altogether according to the individual drop of dew. The refracted light is the speculative intellect or intellect in habit.

With the disappearance of dewdrops, their glassy surface and their refracted light, that is, the passible intellect and intellect in habit of individual men disappear also. Death, however, cannot touch the agent and the material intellect. The effulgence of the sun, released from the state of bodily differentiation, returns into itself. But men are destined for a second creation, when, again as glassy surfaces, they will reflect the source of all light for all eternity.

CHAPTER V

CONCLUSION

In the light of the foregoing study we can say that our hypothesis is tenable:[1] Averroes' treatment of personal immortality exemplifies the harmony of reason and revelation so firmly defended by medieval Scholasticism. But Averroes' treatment of personal immortality harmonizes philosophical reason with the doctrine of the totality of death and the resurrection, not with a belief in the natural immortality of the soul. We have shown that both Averroes and Scholasticism, singularly Aquinas, emphasize the importance of reason in understanding revelation.[2] Yet we have seen that, while both Averroes and Aquinas admit that the truth arrived at by reason cannot be opposed to the truth of revelation, Averroes' belief in the nature of man and his destiny is not the same as Aquinas'. We may therefore preliminarily conclude that one can interpret Averroes' great commentary on the De Anima with respect to the soul without ascribing to him that kind of rationalism associated with the Latin Averroists. His doctrine of the soul, including its immortality, like that of Aquinas, is what "faith proposes and reason investigates." But what follows from this, in the light of the evidence we have reviewed in this study, for one's understanding of the history of Christian thought?

Let us recall that though Aristotle teaches that man is mortal, his exposition of the relation of the soul to the body in the De Anima is ambiguous.[3] One can certainly use elements of his thought to establish the natural immortality of the soul as, for example, Aquinas has done. Yet, on the other hand, it is also possible to maintain that for Aristotle death is total, since for him body and soul are two aspects of the one reality that is man. It is this latter position that Averroes had adopted and defended, since he knew that he was not taking over anything foreign to revelation, but rather championing the monistic, and in fact biblical, idea that man is an animated body, not an incarnated soul. In such a conception man's spirituality is supernatural. Thus, when Averroes says that man is a besouled body, he is not demeaning man. He is saying what man is as a historical being. He is saying that man is not a substantial composite, half corporeal and half incorporeal, but a being who belongs wholly to the physical universe. And, granted that man is a physical being, not only man, but the soul itself must in some sense be corporeal.

It is reasonable to infer that for Averroes the doctrine of the natural immortality of the soul is tantamount to a spiritualistic minimizing of death; rather, death involves both body and soul. This does not mean that for Averroes the soul is extinguished at death. What it implies is that the soul is not a carrier of an immortal human nature through the process of death. What it means is that because man is a psychophysical organism forming a unity, the question of whether the soul is naturally immortal is not any more important than the question of whether the body is naturally immortal. What it affirms is that it is not man's body nor his soul that dies, but man himself. What it connotes is that if there is to be any discussion of immortality which remains faithful to revelation, such immortality must be attributed not to the soul, but to the whole man, body and soul. In fact, Averroes does not deny the survival of the soul after death.[4] What he does, as we have seen, is to refrain from speculating on the soul on the other side of death. Like St. Paul in the New Testament, he speaks of death as the sleep of souls.[5]

To put it another way, for Averroes the human body and the human soul are distinct and constituent parts of man. Death is the separation of these component parts, that is, the corruption or break-up of the one man into his component parts. But it is clear that the component parts, when they exist separately, are no longer actually human, since they no longer actually compose the man. Therefore, body and soul are separable. But this is only to say that man is mortal. A separately existing soul is no more a man, or even an actually human reality than is the separately existing corpse which remains after death. Thus,

Conclusion

the body is dependent on the soul, and the soul is dependent on the body for their activities. And since body and soul constitute the unitary being man, death is necessarily a disaster. For if man exists only as a unity of body and soul, once these elements are separated, man no longer exists. That is to say, Averroes seems to recognize that after death there no longer exists anything which can, strictly speaking, be called human. For him, since the soul is an integral part of man, the future life cannot be centred on it, but on God and His promise of the resurrection.

Averroes' account of personal immortality may be described as a reasonable and viable attempt to reconcile Aristotle's ambiguity concerning soul and intellect with a monistic, rather than with a dualistic, doctrine of man and his destiny. Moreover, as we have illustrated, his attempt was successful to the extent that his exposition can account for a system of reward and punishment in harmony with reason and revelation. In the absence of any explicit denial of personal immortality in Averroes available to the medieval scholastics, it is hard today to see how his position is entirely incompatible with Christian thought, particularly since there is a growing consensus among modern scholars that the biblical view of man is monistic.

We have seen above, however, that dualism -- whether the unmitigated sort of dualism of which Plato's is the archetype, or the mitigated kind which harks back to the Aristotelian doctrine of the soul as the form of the body -- was adopted since early times by Christian theology. To be sure, Aquinas attenuated this dualism to an unusually high degree; we shall deal with this in more detail in a moment. In fact, not a few scholars would maintain that his anthropology should not be called dualistic. On the other hand, for Aquinas the human soul remains, in the last analysis, a spiritual substance properly so-called. It may be the kind of spiritual substance which for its own proper perfection is substantially united to the body as its form and thus makes man into one substance rather than an amalgam of two parts. Nevertheless, this doctrine, whether it be properly called dualistic or not, should in either event be contrasted with the assumption which, according to biblical scholars, runs throughout the Bible, which does not construe man's unity as the result of a composition, and which does not suggest that the soul is a spiritual substance. Thus, if one should postulate that the anthropology of Aquinas should not be called dualistic, but monistic, it would be necessary to add that this "monism" is at very least a qualified monism; it is a monism which differs noticeably from the biblical monism, which is a pure and simple monism. By whatever name, however, it was the doctrine of the soul of Christian theology, particularly as developed by Aquinas, rather than the doctrine of man assumed by the Bible, which prevailed in the history of Christian thought. Indeed, the latter has gained such ascendancy that is has become difficult for Christians today to grant their full weight to the monistic implications found in both the Old and New Testament. For instance, it is difficult for Christians today, who are heirs to a long tradition according to which there is an essential difference in the natural order between men and beasts which is the natural basis of their different ultimate destinies, to read the Bible and take at face value its assumption that men and beasts are differentiated only by supernatural considerations. By the same token, Averroes was bound to be misunderstood by the Middle Ages to the extent that by the Middle Ages Christianity had diverged from the original monistic anthropology of the Bible. Conversely, to understand Averroes' doctrine of the soul as a viable harmonization of Aristotle and the Qur'an is to understand not only the processes involved in the medieval Christian ascription to him of a denial of personal immortality, but also to understand how medieval Scholasticism brought to culmination certain prior developments in the history of Christian thought.

As we have noted, modern scholarship converges on the conclusion that the New Testament does not speak of a purely disembodied soul of man.[6] The biblical hope is not based on the nature of man, but on the power and goodness of God. Man's only hope of victory over death is God's promise of the resurrection. The New Testament promise is not that from man's mortal nature something immortal will survive, but that through the resurrection of the dead mortal man will put on immortality. In this view, according to the Bible there is no element in man which guarantees immortality after death. Since the biblical conception of man is monistic, there is no true life without the body. This explains why man's hope in the resurrection is a hope in a new creation, not in the natural immortality of the soul. It is because the New Testament view of man is monistic that it does not conjecture about the condition of the dead after death and before the Last Day. We recall that Paul does not comfort his questioners with a disembodied existence for the soul after death.[7] Instead, he insists that man's destiny lies not in the nature of his soul, but with the returning Lord. For him, as for Averroes, death is a sleep of souls.

The conclusion to which we arrive is therefore that the medieval Christian ascription to Averroes of a denial of the future life is part of a much broader phenomenon and is intelligible only in the context of that development: namely a shift from understanding the Christian hope as the resurrection of the dead without a belief in the natural immortality of the soul to that of the resurrection of the body linked to a belief in the natural immortality of the soul. As was suggested earlier,[8] this shift in doctrine is partly the result of the transfer of the centre of Christianity from Semitic to Greek soil. As a consequence, the church fathers, who were Greek in their mentality, were inevitably caught up in the cross-cultural processes of assimilating the biblical doctrine of death and the afterlife to the Platonic view of the natural immortality of the soul, which was more comprehensible to them and their converts. That is to say, the church fathers did not affirm a belief in the natural immortality of the soul to establish the plausibility of the resurrection for themselves and their followers. In fact, they recognized that any dualism of body and soul is contrary to a Christian anthropology.

Long before the end of the patristic period, however, while a belief in the resurrection of the dead as man's only hope of conquest over death was prominent, the idea of a disembodied afterlife for the soul was also in vogue. That is, from a picture of death as sleep which would last until the day of the resurrection and the second coming of Christ, an alternative conception of death developed in which there was an active life for the soul during the interim between death and the resurrection. The tension between these two views of the destiny of the soul after death, the biblical and the Platonic, continued into the early Middle Ages, though there seems to have been a growing acceptance of the idea that the soul is naturally immortal, a view perhaps popularized by Augustine who, influenced by Plato, regarded the soul as the real man. At any rate, by the thirteenth century the orthodox theologians had come to hold such an opinion.

It was because the Platonic conception of the soul was widely, if not exclusively, accepted by Christian scholars up to the thirteenth century that Averroes' great commentary on Aristotle's De Anima was significant for Christian eschatology. For while it is true that the translation of Aristotle's De Anima into Latin threatened the prevailing anthropology, because its doctrine of the soul is ambiguous, the orthodox theologians were able to accommodate their belief in the natural immortality of the soul to the Aristotelian view that the soul is not the real man, but the form of the body. It was Averroes' interpretation of Aristotle's De Anima as understood by the Latin Averroists that made Aristotle dangerous. In any case, it was because Averroes' interpretation of Aristotle's De Anima does not allow for a doctrine of the natural immortality of the human soul as an intellectual substance that the orthodox reaction to him was so spirited and vehement. Besides, it logically followed from Averroes' doctrine of the totality of death that man's only hope for a future life is the resurrection of the dead. However, as previously stated,[9] this view was also in conflict with the common Christian belief at that time that the soul of man went directly to its reward and punishment

Conclusion

before the corporate triumph of Christ at the last judgment.

Since Aquinas' refutation of Averroes was most influential in establishing the basic cast of Christian eschatology until the twentieth century, at this point it is perhaps proper to consider how his doctrine of the soul is related to revelation. In refuting Averroes, as we have seen,[10] Aquinas maintains that though man is a unity of body and soul, the soul is a substance in its own right. However, when Aquinas posits a distinction between man as a substance and soul as a substance as part of his attempt to harmonize Aristotle and the Gospel, does this doctrine really define a biblical view of man, of man's death, and of man's hope in God despite death, or is it not rather a reflection of the prevailing medieval opinion that the natural immortality of the soul is part of the Christian faith? If the soul is a substance in its own right, how does what happens in death affect our core? If the soul can have an active existence apart from the body after death, is not the soul the real man? And if the soul is the real man, why is the resurrection of the body essential to the future life promised by the New Testament? It is fitting to point out once more that if the soul is an intellectual substance, even if the body is necessary for the complete perfection of the soul, such a conception would in some way reflect a dualistic conception of man. For in Aquinas' view the soul is recognized as a reality distinct from the body, and indeed is able to subsist and be saved by itself, even though the body is united to it before death, and even though it eventually participates in the salvation of the soul. Indeed, the anthropology of Aquinas cannot be said to be monistic in the same sense and with the full justification in which the term applies to the anthropology of the New Testament.

The medieval belief that the natural immortality of the soul was essential to the Christian faith is what prevented Aquinas and the orthodox theologians from seeing that Averroes' doctrine of the soul does allow for a personal immortality for man. Indeed, the controversies surrounding Averroes' monistic conception of man in the Middle Ages really stem from the confrontation of Christian thought with the view that man's death is total, that man's assurance of a future life is not based on the nature of his soul, but on his hope in God. For, as we have shown, once it is granted that the future life is centred on God's promise of the resurrection, and not on the natural immortality of the soul, Averroes' doctrine of the soul as found in his great commentary on the De Anima can be more adequately and coherently interpreted than was done in the Middle Ages. It is true that Averroes' explanation of how his theory of the soul is related to a belief in the resurrection was available to Western scholars only after the medieval controversy on the soul was already over. Nevertheless, it must be conceded that the writings of Averroes available to the medieval scholastics do not contain a denial of personal immortality. Furthermore, if Averroes is an Aristotelian, and Aristotle has no doctrine of the personal destiny of man after death, Averroes cannot be called a perverter of peripatetic philosophy for not finding a doctrine of the natural immortality of the soul in the De Anima.

However, it was not only the orthodox scholastics who misunderstood Averroes. The Latin Averroists themselves shared the view that the doctrine of Averroes was incompatible with the Christian revelation. Indeed, it is because the Latin Averroists professed a belief in the natural immortality of the soul that in defending their view of the destiny of man they claimed that they were merely defending the truth of philosophy, represented by Aristotle, as interpreted by Averroes, and not denying the truth of revelation. That is to say, even for the Latin Averroists a doctrine of the totality of death meant that reason and revelation were in conflict. Ironically, it was the truth of revelation that Averroes was defending, the truth that since it is only man who truly exists, his only hope of overcoming death is the resurrection of the dead.

The failure of the Latin Averroists to understand the thought of Averroes is rooted in the medieval assumption that the intellect is a power of the soul. It is for this reason that they interpreted Averroes' doctrine of the unicity of the intellect to mean that there is one immortal soul for all men. However, as we have seen, Averroes made no such assumption. He excluded the intellect from the soul in order to affirm that man is a mere creature dependent on God for his every activity, and in order to ensure that the future life is consistent with revelation. If soul and intellect are distinct, the future life cannot be interpreted as the spiritual survival of the soul as an intellectual substance, as taught by Plato and those influenced by him. Averroes' doctrine of the soul is not monopsychist.

Finally, it may be pertinent to remark that the medieval view of the immortality of the soul should not be formally so-called, since it is not a doctrine of the immortality of either a Platonic or an Aristotelian soul; it is not a doctrine of the immortality of the real man who is to be identified with his soul, or of the human form of the human body which determines the composite to be a man; it is really a doctrine of the immortality of the subject of consciousness, or at least, of the subject of intellectual operations. Furthermore, as noted above,[11] if the Christian understanding that the intellect is a power of the soul common in the Middle Ages did not originate with Christianity, but like the doctrine of the immortality of the soul is the result of the influence of Greek philosophy, and if it is Averroes' view that the soul can have no activity without a body rather than the medieval view that the soul is an intellectual substance in its own right which is faithful to the Scriptural tradition, we may have found the principal reason for the failure of medieval scholars to appreciate what Averroes was trying to achieve in his attempt to reconcile philosophy with revelation with respect to the soul.

In any event, we have seen that, despite Aquinas' refutation of Averroes, the tension between resurrection and immortality continued into the fourteenth century. Benedict XII, in his Bull <u>Benedictus Deus</u> of 1336, tried to silence the view that death is a sleep of souls until the Last Day.[12] Yet in 1439 the Council of Forence found it necessary to proclaim for the benefit of the Greeks that the soul goes to its reward before the resurrection.[13] And even after that the issue was so heatedly debated that in 1513 the Fifth Lateran Council, in condemning the Averroists and the Alexandrists, made belief in the personal immortality of the soul an article of faith.[14] With this promulgation, the Averroist controversy had come full circle.

As for the modern reaction, Hourani, Fakhry, Rosenthal, and others[15] are quite right to point out that the Commentator does profess a belief in the resurrection of the dead in his treatises on reason and revelation. Nevertheless, the persistence of the idea that the soul is naturally immortal has led them to regard Averroes as a fideist. Their position implies that his philosophical doctrine of the soul is not in harmony with revelation. But, as we have shown, Averroes' doctrine of the soul is in harmony with revelation if we concede that the future life is centred on God and the promise of the resurrection, and not on the natural immortality of the soul. Indeed, his theory of the soul, including its immortality, is a reasonable and viable attempt to reconcile Aristotle and the Qur'an. His doctrines of soul and intellect, even though they are distinct, allow for a system of reward and punishment. In short, his doctrine of man and his destiny is not only what faith proposes, but also what he has succeeded in explaining within the Aristotelian framework.

It is the persistence of the idea that the soul is naturally immortal that has led others to regard Averroes' admission of a future life in his works on reason and revelation as evidence that he is a rationalist.[16] Unable to harmonize this finding with their own conception of the future life, they have resorted to alleging that Averroes is guilty of dissimulation. Arnaldez is right in saying to them that it is methodologically unsound to resort to an analysis of motives to resolve an apparent conflict of ideas.[17] More particularly, the charge of Gauthier,[18] Mandonnet,[19] and de Wulf[20] that Averroes invented the doctrines of the allegorical interpretation of Scripture and the three classes of men to disguise his rationalism is unfair to say the least. Al-Kindi,[21] Alfarabi,[22] Avicen-

Conclusion   141

na,[23] and Algazali[24] used the same doctrines. Moreover, the use of these doctrines is permitted by the Qur'an itself.[25] Nor must we forget that the use of allegorical interpretation of Scripture to meet the needs of men was well established in Christianity long before the birth of Islam.

Gilson's view that the Qur'an was an embarrassment to Averroes is based on a defective exegesis of his thought.[26] Averroes did not substitute the thought of Aristotle for revelation, as the same writer claims.[27] There is no question of substitution. Philosophy, understood as a demonstrative science, is one of the three ways recognized by the Qur'an for interpreting revelation.[28] Moreover, our study has shown that Averroes' veneration for Aristotle is merely his respect for philosophy as a medium of truth about the world. He thought that he could learn something from a heathen. According to Averroes, if a predecessor had made progress in the knowledge of reality, he would be foolish to ignore his findings, though, as a religious philosopher, he has a responsibility to go beyond his findings. In this viewpoint, we have the key to Averroes' whole outlook, an outlook identical with that of Aquinas,[29] as Asín has acknowledged.[30]

Mandonnet's objection to the use of the Arabic text of the Tahafut al-Tahafut for showing that the Western understanding of Averroes is wrong is untenable,[31] since there is no difference in the thought expressed in the Arabic and Latin versions of the treatise. Furthermore, not only is Averroes' doctrine of the soul found in the great commentary on the De Anima not different from that found in the Tahafut al-Tahafut, but also Averroes' doctrine of the future life can be reconstructed from his great commentary on the De Anima alone if Western scholars accept a monistic conception of man and the future life as dependent on God, as we have shown.

Modern scholars who have restudied the problem of man and his destiny in the thought of Averroes by restudying his doctrine of the soul have also failed to understand the point of Averroes' exposition. Thus, although Sweetman[32] and de Vaux[33] recognize that the soul is not an intellectual substance for Averroes, they do not recognize this finding as compatible with Aristotle and revelation. The criticism of others is influenced by their own belief that the soul is naturally immortal. It is for this reason that Tallon[34] and Pegis[35] consider Averroes to have an inadequate conception of man. It is for this reason that Teske[36] concludes that Averroes' theory of the intellect does not allow for a personal immortality for man. It is for this reason that Nogales[37] does not even entertain the possibility that soul and intellect are distinct for Averroes. It is for this reason that Zedler[38] observes that Averroes failed to prove the natural immortality of the soul, unlike Aquinas, who was able to do so. It is for this reason that Alonso[39] finds Averroes unable to explain how the soul exercises its faculties without a body.

In sum, both the medieval scholastics and modern Christian scholars have failed to recognize that Averroes' doctrine of the totality of death is in accordance with the doctrine of the New Testament. That is to say, they have failed to remember that in the Christian tradition man is mortal, and God alone can offer him the opportunity to overcome his mortality. Like the New Testament, Averroes affirms that the future life is not a survival over death. It is grounded entirely in God and not in the natural immortality of the soul.

NOTES

Introduction

¹II Sent., d. 18, a. 2, q. 1, in Opera Omnia (Quaracchi: Ex Typographia Colegii S. Bonaventurae, 1885), II, 444-446.

²In Hexaemeron, in Opera Omnia (Quaracchi: Ex Typographia Colegii S. Bonaventurae, 1891), V, 329-454.

³De Unitate Intellectus Contra Averroem, in Opera Omnia, ed. A. Borgnet (Paris: Vivès, 1899), IX, 437-476.

⁴E. Renan, Averroès et l'Averroisme, in Oeuvres Complètes de Ernest Renan (Paris: Calmann-Lévy, 1949), III, 233.

⁵Thomas Aquinas, De Unitate Intellectus Contra Averroistas, ed. L. Keeler (Rome: Gregorian University Press, 1946), cap. 1, 14, pp. 10-11. Cf. also ibid., cap. 1, 16-17, pp. 12-13.

⁶Summa Theologiae, I, q. 3, art. 5, obj. 2.

⁷Summa Contra Gentiles, I, c. 2, in ed. Leon. (Rome 1934), p. 2.

⁸Ibid., I, c. 6, in ed. Leon., p. 6.

⁹In II Sent., d. 17, q. 2, art. 2, in Opera Omnia, eds. S. E. Fretté and P. Maré (Paris: Vivès, 1873), VIII, 226.

¹⁰Cf. Summa Contra Gentiles, II, c. 69; De Anima, art. 1; De Spiritualibus Creaturis, art. 9; De Unitate Intellectus Contra Averroistas, proem; In II Sent., d. 17, q. 2, art. 1.

¹¹For a summary of Aquinas' doctrine of the soul, cf. E. Gilson, History of Christian Philosophy in the Middle Ages (New York: Random House, 1955), p. 714, n. 114; A. C. Pegis, "The Separated Soul and its Nature in St. Thomas," in St. Thomas Aquinas (1274-1974) Commemorative Studies (Toronto: Pontifical Institute of Mediaeval Studies, 1974), I, 131-158; H. Blumberg, "The Problem of Immortality in Avicenna, Maimonides and St. Thomas Aquinas," in Harry Austryn Wolfson Jubilee Volume (Jerusalem: The American Academy of Jewish Research, 1965), I, 180-184. For the position of Aquinas relative to that of Averroes, cf. A. C. Pegis, At the Origins of the Thomistic Notion of Man (New York: Macmillan, 1963); A. C. Pegis, "Some Reflections on the Summa Contra Gentiles II, 56," in An Etienne Gilson Tribute, ed. C. J. O'Neil (Milwaukee: Marquette University Press, 1959), pp. 169-188; A. C. Pegis, St. Thomas and the

Problem of the Soul in the Thirteenth Century (Toronto: Pontifical Institute of Mediaeval Studies, 1934), especially pp. 159-165; A. C. Pegis, "St. Thomas and the Unity of Man," in Progress in Philosophy, ed. J. A. McWilliams (Milwaukee: Marquette University Press, 1955), pp. 153-173; B. H. Zedler, "Averroes on the Possible Intellect," Proceedings of the American Catholic Philosophical Association, XXV (1951), 176-178; A. Badawi, Histoire de la philosophie en Islam (Paris: J. Vrin, 1972), II, 849-856.

[12] Cf. M. Asín y Palacios, "El Averroismo teológico de Santo Tomás de Aquino," in Homenaje á D. Francisco Codera (Zaragoza: Escar, 1904), pp. 317-324; Thomas Arnold and Alfred Guillaume, eds. The Legacy of Islam (Oxford: Clarendon Press, 1931), pp. 273-274, 276; André Berthier, "Un maître orientaliste de XIIIe siècle: Raymond Martin, O. P.," Archivum Fratrum Praedicatorum, VI (1936), 267-311; B. H. Zedler, ed. Averroes Destructio Destructionum Philosophiae Algazelis (Milwaukee: Marequette University Press, 1961), pp. 21-22.

[13] Cf. Pugio Fidei Adversus Mauros et Judaeos, ed. Jo. Benedictus Carpozovus (Lipsiae et Francofurti: Typis Viduae Johannis Wittigav, 1687), Part I, cap. 12, pp. 226-227.

[14] The condemnation of 1277 has been translated into English by E. L. Fortin and P. D. O'Neill and can be found in Medieval Political Philosophy: A Sourcebook, eds. R. Lerner and M. Mahdi (Glencoe, Ill.: The Free Press, 1963), pp. 335-354.

[15] Errores Philosophorum ed. J. Koch, trans. J. Riedl (Milwaukee: Marquette University Press, 1944), pp. 2-25.

[16] Cf. Alexander, De Intellectu et Intellecto, in G. Théry, Alexandre d'Aphrodise (Kain, Belgium: Le Saulchoir, 1926), pp. 74-82.

[17] H. Denzinger and H. Schonmetzer, eds. Enchiridion Symbolorum (32nd ed.; Rome: Herder and Herder, 1963), pp. 353-354, nos. 1440 and 1441.

[18] Nifo, quoted by Renan, III, 281.

[19] An English translation of the De Immortalitate Animae by W. H. Hay II, revised by J. H. Randall, Jr., can be found in E. Cassirer, P. O. Kristeller and J. H. Randall, Jr., eds. The Renaissance Philosophy of Man (Chicago: University of Chicago Press, 1948), pp. 280-393.

[20] On the problem of the soul according to Pomponazzi, cf. E. Gilson, Autour de Pomponazzi, Problématique de l'immortalité de l'âme en Italie au debut du XVIe siècle," Archives d'histoire doctrinale et littéraire du moyen âge, XXXVI (1961), 163-279; Domenic A. Iorio, "The Problem of the Soul and the Unity of Man in Pietro Pomponazzi," The New Scholasticism, XXXVII (1963), 293-311; Martin Pine, "Pomponazzi and the Problem of 'Double Truth,'" Journal of the History of

Ideas, XXIX (1968), 163-178; Lynn Thorndike, A History of Magic and Experimental Science, Vol. V: Sixteenth Century (New York: Columbia University Press, 1941), 94-99; Randall, Jr., in Cassirer, Kristeller, and Randall, Jr., pp. 274-276.

[21] For a recent and clear discussion of the three Calonymoses, cf. Zedler, Destructio Destructionum Philosophiae Algazelis, pp. 22-31, 46-50.

[22] Ibid., pp. 45-46.

[23] Cf. Mohammed Iqbal, The Reconstruction of Religious Thought in Islam (Lahore: Shaikh Muhammed Ashraf, 1962), pp. 111-112; J. Windrow Sweetman, Islam and Christian Theology, Part I, Vol. II (London: Lutterworth Press, 1967), p. 183; S. van den Bergh, trans. Averroes' Tahafut al-Tahafut (London: Luzac and Co. Ltd., 1954), I, xxxi-xxxiii.

[24] Cf. A. Hyman and J. Walsh, eds. Philosophy in the Middle Ages (New York: Harper and Row, 1967), p. 3.

[25] Among such scholars are F. Mehren, "Études sur la philosophie d'Averroès concernant son rapport avec celle d'Avicenne et de Gazzali," in Muséon, VII (1888), 613-627; VIII (1889), 5-20; Asín, pp. 271-331; A. J. Rahilly, "Averroism and Scholasticism," Studies: An Irish Quarterly Review of Letters, Philosophy and Science, III (1914), 686-713; Arnold and Guillaume, pp. 276-282; E. I. J. Rosenthal, Political Thought in Medieval Islam (Cambridge: Cambridge University Press, 1956), pp. 175-209; G. F. Hourani, Averroes' On the Harmony of Religion and Philosophy (London: Luzac, 1961), pp. 1-43; M. Fakhry, "Philosophy and Scripture in the Theology of Averroes," Mediaeval Studies, XXX (1968), 78-89; M. Fakhry, A History of Islamic Philosophy (New York: Columbia University Press, 1970), pp. 313-316, Badawi, Histoire de la philosophie en Islam, II, 766-789; W. Montgomery Watt, Islamic Philosophy and Theology (Edinburgh: Edinburgh University Press, 1972), pp. 139-142; M. Hernandez, Filosofía Hispano-Musulmana (Madrid: Asociacion Española para el Progreso de la Ciencias, 1957), II, 81-103; A. Ruibal, Problemas Fundamentales de la Filosofía y la Dogma, IV, note 371, cited by M. Alonso, Teología de Averroes (Madrid and Granada: Maestre, 1947), pp. 111-112 and passim.

[26] Asín, p. 272.

[27] P. Mandonnet, Siger de Brabant et l'Averroisme Latin au XIIIe siècle (Louvain: Institut Supérieur de Philosophie, 1911), I, 149.

[28] Hourani, Averroes' On the Harmony of Religion and Philosophy, pp. 22-27.

[29] Fakhry, "Philosophy and Scripture in the Theology of Averroes," 88, 82.

[30] Among such scholars are Renan, III, 139-140; S. Munk, Mélanges de philosophie juive et arabe (Paris: Franck,

1859), pp. 454-455; Mandonnet, I, 148-150; T. J. De Boer, The History of Philosophy in Islam translated by E. R. Jones (New York: Dover Publications, Inc., 1969), pp. 198-199; D. B. Macdonald, The Development of Muslim Theology, Jurisprudence and Constitutional Theory (New York: Russell and Russell, 1966), pp. 257, 286; L. Gauthier, Ibn Rochd (Averroès) (Paris: Presses Universitaires de France, 1948), pp. 17-46; L. Gauthier, La théorie d'Ibn Rochd (Averroès) sur les rapports de la religion et la philosophie (Paris: Leroux, 1909), pp. 31-111, 177-182; E. H. Weber, L'homme en discussion à l'université de Paris en 1270 (Paris: J. Vrin, 1970), pp. 23-24; Philip Merlan, Monopsychism, Mysticism, Metaconsciousness: Problems of the Soul in the Neoaristotelian and Neoplatonic Tradition (The Hague: M. Nijhoff, 1969, pp. 102-113; S. W. Baron, Essays on Maimonides (New York: Columbia University Press, 1941), p. 111; M. de Wulf, Histoire de la philosophie médiévale (Paris: J. Vrin, 1934), I, 305-309; E. Gilson, Reason and Revelation in the Middle Ages (New York: Charles Scribner's Sons, 1948), pp. 37-66.

[31]Though there has been much debate through the ages as to whether the soul is mortal or immortal in the thought of Aristotle, many modern scholars are prepared to grant that Aristotle did not teach a doctrine of personal immortality; for example, Gilson, Reason and Revelation in the Middle Ages, p. 6.

[32]Gauthier, La théorie d'Ibn Rochd sur les rapports de la religion et de la philosophie, pp. 108, 126, 131, 148-149.

[33]Mandonnet, I, 150.

[34]De Wulf, Histoire de la philosophie médiévale, I, 308.

[35]Gilson, Reason and Revelation in the Middle Ages, pp. 39-40, 50-51.

[36]Gilson, History of Christian Philosophy in the Middle Ages, p. 219.

[37]R. Arnaldez, "L'immortalité de l'âme dans le Tahâfut," Studia Islamica, X (1959), 35-36.

[38]L. Gardet, reviewer of Gauthier's Ibn Rochd (Averroès), in Bulletin Thomiste (1947-53), pp. 248-252; G. F. Hourani, Islamic Rationalism (Oxford: Clarendon Press, 1971), p. 129; Hendrick Kraemer, World Cultures and World Religions (Philadelphia: Westminster, 1960), pp. 102, 108-109; Sayyed Hossein Nasr, Ideals and Realities of Islam (New York: Frederick A. Praeger, 1967), pp. 92-119; Dominique Sourdel, Islam (New York: Walker, 1962), Chapter II; L. Strauss, Persecution and the Art of Writing (Glencoe, Ill.: Free Press, 1952), pp. 8-11; W. M. Watt, Islamic Revelation in the Modern World (Edinburgh: Edinburgh University Press, 1969, pp. 1-11, 94-98.

[39] Rosenthal, *Political Thought in Medieval Islam*, p. 116.

[40] Sweetman, Part II, Vol. II, 179-180.

[41] Cf. A. Tallon, "Personal Immortality in Averroes' *Tahafut al-Tahafut*," *The New Scholasticism*, XXXVIII (1964), 341-351. For his faulty citations from the text see, for example, p. 343: Tallon states that Averroes says "the soul does not die when the body dies;" the correct citation reads "*if* the soul does not die when the body dies." Averroes does not say "matter is not a condition for the existence of the soul;" he says, "*he who* concedes that matter is not a condition for the existence of the soul." Averroes does not say "the soul does not receive its existence through the body;" he says, "*If* the body serves as an instrument for the soul, the soul does not receive its existence through the body." Averroes does not say of the soul that "it is false that it can perish through the corruption of the body;" he merely reports this as the opinion of Ghazali concerning the philosophers. For the most part, Tallon does not confine his citations from the text to statements in which Averroes voices his own views, but treats conditional sentences, used to clarify a position, as if they are declarative expressions of Averroes' own understanding of the soul.

[42] Alonso, pp. 317, n. 1; 343, n. 1; 347, n. 1. Cf. also the discussion of Ruibal, cited by Alonso, pp. 111-112.

[43] Arnaldez, "L'immortalité de l'âme dans le *Tahâfut*," 40.

[44] R. J. Teske, "The End of Man in the Philosophy of Averroes," *The New Scholasticism*, XXXVII (1963), 460.

[45] S. Gomez Nogales, "La immortalidad del alma a la luz de la noetica d'Averroes," *Pensamiento*, XV (1959), 162.

[46] Carra de Vaux, "Averroes, Averroism," *Encyclopedia of Religion and Ethics*, ed. James Hastings (New York: Charles Scribner's Sons, 1918), II, 264.

[47] Pegis, "St. Thomas and the Unity of Man," p. 160.

[48] J. Riordan, "Form and Intellect in Averroes," (unpublished Ph.D. dissertation, University of Toronto, 1960), p. 186.

[49] Zedler, "Averroes on the Possible Intellect," 178.

[50] B. H. Zedler, "Averroes and Immortality," *The New Scholasticism*, XXVIII (1954), 446-447.

[51] *Summa Contra Gentiles*, I, c. 7, in ed. Leon., p. 6.

[52] *Ibid.*, I, c. 9, in ed. Leon., p. 8.

⁵³See above, note 27.

⁵⁴The findings of Steinschneider can be read in Zedler, Destructio Destructionum Philosophiae Algazelis, pp. 29-31. On page 30, Zedler lists some of the minor deviations:

In English translation by Van den Bergh made directly from Arabic text:	In Latin translation by Calo Calonymos, a Jewish scholar working from the Hebrew version:
Disp. I. Explicit reference to Koran (Van den Bergh, p. 30)	Omits reference to Koran (in 1550 ed., fol. 12ra)
Disp. VIII. Reference to Koran (p. 239)	Omits reference to Koran; includes reference to Talmud (fol. 43vb)
Disp. XI. "in our Divine Revelation" (p. 239)	Reads "in lege Mosaica divina" (fol. 46vb)
Disp. XVI. Reference to road to Mecca (p. 307)	Refers instead to Jerusalem (fol. 54va)
In Phys. IV has the phrase "prophets of Israel after Moses, as is evident from the Psalms." (p. 359)	Inserts after mention of Moses: "principem prophetarum" (fol. 63rb)
In Phys. IV says "bodily resurrection is also affirmed in the New Testament and attributed by tradition to Jesus." (p. 359)	Omits the phrase containing the reference to Jesus. (fol. 63rb).

⁵⁵Rahilly, II (1913), 306-307.

⁵⁶Cf. B. H. Zedler, trans., Saint Thomas Aquinas On the Unity of the Intellect Against the Averroists (Milwaukee: Marquette University Press, 1968), pp. 1-17; Zedler, "Averroes on the Possible Intellect," 165 and 178; A Seth Pringle Patterson, The Idea of Immortality (Oxford: Clarendon Press, 1922), pp. 63-68; Pegis, St. Thomas and the Problem of the Soul in the Thirteenth Century, pp. 160-165; Pegis, "St. Thomas and the Unity of Man," pp. 158-161; Pegis, At the Origins of the Thomistic Notion of Man, pp. 68-70; Pegis, "Some Reflections on the Summa Contra Gentiles II, 56," pp. 169-188; K. Foster and St. Humphries, trans., Aristotle's De Anima, in the Version of William of Moerbeke and the Commentary of St. Thomas Aquinas (New Haven: Yale University Press, 1954), pp. 18-24; Randall, Jr., in Cassirer, Kristeller, and Randall, Jr., pp. 260-261; D. Knowles, The Evolution of Medieval Thought (Baltimore: The Helicon Press, 1962), pp. 210-211; C. C. J. Webb, Studies in the History of Natural Theology (Oxford: Clarendon Press, 1915), pp. 264-273.

⁵⁷De Unitate Intellectus Contra Averroistas, ed. Keeler, prooemium 2, p. 2.

Notes

⁵⁸Ibid., p. 3. See also note 5 above.

⁵⁹In IV Sent., d. 49, q. 2, art. 1, in Opera Omnia, ed. S. E. Fretté (Paris: Vivès, 1874), XI, 483.

Chapter I

¹For references to the Qur'an, consult Mohammed M. Pickthall, The Meaning of the Glorious Koran (New York: The New American Library, 1958) and E. H. Palmer, trans., The Qur'an (Oxford: Clarendon Press, 1949).

²For a full treatment of nafs and rūh in the Qur'an and in later Islamic thought, see D. B. Macdonald, "The Development of the Idea of Spirit in Islam," Muslim World, 22, no. 1 (January-April, 1932), 25-42.

³E. E. Calverly, "Nafs," Shorter Encyclopedia of Islam, edited by H. A. R. Gibb and J. H. Kramers (Leiden: E. J. Brill, 1953), p. 434.

⁴M. Mahmud Hijazi, Al-Tafsir al-wadih (Cairo, 1952), XXIV, 7: cited by J. I. Smith in "The Understanding of nafs and rūh in Contemporary Muslim Considerations of the Nature of Sleep and Death," Muslim World, 49, no. 3 (July, 1979), 158.

⁵Cited by Smith, 159, from a private communication.

⁶E. E. Calverly, "Doctrines of the Soul (nafs and ruh) in Islam," Muslim World, 33, no. 4 (October, 1943), 261.

⁷Calverly, Shorter Encyclopedia of Islam, p. 434.

⁸Cited by Smith, 152, from a private communication.

⁹Mahmud b. 'Umar al-Zamakhshari, Al-Kashshaf 'an haqa'iq ghawamid al-tanzil (Beirut, 1966), IV, 130-131; Smith, 153-154.

¹⁰al-Fadl b. al-Hasan al-Tabarsi, Majma' al-bayan fi tafsir al-Qur'an (Beirut, 1961), XIX, 159-160; Smith, 154.

¹¹Fakhr al-Din al-Razi, Tafsir al-Kabir (Cairo, 1934-1962), XXVI, 283-284; Smith, 154.

¹²Ahmad Mustafa al-Maraghi, Tafsir al-Maraghi (Cairo, 1953), XXIV, 11-12; Smith, 158.

¹³Muhammad 'Abd al-Mun'im al-Jammal, Al-Tafsir al-farid (Cairo, 1973), IV, 2682; Smith, 158.

¹⁴Muhammad Husayn al-Tabataba'i, Al-Mizan fi tafsir al-Qur'an (Beirut, 1970-   ), XVII, 268-269; Smith, 158.

[15] M. M. Sharif, "Philosophical Teachings of the Qur'an," in History of Islamic Philosophy, ed. M. M. Sharif (Weisbaden: Otto Harrasowitz, 1963), I, 152; L. Gardet, L'Islam: Religion et communauté (Paris: Desclée de Brower, 1967), p. 96; D. Masson, Le Coran et la révélation Judéo-Chrétienne (Paris: Libraire d'Amérique et d'Orient Adrien-Maissoneuve, 1958), II, 698.

[16] Thomas O'Shaughnessy, Muhammad's Thoughts on Death (Leiden: E. J. Brill, 1969), p. 69.

[17] S. G. F. Brandon, The Judgment of the Dead (London: Weidenfeld and Nicolson, 1967), p. 144.

[18] T. Andrae, Mohammed: The Man and His Faith, trans. T. Menzel (New York: Harper and Row, 1960), pp. 57-59. The Qur'an makes one exception to this, martyrs who died in the cause of Islam. They are alive and already enjoy God's favour. However, they are never called spirits or souls. See S. 2:154; 3:169; 22:58-59; 3:170-171.

[19] Ibid., pp. 58-59.

[20] W. Montgomery Watt, Bell's Introduction to the Qur'an (Edinburgh: Edinburgh University Press, 1970), pp. 159-160.

[21] Sweetman, Part I, Volume II, 189.

[22] Dominique Sourdel, Islam (New York: Walker, 1962), p. 11; see also T. F. Glasson, His Appearing and His Kingdom (London: Epworth Press, 1953), p. 72.

[23] W. Montgomery Watt, What is Islam? (London: Longmans, Green, 1968), p. 49.

[24] The translation of the Bible used in this study is that of the Revised Standard Version.

[25] 80c-80d, 64c, 66d, 70a, 72e. The translation of the Phaedo used is that of Hugh Tredennick, in Edith Hamilton and Huntington Cairns, eds., The Collected Dialogues of Plato, Including the Letters (New York: Pantheon Books, 1961).

[26] On the Platonic conception of immortality, see M. McC. Gatch, Death: Meaning and Mortality in Christian Thought and Contemporary Culture (New York: Seabury Press, 1969), pp. 26-34; E. O. James, Comparative Religion (London: Methuen, 1961), pp. 288-291; J. Choron, Death and Western Thought (New York: Collier Books, 1963), pp. 47-52; Pringle-Patterson, pp. 33-61.

[27] J. L. McKenzie, "Aspects of Old Testament Thought," in The Jerome Biblical Commentary, eds. R. E. Brown, J. A. Fitzmyer, R. E. Murphy (New Jersey: Printice-Hall, Inc., 1968), II, 765. See also M. Delcor, "L'immortalité de l'âme dans le livre de la Sagesse et dans les documents de

Qumrân," Nouvelle revue théologique, LXXVII (1955), 614-630; R. H. Charles, Eschatology: The Doctrine of the Future Life In Israel, Judaism, and Christianity (New York: Schocken Books, 1970), pp. 1-50. For a dissenting view, see M. Dahood, "On Death, Resurrection, and Immortality in the Old Testament," The Anchor Bible: Psalms III (New York: Doubleday, 1970), pp. XLI-LII.

[28] J. H. Eaton, Psalms: Introduction and Commentary (London: SCM Press, 1967), p. 40.

[29] Cf. C. Tresmontant, A Study of Hebrew Thought (New York: Desclée Company, 1960), pp. 87-106; D. S. Russell, The Method and Message of Jewish Apocalyptic (London: SCM Press, 1964), pp. 140-157, 353-390.

[30] Dom Wulstan Mork, The Biblical Meaning of Man (Milwaukee: The Bruce Publishing Company, 1967), p. x; see also pp. 14-18, 33-34.

[31] N. W. Porteous, "The Nature of Man in the Old Testament," in The Interpreter's Dictionary of the Bible, eds. G. A. Buttrick et al. (New York: Abingdon Press, 1962), III, 243.

[32] A. Deissler, "Man," in Sacramentum Verbi, ed. J. B. Bauer (New York: Herder and Herder, 1970), II, 543. See also O. Schelling, "Resurrection," in Sacramentum Verbi, II, 754.

[33] Porteous, III, 243.

[34] A New Catechism (New York: Herder and Herder, 1969), p. 473. See also E. Jacob, "Death," in The Interpreter's Dictionary of the Bible, I, 802; J. Schmid, "Resurrection of the Body," in Sacramentum Mundi, eds. K. Rahner et al. (Montreal: Palm Publishers, 1970), V, 334.

[35] Schmid, V, 334.

[36] Russell, p. 366.

[37] W. G. Kummel, Promise and Fulfillment: The Eschatological Message of Jesus, trans. D. M. Barton (London: SCM Press, 1957), p. 153. See also L. G. Patterson, God and History in Early Christian Thought (New York: Seabury Press, 1967), pp. 1-15.

[38] "Immortality of the Soul or Resurrection of the Dead," in Immortality or Resurrection, ed. K. Stendahl (New York: Macmillan, 1965), p. 18.

[39] José-Maria Gonsález-Ruiz, "Should We De-Mythologize the 'Separated Soul'?" in Concilium, XLI (1969), 88.

[40] Schmid, V, 336.

[41] Cullman, p. 29.

[42] Cf. Schmid, V, 338-339; J. A. T. Robinson, In the End God (New York: Harper and Row, 1968), pp. 95-109.

[43] On New Testament eschatology, consult E. Earle Ellis, "II Corinthians V:1-10 in Pauline Eschatology," New Testament Studies, VI (1959-1960), 211-224; Charles, pp. 362-473; D. E. H. Whiteley, The Theology of St. Paul (Oxford: Basil Blackwell, 1970), pp. 262-269; Schmid, V, 338-339; J. Kremer, "The Resurrection of Jesus, the Cause and Exemplar of our Resurrection," Concilium, LX (1970), 78-91; M. Carrez, "With What Body do the Dead Rise Again?" Concilium, LX (1970), 97-102; P. Benoît, "Resurrection: At the End of Time or Immediately After Death?" Concilium, LX (1970), 103-126; J. Gnilka, "Contemporary Exegetical Understanding of 'the Resurrection of the Body,'" Concilium, LX (1970), 129-141.

[44] J. Baillie, ... And the Life Everlasting (London: Epworth, 1961), pp. 191-192.

[45] Cf. A New Catechism, p. 473; J. L. Price, The Interpreter's One-Volume Commentary on the Bible, ed. C. M. Laymon (New York: Abingdon, 1971), p. 816; Cullman, p. 39.

[46] Gatch, p. 46; cf. also P. Müller-Goldkuhle, "Post-Biblical Developments in Eschatological Thought," Concilium, XLI (1969), 24-30; D. M. Stanley, "The Greco-Roman Background of the New Testament," The Interpreter's One-Volume Commentary on the Bible, pp. 1037-1044; Whiteley, pp. 2-8.

[47] Cf. H. A. Wolfson in Stendahl, pp. 54-96; Dahood, pp. XLI-LII; Whiteley, pp. 2-8, 262-269.

[48] Cf. J. Pelikan, The Shape of Death: Life, Death and Immortality in the Early Fathers (New York: Abingdon, 1961), especially pp. 33-34.

[49] C. Tresmontant, The Origins of Christian Philosophy, trans. M. Pontifex (New York: Hawthorn Books, 1963), pp. 75-118; C. Tresmontant, Christian Metaphysics (New York: Sheed and Ward, 1965), pp. 71-81.

[50] Gatch, p. 78.

[51] Cf. J. Leclercq, The Love of Learning and the Desire for God, trans. C. Misrahi (New York: Fordham University Press, 1961), p. 283; also pp. 65-184, especially pp. 135-137; p. 252.

[52] P. O. Kristeller, Renaissance Philosophy and the Medieval Tradition (Latrobe, Pennsylvania: Archabbey Press, 1966), p. 61; also pp. 18-19, 34-36, 62.

[53] Gatch, p. 92.

[54] Knowles, p. 75. On the problem of eschatology in the Middle Ages, see also Müller-Goldkuhle, 30-36; H. De Lubac, Catholicism: A Study of Dogma in Relation to the

Corporate Destiny of Mankind (London: Burns, Oates & Washbourne, 1950), pp. 51-53; Pegis, "St. Thomas and the Unity of Man," pp. 153-173; Introduction, note 11.

[55] See Introduction, note 55.

[56] Gatch, p. 101.

[57] G. F. Kreyche, "The Soul-Body Problem in St. Thomas," The New Scholasticism, XLVI (1972), 474; also M.-D. Chenu, Toward Understanding St. Thomas, trans. A. M. Landry and D. Hughes (Chicago: Henry Regnery, 1964), pp. 289-292.

[58] "St. Thomas and the Unity of Man," p. 153.

[59] Ibid., p. 156. Pegis cites In III Sent., d. 5, q. 3, a 2; ed. M. F. Moos (Paris: P. Lethielleux, 1933), pp. 206-207 in support of his view.

[60] Ibid., Moos, p. 207.

[61] De Unitate Intellectus Contra Averroistas, ed. Keeler, cap. 2, 59, p. 38.

[62] Ibid., cap. 3, 84, p. 53.

[63] De Spiritualibus Creaturis, q. 1, art. 2, in Quaestiones Disputatae et Quaestiones Duodecim Quodlibetales (Rome: Marietti Edition, 1927), II, 318.

[64] Ibid., II, 320.

[65] "It follows therefore that the soul is a particular thing, having of itself the power to subsist; not as a thing having a complete species of its own, but as completing the human species as the form of the body." De Anima, q. 1, art. 1, in Quaestiones Disputatae et Quaestiones Duodecim Quodlibetales, II, 369.

[66] Kreyche, p. 475 and p. 479.

[67] De Lubac, p. 55; cf. also J. Ratzinger, "Resurrection," in Sacramentum Mundi, V, 340; Müller-Goldkuhle, 35; H. Schwarz, On the Way to the Future (Minneapolis: Augsburg, 1972), p. 191.

[68] Gatch, p. 115; cf. also pp. 112-115, 206; Schwarz, pp. 14, 64, 105, 137-140, 149-150, 168, 174, 191-192.

[69] Gatch, p. 119; cf. also pp. 115-120; Schwarz, pp. 139, 157, 171, 174.

[70] Cullman, pp. 46-47.

[71] R. W. Gleason, The World to Come (New York: Sheed and Ward, 1958), p. 58.

[72] Ratzinger, 340.

[73] K. Rahner, Theological Investigations, trans. K. Smyth (Baltimore: Helicon Press, 1966), IV, 347.

[74] G. Marcel, Searchings (New York: Newman Press, 1967), p. 57.

[75] W. Kunneth, The Theology of the Resurrection (London: SCM Press, 1965), pp. 33-40. See also Robinson, pp. 91-94.

[76] González-Ruiz, 92-93.

[77] Kunneth, p. 40.

[78] Schwarz, p. 172.

[79] De Anima, I, 1 (402a 22-b6).

[80] Ibid., I, 1 (402b 10). The translation of Aristotle's De Anima used in this study is that of J. A. Smith, in The Works of Aristotle, ed. W. D. Ross (Oxford: Clarendon Press, 1931), III.

[81] Ibid., I, 1 (404a 25-b6).

[82] Ibid., I, 1 (405a 14-16).

[83] Ibid., I, 4 (408b 21).

[84] Ibid., I, 4 (408b 18).

[85] "Some hold that the soul is divisible, and that one part thinks, another desires. If, then, its nature admits of its being divided, what can it be that holds the parts together? Surely not the body; on the contrary it seems rather to be the soul that holds the body together; at any rate when the soul departs the body disintegrates and decays. If, then, there is something else which makes the soul one, this unifying agency would have the best right to the name of soul." Ibid., I, 5 (411b 5-10).

[86] Ibid., I, 5 (411b 18).

[87] Ibid., II, 1 (412a 19-21).

[88] Ibid., II, 1 (412a 27-28).

[89] Ibid., II, 2 (412b 4-6).

[90] Ibid., II, 2 (414a 21).

[91] Ibid., II, 1 (412b 6-7).

[92] On the psychology of Aristotle, cf. Pringle-Patterson, pp. 62-66; Choron, pp. 53-57; C. Shute, The Psychology of Aristotle (New York: Columbia University Press, 1941), especially pp. 129-131; M. De Corte, La Doctrine de l'Intelligence chez Aristote (Paris: J. Vrin, 1934); R. D.

Hicks, ed. and trans. Aristotle's De Anima (London: Cambridge University Press, 1965), pp. xlii-xliv, lxiv-lxix; F. Nuyens, L'Evolution de la Psychologie d'Aristote (Louvain: Institut Supérieur de Philosophie, 1948); Pegis, "St. Thomas and the Unity of Man," pp. 153-173; Riordan, pp. 7-19; W. D. Ross, Aristotle (London: Methuen, 1930), pp. 131-135, 148-153; Webb, pp. 264-273.

[93] De Anima, II, 2 (413a 4-9).

[94] "At present we must confine ourselves to saying that the soul is the source of these phenomena and is characterized by them, viz. by the powers of self-nutrition, sensation, thinking, and motivity. Is each of these a soul or part of a soul? And if a part, a part in what sense? A part merely distinguishable by definition or a part distinct in local situation as well? In the case of certain of these powers, the answers to these questions are easy, in the case of others we are puzzled what to say." Ibid., II, 2 (413b 11-16).

[95] Ibid., II, 2 (413b 24-25).

[96] "The thinking part of the soul must therefore be, while impassible, capable of receiving the form of an object; that is, must be potentially identical in character with its object without being the object. Mind must be related to what is thinkable as sense is to what is sensible." Ibid., III, 4 (429a 15-17).

[97] "Therefore, since everything is a possible object of thought, mind in order, as Anaxagoras says, to dominate, that is, to know, must be pure from all admixture; for the co-presence of what is alien to its nature is a hindrance and a block: it follows that it too, like the sensitive part, can have no nature of its own, other than that of having a certain capacity. Thus that in the soul which is called mind (by mind I mean that whereby the soul thinks and judges) is before it thinks, not actually any real thing. For this reason it cannot reasonably be regarded as blended with the body." Ibid., III, 4 (429a 18-24).

[98] Ibid., III, 4 (429a 27).

[99] Cf. Smith's footnote in Ross, The Works of Aristotle, p. 429a.

[100] Cf. Introduction, note 13; cf. also Munk, p. 443; Weber, pp. 23 24.

[101] De Anima, III, 4 (429b 4-5).

[102] Ibid., III, 5 (430a 10-19).

[103] Ibid., III, 5 (430a 20-25).

[104] Ibid., II, 4 (415b 4).

[105] Ibid., II, 4 (415b 6). Cf. also De Generatione et Corruptione, II, 2 (338a 15 - 338 b 24) and II, 10 (336b - 337a 1).

[106] De Anima, III, 10 (433a 12).

[107] Ibid., III, 7 (431a 16).

[108] De Generatione Animalium, II, 3 (736b 27-29).

[109] "And thinking in itself deals with that which is best in itself, and that which is thinking in the fullest sense with that which is best in the fullest sense. And thought thinks on itself because it shares the nature of the object of thought; for it becomes an object of thought in coming into contact with and thinking its objects, so that thought and the object of thought are the same. For that which is capable of receiving the object of thought, i.e. the essence, is thought. But it is active when it possesses this object," Metaphysica, XI, 7 (1072b 18-22); translation in Ross, The Works of Aristotle, VIII. Cf. also XII, 9 (1074b 15 - 1075a 11).

[110] "If reason is divine, then, in comparison with man, the life according to it is divine in comparison with human life.... And what we have said before will apply now; that which is proper to each thing is by nature best and most pleasant for each thing; for man, therefore, the life according to reason is best and pleasantest, since reason more than anything else is man. This life is therefore also the happiest." Ethica Nicomachea, X, 7 (1177b 30 - 1178a 7); translation by W. D. Ross in The Basic Works of Aristotle, ed. Richard McKeon (New York: Random House, 1941).

[111] For summaries of various interpretations of Aristotle's theory of the intellect, see Hicks, pp. lxiv-lxix; Webb, pp. 264-273.

[112] Nuyens, pp. 317-318, acknowledges that the relation of the intellect to the soul is a problem that Aristotle never resolves.

[113] Theophrastus, Fragments Ia and XII in E. Barbotin, La Théorie Aristotélicienne de l'Intellect d'après Théophraste (Louvain: Publications Universitaires de Louvain, 1954), pp. 248-249; 270-271.

[114] Themistius, Paraphrasis eorum quae de Anima Aristotelis, in Themistius, Commentaire sur le Traité de l'Âme d'Aristote: Traduction de Moerbeke, ed. G. Verbake (Louvain: Publications Universitaires de Louvain, 1957), pp. 224-225, 235.

[115] See Introduction, note 16.

Chapter II

[1] Cf. Muzaffar-ud-Din Nadvi, Muslim Thought and its Source (Lahore: Shaikh Muhammed Ashraf, 1953), pp. 45-46. Irenaeus makes the same point in Against Heresies, II, 6 and IV 6. Contrast with the Christian view of the relation of faith to reason from a Thomistic standpoint: "I know by reason that something is true because I see that it is true; but I believe that something is true because God has said it. In these two cases the cause of my assent is specifically different, consequently science and faith should be held as two specifically different kinds of assent. If they are two distinct species of knowledge, we should never ask one of them to fulfil what is the proper function of the other.... According to its very definition, faith implies assent of the intellect to that which the intellect does not see to be true.... Consequently, an act of faith cannot be caused by a rational evidence, but entails an intervention of the will." Gilson, Reason and Revelation in the Middle Ages, pp. 72-74. For a criticism of Gilson's view from an Islamic standpoint, cf. Rosenthal, Political Thought in Medieval Islam, p. 17 and Hyman and Walsh, p. 5.

[2] See also S. 16:65, 16:67, 30:21-25. Compare with Psalm 19:1: "The heavens are telling the glory of God; and the firmament proclaims his handiwork."

[3] Cf. A. J. Arberry, Revelation and Reason in Islam (London: George Allen and Unwin Ltd., 1965), pp. 12-15; Sharif, I, 146-150.

[4] Compare with Hebrews 1:1-2: "In many and various ways God spoke of old to our fathers by the prophets; but of these last days he has spoken to us by a Son."

[5] See note 3 above.

[6] Arberry, p. 15; cf. also Hourani, Averroes' On the Harmony of Religion and Philosophy, p. 92, note 56; S. Van den Bergh, trans. Averroes' Tahafut al-Tahafut (London: Luzac, 1954), II, 1, note 1 and II, 98; Rosenthal, Political Thought in Medieval Islam, p. 298, note 92.

[7] Cf. Arberry, pp. 16-17.

[8] On the Mu'tazilites, cf. Rosenthal, Political Thought in Medieval Islam, pp. 114-115; W. M. Watt, Islamic Philosophy and Theology (Edinburgh: Edinburgh University Press, 1962), pp. 58-70; Fakhry, A History of Islamic Philosophy, pp. 58-81; A. J. Wensinck, The Muslim Creed (London: Frank Cass, 1965), pp. 68-70; Hyman and Walsh, pp. 205-206; Badawi, Histoire de la philosophie en Islam, I, 25-33; Hernandez, I, 46-50; Gilson, History of Christian Philosophy in the Middle Ages, pp. 182-183.

[9] Watt, Islamic Philosophy and Theology, p. 67; cf. also Fakhry, A History of Islamic Philosophy, pp. 64-68.

[10] Arberry, p. 21.

[11] Fakhry, A History of Islamic Philosophy, p. 231.

[12] On the Ash'arites, cf. ibid., pp. 72-73, 230-235; Wensinck, pp. 90, 116; Watt, Islamic Philosophy and Theology, pp. 86-88; Hernandez, I, 53-58; Badawi, Histoire de la philosophie en Islam, I, 292-298; Hyman and Walsh, p. 206; Gilson, History of Christian Philosophy in the Middle Ages, pp. 184-185. Note also the following on the structure of religious thought in Islam: "Islamic theology is thus always forced into extreme positions. There can be no agent of any kind in the universe except God, since the existence of an agent implies the possibility of an action independent of God, and therefore a theoretical limitation on the absolute power of God." H. A. R. Gibb, Studies in the Civilization of Islam (Boston: Beacon Press, 1962), p. 205.

[13] De Boer, p. 62.

[14] Nadvi, p. 40.

[15] On the falasifa, cf. Rahilly, III (1914), 688; L. Gardet, Dieu et la destinée de l'homme (Paris: J. Vrin, 1967), pp. 276-278; Hourani, Averroes' On the Harmony of Religion and Philosophy, pp. 20-21; Rosenthal, Political Thought in Medieval Islam, pp. 3-8, 14, 113-121; Arberry, pp. 7-11.

[16] Rosenthal, Political Thought in Medieval Islam, p. 4.

[17] E. Gilson, God and Philosophy (New Haven: Yale University Press, 1946), p. 47.

[18] R. Walzer, "Islamic Philosophy," in S. Radhakrishnan, ed., History of Philosophy: Eastern and Western (London: George Allen and Unwin, 1953), II, 131.

[19] Arberry, pp. 16-17.

[20] Abu Rida, Rasa'il al-Kindi al-falsafiya, p. 50; trans. by Arberry, p. 34.

[21] Abu Rida, pp. 102-103; trans. by Walzer, II, 121; cf. also Arberry, p. 34.

[22] Abu Rida, p. 103; trans. by Walzer, II, 121.

[23] Abu Rida, p. 244; trans. by Arberry, p. 35.

[24] Fakhry, A History of Islamic Philosophy, p. 86.

[25] Cf. Walzer, II, 128; Gilson, A History of Christian Philosophy in the Middle Ages, p. 184. On Al-Kindi, cf. also Hyman and Walsh, p. 207; Fakhry, A History of Islamic Philosophy, pp. 102-103; Hernandez, I, 71; Badawi, Histoire de la philosophie en Islam, II, 427-437.

Notes

[26] Walzer, II, 131-132; Arberry, pp. 36-37.

[27] On Alfarabi, cf. Arberry, pp. 40-42; De Boer, pp. 118-121, 127-128; Fakhry, A History of Islamic Philosophy, pp. 145-147; Rosenthal, Political Thought in Medieval Islam, pp. 128-130; Hyman and Walsh, pp. 213-214; I. Madkour, La place d'al Fârâbî dans l'école philosophique musulmane (Paris: Librairie d'Amerique et d'Orient, 1934), pp. 122-180. Cf. also Hernandez, I, 90-97; Badawi, Histoire de la philosophie en Islam, II, 529, 545-555; Gilson, History of Christian Philosophy in the Middle Ages, pp. 186-187; Strauss, pp. 9-21.

[28] Avicenna, al-Risalat al-adhawiya fi amr al-ma'ad, ed. S. Dunya (Cairo, 1949), pp. 62, 117-118; trans. by Arberry, pp. 53, 54-55.

[29] On Avicenna, cf. Hyman and Walsh, pp. 233, 235; De Boer, pp. 139-145; Arberry, pp. 48-57; Rosenthal, Political Thought in Medieval Islam, pp. 151-152; Fakhry, A History of Islamic Philosophy, pp. 165-167; Hernandez, I, 140-147; Badawi, Histoire de la philosophie en Islam, II, 660-695; Gilson, History of Christian Philosophy in the Middle Ages, pp. 187-188, 197-205; Blumberg, "The Problem of Immortality in Avicenna, Maimonides and St. Thomas Aquinas," I, 166-174.

[30] Algazali, Tahafut al-falasifa, p. 282; trans. by Arberry, p. 62.

[31] Algazali, Mishkat ul Anwar, trans. by Sweetman, Part I, Vol. I, 55. On Algazali, cf. also Hyman and Walsh, pp. 263-264; Fakhry, A History of Islamic Philosophy, pp. 249-250, 260-261; De Boer, pp. 158-159, 163-166; Arberry, pp. 61-64; Hernandez, I, 165.

[32] Cf. Hyman and Walsh, pp. 206, 208; Knowles, p. 200.

[33] See Introduction, p. 4.

[34] Gilson, God and Philosophy, pp. 33-34, 41.

[35] Aristotle, Ethica Nicomachea, X, 7 (1177b 30 - 1178a 7), quoted in the previous chapter, note 110.

[36] Arberry, pp. 67-69; Watt, Islamic Philosophy and Theology, p. 140; Gilson, A History of Christian Philosophy in the Middle Ages, p. 183.

[37] Translation by Hourani, Averroes' On the Harmony of Religion and Philosophy, p. 44.

[38] See Introduction, notes 38 and 39.

[39] Averroes, Fasl al-maqal, trans. by Hourani, Averroes' On the Harmony of Religion and Philosophy, p. 45.

[40] See note 3 above.

[41] See note 1 above.

[42] Psalm 19:1, quoted in note 2 above.

[43] Hourani, Averroes' On the Harmony of Religion and Philosophy, pp. 20-21 and p. 45.

[44] Ibid., pp. 46-47. See also note 21 above; Arberry, pp. 67-68; Walzer, II, 131.

[45] Averroes, Fasl al-maqal, trans. by Hourani, Averroes' On the Harmony of Religion and Philosophy, p. 49. Cf. also Fakhry, A History of Islamic Philosophy, p. 312; Fakhry, "Philosophy and Scripture in the Theology of Averroes," 78-89.

[46] Averroes, Fasl al-maqal, trans. by Hourani, Averroes' On the Harmony of Religion and Philosophy, p. 49; see also ibid., p. 92, note 56; Arberry, p. 15; Van den Bergh, II, 1 and II, 98; Rosenthal, Political Thought in Medieval Islam, p. 298, note 92. The Qur'anic reference is to S. 16:125.

[47] Averroes, Fasl al-maqal, trans. by Hourani, Averroes' On the Harmony of Religion and Philosophy, p. 50. Underlining mine. See also, ibid., pp. 22-23.

[48] Cf. Sura 3:7; Gauthier, Ibn Rochd (Averroès), pp. 30-33; H. A. R. Gibb, Modern Trends in Islam (Chicago: The University of Chicago Press, 1947), pp. 11-16; L. Gardet, Mohammedanism, trans. from the French by William Burridge (New York: Hawthorn, 1961), pp. 84-86; Hourani, Averroes' On the Harmony of Religion and Philosophy, pp. 19-20, 28-32; Fakhry, A History of Islamic Philosophy, pp. 310-333; Arnold and Guillaume, p. 278.

[49] Averroes, Fasl al-maqal, trans. by Hourani, Averroes' On the Harmony of Religion and Philosophy, pp. 50, 51, 59; cf. also pp. 24 and 104, note 128.

[50] Ibid., p. 24; cf. also pp. 23-24.

[51] Cf. H. A. Wolfson, "The Double Truth Theory in Clement, Saadia, Averroes and St. Thomas, and its Origin in Aristotle and the Stoics," Jewish Quarterly Review, N. S. XXXIII (1942), 213-264, especially 243-251. Wolfson refers to Ethica Nicomachea, VI, 2 (1139a 21-26) and De Anima, III, 10 (433a 22-25). Note also: "The question of whether an act of intellect or that of will is more fundamental, which became an important point of difference between Thomists and Scotists, seems to have no precise analogue in Jewish and Muslim thought. In the latter traditions, willing is often viewed simply as the decision-making of the intellect, rather than as a distinct act of a distinct faculty, as it is among the Latins." Hyman and Walsh, p. 3.

[52] Averroes, Fasl al-maqal, trans. by Hourani, Averroes' On the Harmony of Religion and Philosophy, p. 57 and p. 102, note 116.

[53] Ibid., pp. 59-61.

[54] Ibid., p. 61.

[55] Cf. Origen, Contra Celsum, VI, 2 and VII, 60; Origen, De Principiis, I, 3; Clement, Stromata, I, 12; For Cyril of Jerusalem and St. John Chrysostom consult J. Quasten, Patrology (Westminster: Newman Press, 1960), III, 363, 364, 445.

[56] Averroes, Fasl al-maqal, trans. by Hourani, Averroes' On the Harmony of Religion and Philosophy, p. 66 and p. 68.

[57] Ibid., p. 70.

[58] Rosenthal, Political Thought in Medieval Islam, p. 116.

[59] Cf. Ibid., p. 8; Introduction, note 38; Hyman and Walsh, pp. 4-5.

[60] E. I. J. Rosenthal, ed. and trans. Averroes' Commentary on Plato's Republic (Cambridge: Cambridge University Press, 1956), p. 185; cf. also Rosenthal, Political Thought in Medieval Islam, p. 179.

[61] For an analysis of Averroes' commentary on Plato's Republic, cf. Rosenthal, Political Thought in Medieval Islam, pp. 116-118, 175-209.

[62] Cf. Ibid., pp. 205-208; Hourani, Averroes' On the Harmony of Religion and Philosophy, p. 92, note 56.

[63] Rosenthal, Political Thought in Medieval Islam, p. 205 and p. 117.

[64] Rosenthal, Averroes' Commentary on Plato's Republic, p. 250; see also p. 300.

[65] Cf. S. 5:44, 5:46, 5:48, 2:136, 33:40.

[66] Van den Bergh, I, 360-361; Zedler, Destructio Destructionum, In Physicis, Disp. IV, p. 454. For the convenience of the reader and in support of the findings of Steinschneider and Rahilly (see Introduction, notes 53 and 54) that the Destructio Destructionum is a faithful rendering of the Tahafut al-Tahafut, references to the Latin text will be given as well.

[67] Van den Bergh, I, 322; Zedler, Destructio Destructionum, In Physicis, Disp. I, p. 410.

[68] Van den Bergh, I, 152; Zedler, Destructio Destructionum, In Metaphysicis, Disp. III, p. 223.

[69] "This inability to comprehend things the knowledge of which is, however, necessary in the life and existence of man, is either absolute -- i.e. it is not in the nature of the intellect, in so far as it is intellect, to comprehend such a thing -- or it is not in the nature of a certain class of man, and this kind of weakness is either a fundamental character of his disposition or something accidental through a lack of education. Revelation is a mercy bestowed on all these classes of men." Ibid.

[70] Van den Bergh, I, 307; Zedler, Destructio Destructionum, In Metaphysicis, Disp. XVI, pp. 392-393.

[71] Van den Bergh, I, 322; Zedler, Destructio Destructionum, In Physicis, Disp. I, p. 410.

[72] Van den Bergh, I, 315; Zedler, Destructio Destructionum, In Physicis, Disp. I, p. 402.

[73] See note 43 above.

[74] Van den Bergh, I, 361; Zedler, Destructio Destructionum, In Physicis, Disp. IV, p. 454.

[75] Van den Bergh, I, 360; Zedler, Destructio Destructionum, In Physicis, Disp. IV, p. 453.

[76] See note 63 above.

[77] Van den Bergh, I, 360; Zedler, Destructio Destructionum, In Physicis, Disp. IV, p. 453.

[78] Van den Bergh, I, 360; Zedler, Destructio Destructionum, In Physicis, Disp. IV, pp. 453-454.

[79] Van den Bergh, I, 359-360; Zedler, Destructio Destructionum, In Physicis, Disp. IV, p. 453.

[80] See Introduction, note 26.

[81] See note 44 above.

[82] Commentarium in Aristotelis Librum de Anima, lib. I, lect. 2, ed. A. M. Pirotta (Rome: Marietti Edition, 1948), p. 9; trans. by K. Foster and S. Humphries, p. 59.

[83] In Boethium de Trinitate, q. 2, art. 1, in Opera Omnia, ed. S. E. Fretté (Paris: Vivès, 1875), XXVIII, 496; trans. by Brennan, The Trinity and the Unicity of the Intellect, p. 47.

[84] See note 47 above.

[85] Summa Contra Gentiles, I, 7; trans. by A. C. Pegis, On the Truth of the Catholic Faith, Summa Contra Gentiles, Book I: God (New York: Doubleday, 1962), p. 74.

[86] See note 68 above.

[87] "The investigation of the human reason for the most part has falsity present within it, and this is due partly to the weakness of the intellect in judgment, and partly to the admixture of images. The result is that many, remaining ignorant of the power of demonstration, would hold in doubt those things that have been most truly demonstrated. This would be particularly the case since they see that, among those who are reputed to be wise men, each one teaches his own brand of doctrine. Furthermore, with the many truths that are demonstrated, there sometimes is mingled something that is false, which is not demonstrated but rather asserted on the basis of some probable or sophistical argument, which has yet the credit of being a demonstration. That is why it was necessary that the unshakeable certitude and pure truth concerning divine things should be presented to men by way of faith." Summa Contra Gentiles, I, 4, in ed. Leon., p. 4; trans. by Pegis, On the Truth of the Catholic Faith, I, 68. Cf. also In Boethium de Trinitate, q. 6, art. 1, Resp.

[88] Gilson, Reason and Revelation in the Middle Ages, p. 83. Cf. also Summa Theologiae, IIa-IIae, q. 1, art. 5, ad 3m, in Opera Omnia, eds. S. E. Fretté and P. Maré (Paris: Vivès, 1872), III, 77.

[89] "That God is the author of holy Scripture should be acknowledged, and he has the power, not only of adapting words to convey meanings (which men also can do), but also of adapting things themselves. In every branch of knowledge words have meaning, but what is special here is that the things meant by the words also themselves mean something. That first meaning whereby the words signify things belongs to the sense first mentioned, namely the historical or literal. That meaning, however, whereby the thing specified by the words in their turn also signify other things is called the spiritual sense; it is based on and presupposes the literal sense." Summa Theologiae, Ia, q. 1, art. 10; Latin text ed. and trans. by the English Dominican Fathers (London: Blackfriars, 1964), I, 37-38. Cf. also Summa Theologiae, IIa IIae, q. 110, art. 3, ad 3 and ad 4.

[90] See notes 55 and 56 above.

[91] "If any subtleties are proposed to uncultivated people, these folk may find in the imperfect comprehension of them matter for error; wherefore, in I Cor. 3:1 it is said: "And I, brethren, could not speak to you as unto spiritual, but as unto carnal. As unto little ones in Christ, I gave you milk to drink, not meat." And therefore also, on Exod. 21:33, "If a man open a pit," the gloss of Gregory says: "He who in sacred eloquence now understands lofty things should cover over these truths by silence when in the

presence of those who do not comprehend them, lest through some scandal of mind he cause the loss of some little one among the faithful." In Boethium de Trinitate, q. 2, art. 4, in Opera Omnia, ed. S. E. Fretté, XXVIII, 502; trans. by Brennan, The Trinity and the Unicity of the Intellect, pp. 64-65.

[92] Gilson, Reason and Revelation in the Middle Ages, p. 79.

[93] Cf., for example, Summa Contra Gentiles, I, 3.

[94] Cf., for example, In Boethium de Trinitate, q. 2, art. 3, Resp.; cf. also note 87 above.

Chapter III

[1] See Chapter I, notes 79 and 80.

[2] In I de Anima, comm. 9, p. 13. The citation is from Averrois Cordubensis Commentarium Magnum in Aristotelis De Anima Libros, ed. F. S. Crawford (Cambridge, Mass.: The Mediaeval Academy of America, 1953). This edition of the commentary of the De Anima will be used throughout the study.

[3] See Chapter I, note 82.

[4] In I de Anima, comm. 31, p. 40.

[5] See Chapter I, note 83.

[6] In I de Anima, comm. 65, p. 88.

[7] See Chapter I, note 85.

[8] In I de Anima, comm. 90, p. 121.

[9] See Chapter I, note 86.

[10] In I de Anima, comm. 92, p. 123.

[11] See Chapter I, note 87.

[12] In II de Anima, comm. 4, pp. 133-134.

[13] See Chapter I, note 88.

[14] In II de Anima, comm. 5, pp. 134-135.

[15] See Chapter I, note 89.

[16] In II de Anima, comm. 7, p. 138.

[17] Ibid., pp. 138-139.

[18] See Chapter I, note 93.

[19] _In II de Anima_, comm. 11, p. 147.

[20] _Ibid._, p. 148.

[21] _Ibid._

[22] See Introduction, note 16.

[23] _In II de Anima_, comm. 11, p. 148.

[24] See Chapter I, note 95.

[25] _In II de Anima_, comm. 21, p. 160.

[26] _Ibid._

[27] _Ibid._, pp. 160-161.

[28] See Chapter I, notes 95 and 108.

[29] See Chapter I, notes 96 and 101.

[30] _In III de Anima_, comm. 1, p. 380.

[31] _In III de Anima_, comm. 2, p. 381.

[32] _Ibid._

[33] _In III de Anima_, comm. 3, p. 382.

[34] _In III de Anima_, comm. 4, pp. 383-384; trans. by Hyman and Walsh, p. 314.

[35] _Ibid._, p. 385; trans. by Hyman and Walsh, p. 315.

[36] _Ibid._, pp. 385-386; trans. by Hyman and Walsh, p. 315.

[37] _Ibid._, p. 386; trans. by Hyman and Walsh, pp. 315-316.

[38] _In III de Anima_, comm. 5, pp. 387-388; trans. by Hyman and Walsh, pp. 316-317.

[39] _In III de Anima_, comm. 6, pp. 413-414.

[40] Aristotle, _De Anima_, III, 4 (430a 1).

[41] _In III de Anima_, comm. 14, p. 430.

[42] _In III de Anima_, comm. 5, pp. 393-394.

[43] _In III de Anima_, comm. 14, pp. 430-432.

[44] _Ibid._, pp. 432-433.

[45] _In III de Anima_, comm. 5, p. 399; trans. by Hyman and Walsh, p. 317.

[46] See, for example, Chapter II, notes 47 and 70.

[47] In III de Anima, comm. 36, p. 502.

[48] In III de Anima, comm. 5, p. 393.

[49] Ibid., pp. 411-412; trans. by Hyman and Walsh, pp. 323-324.

[50] Ibid., p. 412; trans. by Hyman and Walsh, p. 324. Cf. also In III de Anima, comm. 5, p. 400.

[51] In III de Anima, comm. 19, pp. 441-442.

[52] In III de Anima, comm. 20, p. 449; trans. by G. P. Klubertanz, The Discursive Power (St. Louis: Modern Schoolman, 1952), p. 118.

[53] In III de Anima, comm. 7, p. 419; trans. by Klubertanz, The Discursive Power, p. 116.

[54] In III de Anima, comm. 20, p. 449; trans. by Klubertanz, The Discursive Power, p. 118.

[55] In III de Anima, comm. 33, p. 475.

[56] In III de Anima, comm. 48, p. 516.

[57] In III de Anima, comm. 57, pp. 529-530; trans. by Klubertanz, The Discursive Power, p. 119.

[58] In II de Anima, comm. 63, pp. 225-226; trans. by Klubertanz, The Discursive Power, p. 120.

[59] In III de Anima, comm. 6, pp. 415-416; trans. by Klubertanz, The Discursive Power, p. 117.

[60] In III de Anima, comm. 33, pp. 476-477; cf. also ibid., comm. 20, p. 451.

[61] In III de Anima, comm. 7, p. 419; trans. by Klubertanz, The Discursive Power, p. 116.

[62] In III de Anima, comm. 33, p. 476; trans. by Klubertanz, The Discursive Power, pp. 120-121.

[63] See Chapter I, notes 89, 95, 108, 110.

[64] Van den Bergh, I, 344; Zedler, Destructio Destructionum, In Physicis, Disp. II, pp. 435-436.

[65] Van den Bergh, I, 356; Zedler, Destructio Destructionum, In Physicis, Disp. II, p. 448.

[66] Ibid.

[67] Ibid.

Notes

⁶⁸Van den Bergh, I, 339; Zedler, <u>Destructio Destructionum</u>, In Physicis, Disp. II, p. 430.

⁶⁹<u>Ibid</u>.

⁷⁰Van den Bergh, I, 339-340; Zedler, <u>Destructio Destructionum</u>, In Physicis, Disp. II, p. 431.

⁷¹Van den Bergh, I, 340; Zedler, <u>Destructio Destructionum</u>, in Physicis, Disp. II, p. 431.

⁷²Van den Bergh, I, 340-341; Zedler, <u>Destructio Destructionum</u>, In Physicis, Disp. II, pp. 431-432.

⁷³Van den Bergh, I, 343; Zedler, <u>Destructio Destructionum</u>, In Physicis, Disp. II, p. 434.

⁷⁴See Chapter I, note 83 and notes 5 and 6 above.

⁷⁵Van den Bergh, I, 343; Zedler, <u>Destructio Destructionum</u>, In Physicis, Disp. II, p. 434.

⁷⁶Qur'an 17:85.

⁷⁷Van den Bergh, I, 343; Zedler, <u>Destructio Destructionum</u>, In Physicis, Disp. II, p. 435. The quotation at the end of the passage is from the Qur'an 39:42.

⁷⁸Van den Bergh, I, 14; Zedler, <u>Destructio Destructionum</u>, In Metaphysicis, Disp. I, p. 84.

⁷⁹Van den Bergh, I, 359; Zedler, <u>Destructio Destructionum</u>, In Physicis, Disp. IV, p. 452.

⁸⁰Van den Bergh, I, 357; Zedler, <u>Destructio Destructionum</u>, In Physicis, Disp. III, p. 450.

⁸¹Van den Bergh, I, 362; Zedler, <u>Destructio Destructionum</u>, In Physicis, Disp. IV, p. 455.

⁸²See Chapter I, note 104.

⁸³See Chapter I, note 105.

⁸⁴Van den Bergh, I, 361; Zedler, <u>Destructio Destructionum</u>, In Physicis, Disp. IV, p. 455.

⁸⁵Averroes, <u>Kashf al-manahidj</u>, trans. by Hourani, Averroes' On the Harmony of Religion and Philosophy, p. 78.

⁸⁶<u>Ibid</u>., p. 77.

⁸⁷<u>Ibid</u>., pp. 76-77.

⁸⁸<u>Ibid</u>., p. 77.

⁸⁹<u>Ibid</u>.

⁹⁰See note 82 above.

⁹¹See note 83 above.

⁹²Averroes, *Kashf al-manahidj*, trans. by Hourani, *Averroes' On the Harmony of Religion and Philosophy*, p. 77.

Chapter IV

¹See Chapter III, notes 50-62.

²*Ibid*., note 27.

³*Ibid*., notes 29-37.

⁴*Ibid*., notes 52-54.

⁵*Ibid*., note 60.

⁶See Chapter I, note 102.

⁷See Chapter II, note 12.

⁸*In III de Anima*, comm. 4, pp. 384-385; trans. by Hyman and Walsh, p. 315.

⁹*In III de Anima*, comm. 5, p. 406; trans. by Hyman and Walsh, p. 321.

¹⁰*In III de Anima*, comm. 18, p. 439.

¹¹*In III de Anima*, comm. 20, pp. 450-451. Cf. also *In III de Anima*, comm. 19, pp. 442-443.

¹²*In III de Anima*, comm. 5, p. 400; trans. by Hyman and Walsh, pp. 317-318. Cf. also Chapter III, note 50.

¹³*Ibid*., p. 401; trans. by Hyman and Walsh, p. 318.

¹⁴*Ibid*., pp. 410-411; trans. by Hyman and Walsh, p. 323.

¹⁵*In III de Anima*, comm. 20, p. 448.

¹⁶*In III de Anima*, comm. 5, p. 408; trans. by Hyman and Walsh, p. 322.

¹⁷*Ibid*., pp. 411-412; trans. by Hyman and Walsh, pp. 323-324. See also Chapter III, note 50.

¹⁸See Chapter I, notes 95 and 108.

¹⁹See Chapter I, note 109.

²⁰*In III de Anima*, comm. 36, pp. 480-481.

[21] In III de Anima, comm. 18, p. 438. See Aristotle, De Anima, 4 (429b 5-10). See also Chapter II, note 51.

[22] In III de Anima, comm. 20, pp. 453-454.

[23] Ibid., p. 448.

[24] In III de Anima, comm. 36, p. 496.

[25] Ibid., p. 498.

[26] Ibid.

[27] Ibid., p. 499.

[28] Ibid., p. 498.

[29] Ibid., p. 499.

[30] Ibid.

[31] Ibid., p. 497.

[32] Ibid.

[33] Ibid., p. 499.

[34] Ibid., pp. 497-498.

[35] Ibid., pp. 499-500.

[36] Ibid., p. 500.

[37] Ibid., p. 499.

[38] Ibid., p. 500.

[39] In III de Anima, comm. 5, p. 411.

[40] In III de Anima, comm. 36, p. 500.

[41] Ibid., (critical apparatus).

[42] Ibid., p. 501 (critical apparatus).

[43] Ibid., p. 502.

[44] Ibid., p. 501.

[45] This simile is an adaptation of that used by S. C. Tornay, "Averroes' Doctrine of the Mind," Philosophic Review, LII (1943), 278, where he concludes that Averroes' theory of the intellect allows only for an impersonal immortality for man.

Chapter V

[1] See above, pp. 23-24.

[2] See above, pp. 82-83.

[3] See above, pp. 55-56.

[4] See above, p. 108 and p. 111.

[5] See above, p. 45.

[6] See above, pp. 43-46.

[7] See above, pp. 44-45.

[8] See above, pp. 46-47.

[9] See above, p. 48.

[10] See above, p. 49.

[11] See above, pp. 39-40.

[12] See above, p. 50.

[13] See above, p. 48 and p. 50.

[14] See above, p. 50.

[15] See above, p. 15.

[16] See above, p. 16.

[17] See above, p. 18.

[18] See above, p. 17.

[19] See above, p. 17.

[20] See above, p. 17.

[21] See above, p. 65.

[22] See above, p. 65.

[23] See above, p. 66.

[24] See above, p. 67.

[25] See above, p. 16 and pp. 60-61.

[26] See above, p. 17.

[27] See above, p. 17.

[28] See above, p. 61.

[29] See above, pp. 82-83.

[30] See above, p. 15.

[31] See above, p. 15.

[32] See above, p. 19.

[33] See above, p. 20.

[34] See above, p. 19.

[35] See above, p. 21.

[36] See above, p. 20.

[37] See above, p. 20.

[38] See above, p. 21.

[39] See above, p. 19.

BIBLIOGRAPHY

Albert the Great. De Unitate Intellectus Contra Averroem. Vol. IX of Opera Omnia. Edited by A. Borgnet. Paris: Vivès, 1899.

Alexander of Aphrodisias. De Intellectu et Intellecto, in G. Théry, Alexandre d'Aphrodise. Kain, Belgium: Le Saulchoir, 1926.

Allard, M. "Le rationalisme d'Averroès d'après une étude sur la création," Bulletin d'Études Orientales, XIV (1952-1954), 7-59 (Institut Français de Damas, Damascus, 1954).

Alonso, M. Teología de Averroes. Madrid and Granada: Maestre, 1947.

Anderson, B. W. Understanding the Old Testament. New Jersey: Prentice-Hall, Inc., 1959.

Andrae, T. Mohammed: The Man and His Faith. Translated by T. Menzel. New York: Harper and Row, 1960. First published in 1936.

Arberry, A. J. Reason and Revelation in Islam. London: George Allen and Unwin Ltd., 1956.

Aristotle. De Anima. Edited and translated by R. D. Hicks. London: Cambridge University Press, 1965.

--------. Basic Works of Aristotle. Edited by R. McKeon. New York: Random House, 1941.

--------. The Works of Aristotle. 11 vols. Edited by W. D. Ross. Oxford: At the Clarendon Press, 1908-31.

--------. Traité de l'âme. Edited by G. Rodier. Paris: Leroux, 1900.

Arnaldez, R. "Ibn Rushd," Encyclopedia of Islam. New edition. Vol. III. Leiden: E. J. Brill, 1971.

--------. "L'immortalité de l'âme dans le Tahafût," Studia Islamica, X (1959), 23-41.

Arnold, T., and A. Guillaume, eds. The Legacy of Islam. Oxford: At the Clarendon Press, 1931.

Asín y Palacio, M. "El Averroismo Teológico de Santo Tomás de Aquino," in Homenaje á D. Francisco Codera. Zaragoza: Escar, 1904, pp. 271-331.

Averroes. Averroes' Commentary on Plato's Republic. Edited and translated by E. I. J. Rosenthal. Cambridge: At the University Press, 1956.

Bibliography

Averroes. *Averroes' On the Harmony of Religion and Philosophy*. Edited and translated by G. F. Hourani. London: Luzac and Co. Ltd., 1961.

--------. *Averroes' Tahafut al-Tahafut*. Edited by M. Bouyges. Beyrouth: Imprimerie Catholique, 1922.

--------. *Averroes' Tahafut al-Tahafut (The Incoherence of the Incoherence)*. Translated by S. Van den Bergh. 2 vols. London: Luzac and Co. Ltd., 1954.

--------. *Averrois Cordubensis Commentarium Magnum in Aristotelis de Anima Libros*. Edited by F. S. Crawford. Cambridge, Mass.: The Mediaeval Academy of America, 1953.

--------. *Destructio Destructionum Philosophiae Algazelis*. Edited by B. H. Zedler. Milwaukee: Marquette University Press, 1961.

--------. *The Philosophy and Theology of Averroes*. Translated by Mohammed Jamil-Ur-Rehman. Baroda: Arya Sudharak Printing Press, 1921.

Badawi, A. *Histoire de la philosophie en Islam*. 2 vols. (Études de Philosophie Médiévale, no. 60.) Paris: J. Vrin, 1970.

--------. *La transmission de la philosophie grecque au monde arabe*. Paris: J. Vrin, 1968.

Baillie, J. *... And the Life Everlasting*. London: The Epworth Press, 1961.

Barbotin, E. "Autour de la noétique aristotélicienne. L'interprétation de témoignage de Théophraste par Averroès et Saint Thomas d'Aquin," *Mélanges Auguste Diés*. Paris: J. Vrin, 1956.

--------. *La théorie aristotélicienne de l'intellect d'après Théophraste*. Louvain: Publications Universitaires, 1954.

Baron, S. W. *Essays on Maimonides*. New York: Columbia University Press, 1941.

Benoît, P. "Resurrection: At the End of Time or Immediately After Death?" *Concilium*, LX (1970), 103-126.

Benoît, P., and R. Murphy, eds. *Immortality and Resurrection*. New York: Herder and Herder, 1970.

Berthier, André. "Un maître orientaliste du XIIIe siècle: Raymond Martin, O. P.," *Archivum Fratrum Praedicatorum*, VI (1936), 267-311.

Bettenson, H. *The Early Christian Fathers*. London: Oxford University Press, 1958.

Blumberg, H. Reviewer of G. F. Hourani's Averroes' On the Harmony of Religion and Philosophy, in Speculum, XXXVII, no. 1 (1963), 635-639.

--------. "The Problem of Immortality in Avicenna, Maimonides and St. Thomas Aquinas," in Harry Austryn Wolfson Jubilee Volume. Vol. I. Jerusalem: The American Academy of Jewish Research, 1965.

St. Bonaventure. Opera Omnia. Vols. II and V. Quaracchi: Ex Typographia Collegii S. Bonaventurae, 1885, 1901.

Boros, L. The Mystery of Death. Translated by Gregory Bainbridge. New York: Herder and Herder, 1965.

Bouyges, M. Notes sur les philosophies arabes connus des Latins au moyen âge. Beyrouth: Imprimerie Catholique, 1922.

Brandon, S. G. F. The Judgement of the Dead. London: Weidenfeld and Nicolson, 1967.

--------. Man and His Destiny in the Great Religions. Toronto: University of Toronto Press, 1962.

Brennan, Robert E. Thomistic Psychology. New York: Macmillan, 1941.

Brown, R. E., J. A. Fitzmyer, and R. E. Murphy, eds. The Jerome Biblical Commentary. New Jersey: Prentice-Hall, Inc., 1968.

Brunner, E. Eternal Hope. Philadelphia: The Westminster Press, 1954.

Burckhardt, J. The Civilization of the Renaissance in Italy. Translated by S. G. C. Middlemore. London: Phaidon Press Ltd., 1955.

Busson, Henri. Les sources et le développement du rationalisme dans la littérature française de la Renaissance (1533-1601). Paris: Letouzy et Ané, 1922.

Buttrick, G. A. et al., eds. The Interpreter's Dictionary of the Bible. 4 vols. New York: The Abingdon Press, 1962.

Callus, D. A. Introduction of Aristotelian Learning to Oxford. London: H. Milford, 1944.

Calverly, E. E. "Doctrine of the Soul (nafs and rūh) in Islam," Muslim World, 33, no. 4 (October, 1943), 254-264.

--------. "Nafs," in H. A. R. Gibb and J. H. Kramers, eds., The Shorter Encyclopedia of Islam. Leiden: E. J. Brill, 1954.

Carrez, M. "With What Body do the Dead Rise Again?" Concilium, LX (1970), 97-102.

Casserley, J. V. L. The Christian in Philosophy. London: Faber and Faber Ltd., 1949.

Cassirer, E. The Individual and the Cosmos in Renaissance Philosophy. Translated by Mario Domandi. Oxford: Basil Blackwell, 1963.

Cassirer, E., P. O. Kristeller, and J. H. Randall, Jr., eds. The Renaissance Philosophy of Man. Chicago: University of Chicago Press, 1948.

Charbonnel, J.-Roger. La pensée Italienne au XIVe siècle et le courant libertin. Paris: Honoré Champion, 1919.

Charles, R. H. Eschatology: The Doctrine of a Future Life in Israel, Judaism, and Christianity. New York: Schocken Books, 1970.

Chelhoud, Joseph. Les structures du sacré chez les Arabes. Paris: G.-P. Maisoneuve et Larose, 1964.

Chenu, M.-D. Toward Understanding St. Thomas. Translated by A. M. Landry and D. Hughes. Chicago: Henry Regnery, 1964.

Choron, J. Death and Western Thought. New York: Collier Books, 1963.

Chossat, M. "L'Averroisme de S. Thomas," Archives de philosophie, IX (1932), 129-177.

Christ, P. S. "The Psychology of the Active Intellect of Averroes." Unpublished Ph.D. dissertation, University of Pennsylvania, 1926.

Cochrane, C. N. Christianity and Classical Culture. London: Oxford University Press, 1944.

Copleston, F. A History of Philosophy, Vol. II: Augustine to Scotus; Vol. III: Ockham to Suarez. Westminster: The Newman Press, 1950, 1953.

--------. Medieval Philosophy. London: Methuen and Co. Ltd., 1952.

Corbin, Henri. Creative Imagination in the Sufism of Ibn Arabi. Translated from the French by Ralph Mandheim. Princeton, N. J.: Princeton University Press, 1969.

--------. Histoire de la philosophie Islamique. Paris: Gallimard, 1964.

Cornford, F. M. Plato's Theory of Knowledge. New York: The Liberal Arts Press, 1957.

Cross, F. L., ed. The Oxford Dictionary of the Christian Church. London: Oxford University Press, 1957.

Cullman, O. "Immortality of the Soul or Resurrection of the Dead?" in K. Stendahl, ed., Immortality and Resurrection. New York: The Macmillan Company, 1965.

Dahood, M. The Anchor Bible: Psalms III. New York: Doubleday and Co., Inc., 1970.

Daniel, Norman. Islam and the West. Edinburgh: At the University Press, 1966.

De Boer, T. J. The History of Philosophy in Islam. Translated by E. R. Jones. New York: Dover Publications, Inc., 1967. First published in 1903.

De Corte, M. La doctrine de l'intelligence chez Aristote. Paris: J. Vrin, 1934.

--------. "Thémistius et saint Thomas d'Aquin. Contribution à l'étude des sources et de la chronologie du commentaire de saint Thomas sur le De Anima, Archives d'histoire doctrinale et littéraire du moyen âge, VII (1932), 47-83.

Deissler, A. "Man," in J. B. Bauer, ed., Sacramentum Verbi. Vol. II. New York: Herder and Herder, 1970.

Delcor, M. "L'immortalité de l'âme dans le livre de la Sagesse et des documents de Qumrân," Nouvelle revue théologique, LXXVII (1955), 614-630.

De Lubac, Henri. Catholicism: A Study of Dogma in Relation to the Corporate Destiny of Mankind. London: Burns, Oates and Washbourne, 1950.

Denifle, H., and E. Chatelain, eds. Chartularium Universitatis Parisiensis. Paris: Vivès, 1889-97.

Denzinger, H., and A. Schönmetzer, eds. Enchiridion Symbolorum. 32nd edition. Rome: Herder and Herder, 1963.

De Spinoza, Benedict. Ethic. Translated by W. Hale White. Translation revised by Amelia Hutchison Stirling. London: Oxford University Press, 1923.

De Vaux, C. "Averroes, Averroism," in James Hastings, ed., Encyclopaedia of Religion and Ethics. Vol. II. New York: Charles Scribner's Sons, 1918.

--------. Les penseurs de l'Islam. 5 vols. Paris: P. Geuthner, 1921-26.

De Vaux, R. "La première entrée d'Averroès chez les Latins," Revue des sciences philosophiques et théologiques, XXII (1933), 193-245.

Doyle, John P. "Ipsum Esse as God Surrogate: The Point of Convergence of Faith and Reason for St. Thomas," The Modern Schoolman, L, no. 3 (1973), 293-296.

Doncoeur, P. "La religion et les maîtres de l'averroisme," Revue des sciences philosophiques et théologiques, V (1911), 267-298.

De Wulf, M. Histoire de la philosophie médiévale. Tome I. Louvain: Institut Supérieur de Philosophie, 1934.

--------. History of Mediaeval Philosophy. Vol. I. Translated by E. Messenger. London: Thomas Nelson and Sons Ltd., 1951.

Duhem, P. Le système du monde. Tome IV. Paris: Hermann, 1916.

Duns Scotus. "De Spiritualite et Immortalitate Animae," in Allan Wolter ed. and trans., Duns Scotus: Philosophical Writings. London: Thomas Nelson and Sons Ltd., 1963.

Eaton, J. H. Psalms: Introduction and Commentary. London: SCM Press, 1967.

Eklund, R. Life Between Death and Resurrection According to Islam. Uppsala: Uppsala University Press, 1941.

El-Ehwany, Ahmed Fouad. Islamic Philosophy. Cairo: Anglo-Egyptian Bookshop, 1957.

Ellis, E. Earle. "II Corinthians V: 1-10 in Pauline Eschatology," New Testament Studies, VI (1959-60), 211-224.

El-Saleh, Soubhi. La vie future selon le Coran. Paris: J. Vrin, 1971.

Ermatinger, C. J. "Averroism in Early Fourteenth Century Bologna," Mediaeval Studies, XVI (1954), 35-56.

Evrin, M. Sadeddin. Eschatology in Islam. Istanbul: Institute of Advanced Islamic Studies, 1960.

Fakhry, M. A History of Islamic Philosophy. New York: Columbia University Press, 1970.

--------. Islamic Occasionalism and its Critique by Averroes and Aquinas. London: George Allen and Unwin Ltd., 1958.

--------. "Philosophy and Scripture in the Theology of Averroes," Mediaeval Studies, XXX (1968), 78-89.

Forget, J. "De l'influence de la philosophie arabe sur la philosophie scolastique," Revue néo-scolastique, Oct. 1894, 385-410.

Gardet, L. Dieu et la destinée de l'homme. Paris: J. Vrin, 1967.

--------. L'Islam: Religion et communauté. Paris: Desclée de Brouwer, 1967.

--------. Mohammedanism. Translated from the French by William Burridge. New York: Hawthorn Books, 1961.

--------. Reviewer of L. Gauthier's Ibn Rochd (Averroès), in Bulletin Thomiste (1947-53), 248-252.

Gardet, L., and M.-M. Anawati. Introduction a la théologie musulmane. Paris: J. Vrin, 1948.

Gatch, M. McM. Death: Meaning and Mortality in Christian Thought and Contemporary Culture. New York: The Seabury Press, 1969.

Gauthier, L. Ibn Rochd (Averroès). Paris: Presses Universitaires de France, 1948.

--------. "Scolastique musulmane et scolastique chretienne," Revue d'histoire de la philosophie, II (1928), 221-253, 333-365.

--------. La théorie d'Ibn Rochd (Averroès) sur les rapports de la religion et de la philosophie. Paris: Leroux, 1909.

Gibb, H. A. R. Mohammedanism. New York: Oxford University Press, 1962.

--------. Studies in the Civilization of Islam. Boston: Beacon Press, 1962.

--------. Trends in Modern Islam. Chicago: University of Chicago Press, 1947.

Gibb, H. A. R. and J. H. Kramers, eds. The Shorter Encyclopedia of Islam. Leiden: E. J. Brill, 1953.

Giles of Rome. Errores Philosophorum. Edited by J. Koch; translated by J. Riedl. Milwaukee: Marquette University Press, 1944.

Gilson, E. "L'affaire de l'immortalité de l'âme à Venise au debut de XVIe siècle," In Umanesimo Europeo e Umanesimo Veneziano. Firenze: G. C. Sansoni Editore, 1962.

--------. "Autour de Pomponazzi, Problématique de l'immortalité de l'âme en Italie au debut du XVIe siècle,"

Bibliography

> Archives d'histoire doctrinale et littéraire du moyen âge, XXXVI (1961), 163-279.

Gilson, E. Being and Some Philosophers. Toronto: Pontifical Institute of Mediaeval Studies, 1949.

--------. "Boèce de Dacie et la double vérité," Archives d'histoire et littéraire du moyen âge, XXX (1955), 81-99.

--------. The Christian Philosophy of St. Thomas Aquinas. New York: Random House, 1956.

--------. "L'études de philosophies arabes et son rôle dans l'interprétation de la scolastique," Proceedings of the Sixth International Congress of Philosophy. New York: Longmans, Green and Co., 1927.

--------. God and Philosophy. New Haven: Yale University Press, 1946.

--------. A History of Christian Philosophy in the Middle Ages, New York: Random House, 1955.

--------. La philosophie au moyen âge. Paris: Payot, 1947.

--------. Reason and Revelation in the Middle Ages. New York: Charles Scribner's Sons, 1948.

--------. The Spirit of Mediaeval Philosophy. Translated by A. H. C. Downes. New York: Charles Scribner's Sons, 1936.

--------. Le Thomisme. 6th edition. Paris: J. Vrin, 1965.

--------. The Unity of Philosophical Experience. New York: Charles Scribner's Sons, 1941.

Glasson, T. F. His Appearing and His Kingdom. London: The Epworth Press, 1953.

Gleason, R. W. The World to Come. New York: Sheed and Ward, 1958.

Glenn, P. J. The History of Philosophy. St. Louis: B. Herder Book Co., 1947.

Gnilka, J. "Contemporary Exegetical Understanding of 'the Resurrection of the Body,'" Concilium, LX (1970), 129-141.

Goldziher, I. Le dogme et la loi de l'Islam. Paris: P. Geuthner, 1930.

--------. Muslim Studies. Edited by S. M. Stern; translated from the German by C. R. Barber and S. M. Stern. Chicago: Aldine Publishing Company, 1968.

González-Ruiz, José María. "Should We De-Mythologize the Separated Soul'?" Concilium, XLI (1969), 82-96.

Grabner-Haider, A. "The Biblical Understanding of 'Resurrection' and 'Glorification,'" Concilium, XLI (1969), 68-81.

Grubé, G. M. A. Plato's Thought. London: Methuen and Co. Ltd., 1935.

Hamelin, C. La théorie de l'intellect d'après Aristote et ses commentateurs. Paris: J. Vrin, 1953.

Harnack, Adolph. History of Dogma. 7 vols. Translated from the third German edition by Neil Buchanan. New York: Dover Publications, Inc., 1961.

Haskins, C. H. Studies in the History of Medieval Science. Cambridge, Mass.: Harvard University Press, 1927.

--------. Studies in Mediaeval Culture. Oxford: At the Clarendon Press, 1929.

Hatch, E. The Influence of Greek Ideas on Christianity. New York: Harper and Row, 1966. First published in 1891.

Hernandez, M. Filosofía Hispano-Musulmana. 2 vols. Madrid: Asociacion Española para el Progreso de las Ciencias, 1957.

Hourani, G. F. Islamic Rationalism. Oxford: At the Clarendon Press, 1971.

--------. The Life and Thought of Ibn Rushd. Cairo: American University Press, 1947.

Husik, Isaac. A History of Mediaeval Jewish Philosophy. New York: Macmillan, 1930.

Hyman, A., and J. Walsh, eds. Philosophy in the Middle Ages. New York: Harper and Row, 1967.

Iorio, Domenick A. "The Problem of the Soul and the Unity of Man in Pietro Pomponazzi," The New Scholasticism, XXXVII (1963), 293-311.

Iqbal, Mohammed. The Reconstruction of Religious Thought in Islam. Lahore: Shaikh Muhammed Ashraf, 1962.

Izutsu, Toshihiko. The Concept of Belief in Islamic Theology. Tokyo: Keio Institute, 1965.

--------. Ethico-Religious Concepts in the Qur'an. Montreal: McGill University Press, 1966.

--------. God and Man in the Koran. Tokyo: Keio Institute, 1964.

Bibliography

Jacob, E. "Death," in G. A. Buttrick et al., eds., The Interpreter's Dictionary of the Bible. Vol. I. The Abingdon Press, 1962.

James, E. O. Comparative Religion. London: Methuen and Co. Ltd., 1961. First published in 1938.

Jolif, J.-Y. "Affirmation rationelle de l'immortalité de l'âme chez saint Thomas," Lumière et Vie, XXIV (1955), 59-77.

Keefe, D. J. "Death as Worship," Theology Digest, XXI, no. 4 (1973), 334-341.

Kelly, J. N. D. Early Christian Doctrines. London: Adam and Charles Black, 1960.

Kennedy, L. A. "The Nature of the Human Intellect According to St. Albert the Great," The Modern Schoolman, XXXVII (1959), 121-137.

Khan, Muhammad Zafrulla, trans. The Quran. London and Dublin: Curzon Press, 1971.

Klubertanz, G. P. The Discursive Power. St. Louis: The Modern Schoolman, 1952.

--------. "The Unity of Human Activity," The Modern Schoolman, XXVII (1950), 75-103.

Knowles, D. The Evolution of Medieval Thought. Baltimore: The Helicon Press, 1962.

Koch, R. "Man," in J. B. Bauer, ed., Sacramentum Verbi. Vol. II. New York: Herder and Herder, 1970.

Kraemer, Hendrick. World Cultures and World Religions. Philadelphia: The Westminster Press, 1960.

Kremer, J. "The Resurrection of Jesus, the Cause and Exemplar of Our Resurrection," Concilium, LX (1970), 78-91.

Kreyche, Gerald F. "The Soul-Body Problem in St. Thomas," The New Scholasticism, XLVI (1972), 446-484.

Kristeller, P. O. The Classics and Renaissance Thought. Cambridge, Mass.: Harvard University Press, 1955.

--------. Eight Italian Philosophers of the Italian Renaissance. Standford: Standford University Press, 1964.

--------. Renaissance Philosophy and the Medieval Tradition. Latrobe, Pennsylvania: The Archabbey Press, 1966.

--------. Studies in Renaissance Thought and Letters. Rome: Edizione di Storia e Litteratura, 1956.

Kuksewicz, Zdzislaw. *Averroisme bolonais au XIVe siècle*. Wroclaw: Ossolineum, 1965.

--------. *De Siger de Brabant à Jacques de Plaissance; la théorie de l'intellect chez les Averroistes Latins des XIIIe et XIVe siècles*. Wroclaw: Ossolineum, 1968.

Kummel, W. G. *Promise and Fulfillment: The Eschatological Message of Jesus*. Translated by D. M. Barton. London: SCM Press, 1957.

Kunneth, W. *The Theology of the Resurrection*. London: SCM Press, 1965.

Lacombe, G. et al. *Aristoteles Latinus*. Rome: La Libreria Dello Strato, 1939.

Leclercq, J. *The Love of Learning and the Desire for God*. Translated by C. Misrahi. New York: Fordham University Press, 1961.

Lee, R. W. "Pomponazzi's Criticism of the Thomistic Position on the Immortality of the Soul." Unpublished L.M.S. thesis, Pontifical Institute of Mediaeval Studies, 1961.

Leff, Gordon. *Medieval Thought*. Harmondsworth, Middlesex: Penguin Books, 1961.

Leibnitz, G. W. "Reflections on the Doctrine of a Single Universal Spirit," in L. E. Loemker, ed. and trans., *Gottfried Wilhelm Leibnitz: Philosophical Papers and Letters*. Chicago: University of Chicago Press, 1956.

Lerner, R., and M. Madhi, eds. *Medieval Political Philosophy: A Sourcebook*. Glencoe, Ill.: The Free Press, 1963.

Little, A. *The Platonic Heritage of Thomism*. Dublin: Golden Eagle Books Limited, 1949.

Lonergan, B. "The Natural Desire to See God," in F. E. Crowe, ed., *Collection: Papers by Bernard Lonergan*. New York: Herder and Herder, 1967.

--------. "St. Thomas' Theory of Operation," *Theological Studies*, III (1942), 375-402.

MacClintock, S. *Perversity and Error: Studies in Averroist John of Jandun*. Bloomington: Indiana University Press, 1956.

Macdonald, D. B. "The Development of the Idea of Spirit in Islam," *Muslim World*, 22, no. 1 (January-April), 25-42.

Macdonald, D. B. The Development of Muslim Theology, Jurisprudence and Constitutional Theory. New York: Russell and Russell, 1966. First published in 1903.

--------. "Immortality in Mohammedanism," in E. H. Sneath, ed., Religion and the Future Life. New York: Fleming H. Revell Co., 1922.

--------. The Religious Life and Attitude in Islam. Chicago: University of Chicago Press, 1909.

Macdonald, John. "Islamic Eschatology," Islamic Studies, III (1964), 285-308, 485-519; IV (1965), 55-102, 137-179; V (1966), 129-197, 331-383.

Madkour, I. "The Concept of Man in Islamic Thought," in S. Radhakrishnan and P. T. Raju, eds., The Concept of Man. London: George Allen and Unwin Ltd., 1966.

--------. La place d'al Fârâbî dans l'école philosophique musulmane. Paris: Librairie d'Amerique et d'Orient, 1934.

Malebranche, N. Recherche de la vérité. Paris: J. Vrin, 1962.

Maloney, C. "A Study of St. Thomas Aquinas' Opinion on Divine Communication in the Vision of God." Unpublished S.T.D. dissertation, Gregorian University, 1966.

Mandonnet, P. Siger de Brabant et l'Averroisme Latin de XIIIe siecle. 2 vols. Louvain: Institut Supérieur de Philosophie, 1911.

Mansion, A. "L'immortalité de l'âme et de l'intellect d'après Aristote," Revue philosophique de Louvain, LI (1953), 444-472.

Marcel, G. Searchings. New York: The Newman Press, 1967.

Marmura, M. E. "Avicenna and the Infinite Number of Souls," Mediaeval Studies, XXII (1960), 232-239.

Martin, Raymond. Pugio Fidei Adversus Mauros et Judeos. Leipzig and Frankfurt: Typis Viduae Johannis Wittigav, 1687.

Martin-Achard, R. From Death to Life. Edinburgh and London: Oliver and Boyd, 1960.

Mascarenhas, H. O. "St. Thomas and the Medieval Scholastics," in S. Radhakrishnan, ed., History of Philosophy: Eastern and Western. London: George Allen and Unwin Ltd., 1953.

Masson, D. Le Coran et la révélation Judéo-Chretienne. 2 vols. Paris: Librairie d'Amerique et d'Orient Adrien-Maissoneuve, 1958.

Maurer, A. "Boethius of Dacia and the Double Truth," Mediaeval Studies, XVII (1955), 233-239.

--------. "Form and Essence in the Philosophy of St. Thomas," Mediaeval Studies, XIII (1951), 165-176.

--------. Medieval Philosophy. New York: Random House, 1967.

McCasland, S. V. "The Nature of Man in the New Testament," in G. A. Buttrick et al., eds., The Interpreter's Dictionary of the Bible. Vol. III. New York: The Abingdon Press, 1962.

McKenzie, J. L. "Aspects of Old Testament Thought," in R. E. Brown, J. A. Fitzmyer, and R. E. Murphy, eds., The Jerome Biblical Commentary. Vol. II. New Jersey: Prentice-Hall, Inc., 1968.

Mehren, A.-F. "Études sur la philosophie d'Averroès concernant son rapport avec celle d'Avicenne et Gazzali," Muséon, VII (1888), 613-627; VIII (1889), 5-20.

Merlan, Philip. Monopsychism, Mysticism, Metaconsciousness: Problems of the Soul in the Neoaristotelian and Neoplatonic Tradition. 2nd edition. The Hague: M. Nijhoff, 1969.

Meyer, Hans. The Philosophy of St. Thomas Aquinas. Translated by Frederic Eckhoff. St. Louis: B. Herder Book Co., 1944.

Miller, Robert. "An Aspect of Averroes' Influence on St. Albert," Mediaeval Studies, XVI (1954), 57-71.

Minio-Paluello, L. "Iacobus Veneticus Grecus, Canonist and Translator of Aristotle," Traditio, VIII (1952), 265-304.

--------. Opuscula: The Latin Aristotle. Amsterdam: M. Hockert, 1972.

--------. "Place of Aristotle," A Catholic Dictionary of Theology. Vol. I. London: Thomas Nelson and Sons Ltd., 1962.

--------. "La texte du 'De Anima' d'Aristote: la tradition latine avant 1500," in Autour d'Aristote. Études offertes à M. Mansion. Louvain: Publications Universitaires, 1955.

Moraux, P. Alexandre d'Aphrodise exégète de la noétique d'Aristote. Liège: Faculté de philosophie et lettres, 1942.

Mork, Dom Wulstan. The Biblical Meaning of Man. Milwaukee: The Bruce Publishing Company, 1967.

Müller-Goldkuhle, P. "Post-Biblical Developments in Eschatological Thought," Concilium, XLI (1969), 24-41.

Munk, S. Melanges de philosophie juive et arabe. Paris: Franck, 1859.

Myers, E. A. Arabic Thought and the Western World. New York: Frederick Ungar Publishing Co., 1964.

Nadvi, Muzaffar-Ud-Din. Muslim Thought and its Source. Lahore: Shaikh Muhammed Ashraf, 1953.

Nasr, Seyyed Hossein. Ideals and Realities of Islam. New York: Frederick A. Praeger, 1967.

A New Catechism. New York: Herder and Herder, 1969.

Nogales, S. Gomez. "El destino del hombre a la luz de la noética de Averroes," in L'homme et son destin d'après les penseurs du moyen âge. (Actes du premier congrès international de philosophie médiévale, Louvain-Bruxelles, 28 août - 4 sept. 1958.) Louvain: E. Nauwelaerts, 1960.

--------. "L'immortalidad del alma a la luz de la noética de Averroes," Pensamiento, XV (1959), 155-175.

Nuyens, F. L'evolution de la psychologie d'Aristote. Louvain: Institut Supérieur de Philosophie, 1948.

O'Leary, De Lacy. Arabic Thought and its Place in History. London: Routledge and Kegan Paul Ltd., 1963.

--------. How the Greek Science Passed to the Arabs. London: Routledge and Kegan Paul Ltd., 1948.

Origen. Contra Celsum. Translated by H. Chadwick. Cambridge: At the University Press, 1953.

--------. On First Principles. Translated by G. W. Butterworth. London: Society for Promoting Christian Knowledge, 1936.

--------. Selections from the Commentaries and Homilies of Origen. Edited by R. B. Tollington. London: Society for Promoting Christian Knowledge, 1929.

O'Shaughnessy, Thomas. Muhammad's Thoughts on Death. Leiden: E. J. Brill, 1969.

Owen, John. The Skeptics of the Italian Renaissance. London: Swan Sonnenschein and Co.; New York: The Macmillan Company, 1908.

Palmer, E. H., trans. The Koran. Oxford: At the University Press, 1949.

Pareja, F. M. *Islamologie.* Beyrouth: Imprimerie Catholique, 1964.

Patterson, L. G. *God and History in Early Christian Thought.* New York: The Seabury Press, 1967.

Peghaire, Julien. "A Forgotten Sense, the Cogitative, According to St. Thomas Aquinas," *The Modern Schoolman,* XX (1943), 123-140, 210-229.

Pegis, A. C. *At the Origins of the Thomistic Notion of Man.* New York: The Macmillan Company, 1963.

--------. "The Separated Soul and Its Nature in St. Thomas," in *St. Thomas Aquinas (1274-1974) Commemorative Studies.* Vol. I. Toronto: Pontifical Institute of Mediaeval Studies, 1974.

--------. "Some Reflections on *Summa Contra Gentiles* II, 56," in C. J. O'Neil, ed., *An Etienne Gilson Tribute.* Milwaukee: Marquette University Press, 1959.

--------. *St. Thomas and the Problem of the Soul in the Thirteenth Century.* Toronto: Pontifical Institute of Mediaeval Studies, 1934.

--------. "St. Thomas and the Unity of Man," in J. A. McWilliams, ed., *Progress in Philosophy.* Milwaukee: Marquette University Press, 1955, pp. 153-173.

Pelikan, J. *The Christian Tradition.* Vol. I. Chicago: University of Chicago Press, 1971.

--------. *The Shape of Death: Life and Immortality in the Early Fathers.* New York: The Abingdon Press, 1961.

Persson, P. E. *Sacra Doctrina: Reason and Revelation in Aquinas.* Translated by Ross Mackenzie. Philadelphia: Fortress, 1972.

Peters, F. E. *Aristotle and the Arabs.* New York: New York University Press, 1968.

Pickthal, Mohammed M., trans. *The Meaning of the Glorious Koran.* New York: The New American Library, 1958.

Pieper, J. *Death and Immortality.* New York: Herder and Herder, 1969.

Pine, Martin. "Pomponazzi and the Problem of 'Double Truth,'" *Journal of the History of Ideas,* XXIX (1968), 163-178.

Plato. *The Collected Dialogues of Plato, Including the Letters.* Edited by Edith Hamilton and Huntington Cairns. New York: Pantheon Books, 1961.

--------. *Dialogues.* Translated by B. Jowett. 5 vols. Oxford: At the Clarendon Press, 1892.

Plooij, E. "The Torch of Philosophy, a Smoking Flax (Averroes)," Synthèse (Bussum), IX (1953-1955), Issue 5, no. 6B, 492-498.

Pomponazzi, Pietro. De Immortalitate Animae. Edited by G. Morra. Bologna: Nanni and Fiammenghi, 1954.

--------. "On the Immortality of the Soul." Translated by William Henry Hay II; revised by John Herman Randall, Jr. In E. Cassirer, P. O. Kristeller, and John Herman Randall, Jr., eds., The Renaissance Philosophy of Man. Chicago: University of Chicago Press, 1948.

Porteous, N. W. "The Nature of Man in the Old Testament," in G. A. Buttrick et al., eds., The Interpreter's Dictionary of the Bible, Vol. III. New York: The Abingdon Press, 1962.

Previté-Orton, C. W. The Shorter Cambridge Medieval History. 2 vols. Cambridge: At the University Press, 1952.

Price, J. L. "The First Letter of Paul to the Corinthians," in C. M. Laymon, ed., The Interpreter's One-Volume Commentary on the Bible. New York: The Abingdon Press, 1971.

Pringle-Patterson, A. Seth. The Idea of Immortality. Oxford: At the Clarendon Press, 1922.

Quadri, G. La philosophie arabe dans l'Europe médiévale. Translated from the Italian by R. Huret. Paris: Payot, 1947.

Quasten, J. Patrology. 3 vols. Westminster: The Newman Press, 1960.

Radhakrishnan, S., ed. A History of Philosophy: Eastern and Western. 2 vols. London: George Allen and Unwin Ltd., 1952.

Radhakrishnan, S., and P. T. Raju, eds. The Concept of Man: A Study in Comparative Philosophy. London: George Allan and Unwin Ltd., 1960.

Rahilly, A. J. "Averroism and Scholasticism," Studies: An Irish Quarterly Review of Letters, Philosophy and Science, II (1913), 301-324; III (1914), 686-713.

Rahman, F. Avicenna's Psychology. London: Oxford University Press, 1952.

--------. Islam. New York: Rinehart and Winston, 1966.

--------. "The Status of the Individual in Islam," Islamic Studies, V (1966), 319-330.

Rahner, K. On the Theology of Death. New York: Herder and Herder, 1961.

Rahner, K. Theological Investigations. Vol. IV. Translated by K. Smyth. Baltimore: The Helicon Press, 1966.

Rahner, K., et al., eds. Sacramentum Mundi. Vol. V. Montreal: Palm Publishers, 1970.

Randall, Jr., J. H. "The Development of Scientific Method in the School of Padua," Journal of the History of Ideas, I (1940), 177-206.

--------. The School of Padua and the Emergence of Modern Science. Padova: Editrice Antenore, 1961.

--------. "The Studies of the Philosophies of the Renaissance," Journal of the History of Ideas, II (1941), 449-496.

Rashdall, Hastings. The Universities of Europe in the Middle Ages. Edited by F. W. Powicke and A. B. Emden. London: Oxford University Press, 1936.

Ratzinger, J. "Resurrection of the Body," in K. Rahner et al., eds., Sacramentum Mundi. Vol. V. Montreal: Palm Publishers, 1970.

Riedl, John O., ed. A Catalogue of Renaissance Philosophers (1350-1650). Milwaukee: Marquette University Press, 1940.

Renan, E. Averroès et l'Averroisme, in Oeuvres Complètes de Ernest Renan. Tome III. Paris: Calmann-Lévy, 1949.

Rhode, E. Psyche. London: Kegan Paul, Trench, Trubner and Co. Ltd., 1925.

Riordan, J. "Form and Intellect in Averroes." Unpublished Ph.D. dissertation, University of Toronto, 1960.

Robinson, J. A. T. In the End God. New York: Harper and Harper, 1968.

--------. "Resurrection in the New Testament," in G. A. Buttrick et al., eds., The Interpreter's Dictionary of the Bible. Vol. IV. New York: The Abingdon Press, 1962.

Rosenthal, E. I. J. Political Thought in Medieval Islam. Cambridge: At the University Press, 1958.

Ross, W. D. Aristotle. London: Methuen and Co. Ltd., 1923.

Russell, Bertrand. History of Western Philosophy. London: George Allen and Unwin Ltd., 1963.

Russell, D. S. The Method and Message of Jewish Apocalyptic. London: SCM Press, 1964.

El-Saleh, Soubhi. _La vie future selon le Coran_. Paris: J. Vrin, 1971.

Salman, D. "Algazel et les Latins," _Archives d'histoire doctrinale et littéraire du moyen âge_, X (1935), 103-127.

--------. "Jean de la Rochelle et les débuts de l'Averoisme Latin, _Archives d'histoire doctrinale et littéraire du moyen âge_, XXII (1947), 133-144.

--------. "Note sur la première influence d'Averroès," _Revue néoscolastique de philosophie_, XL (1937), 203-212.

Sarton, George. _Introduction to the History of Science_. Baltimore: Williams and Wilkins Co., 1931.

Schacht, Joseph. _An Introduction to Islamic Law_. Oxford: Oxford University Press, 1964.

--------. _The Origins of Mohammedan Jurisprudence_. Oxford: Oxford University Press, 1950.

Schelling, O. "Resurrection," in J. B. Bauer, ed. _Sacramentum Verbi_. Vol. II. New York: Herder and Herder, 1970.

Schillebeeckx, E. "The Interpretation of Eschatology," _Concilium_, XLI (1969), 42-56.

Schillebeeckx, E., and B. Willems, eds. _Dogma: The Problem of Eschatology_. New York: Paulist Press, 1969.

Schmid, J. "Resurrection of the Body," in K. Rahner et al., eds., _Sacramentum Mundi_. Vol. V. Montreal: Palm Publishers, 1970.

Schmitt, E. "Death," in J. B. Bauer, ed., _Sacramentum Verbi_. Vol. I. New York: Herder and Herder, 1970.

Schoonenberg, P. "I Believe in Eternal Life," _Concilium_, XLI (1969), 97-112.

Schwarz, H. _On the Way to the Future_. Minneapolis: Augsburg Publishing House, 1972.

Searle, Morris S. _Muslim Theology_. London: Luzac and Co. Ltd., 1964.

Serouya, H. _La pensée arabe_. Paris: Presses Universitaires de France, 1960.

Sharif, M. M., ed. _A History of Islamic Philosophy_. 2 vols. Wiesbaden: Otto Harrassowitz, 1963.

--------. "Muslim Philosophy and Western Thought," _Iqbal_, VIII, no. 1 (1959), 1-14.

Shinedling, Abraham. "Kalonymos ben Kalonymos ben Meir," Universal Jewish Encyclopedia. Vol. VI. New York: Universal Jewish Encyclopedia Co., 1962.

Shute, C. The Psychology of Aristotle. New York: Columbia University Press, 1941.

Singer, Charles and Dorothea. "The Jewish Factor in Medieval Thought," in A. R. Becan and Charles Singer, eds., The Legacy of Israel. Oxford: At the Clarendon Press, 1927.

Sleeva, V. E. The Separated Soul in the Philosophy of St. Thomas Aquinas. Washington: Catholic University of America Press, 1940.

Smith, Jane I. "The Understanding of nafs and rūh in Contemporary Muslim Considerations of the Nature of Sleep and Death," Muslim World, 49, no. 3 (July, 1979), 151-152.

Smith, Jane I and Y. Y. Haddad. "Afterlife Themes in Modern Qur'an Commentary," Journal of the American Academy of Religion, Supplement, (December, 1979), 699-720.

--------. The Islamic Understanding of Death and Resurrection. Albany: State University of New York Press, 1981.

Sourdel, D. Islam. New York: Walker & Co., 1962.

Southern, R. W. Western View of Islam in the Middle Ages. Cambridge, Mass.: Harvard University Press, 1962.

Stanley, D. M. "The Greco-Roman Background of the New Testament," in C. M. Laymon, ed., The Interpreter's One-Volume Commentary on the Bible. New York: The Abingdon Press, 1971.

Stendahl, K., ed. Immortality and Resurrection. New York: The Macmillan Company, 1965.

Strauss, L. Persecution and the Art of Writing. Glencoe, Ill.: The Free Press, 1952.

Sweetman, J. Windrow. Islam and Christian Theology. 2 parts, 4 vols. London: Butterworth Press, 1945-67.

Tallon, A. "Personal Immortality in Averroes' Tahafut al-Tahafut," The New Scholasticism, XXXVIII (1964), 341-357.

Tapiéro, E. Le dogme et les rites de l'Islam par les textes. Paris: G. Klincksieck, 1957.

Teske, Roland J. "The End of Man in the Philosophy of Averroes," The New Scholasticism, XXXVII (1963), 431-461.

Themistii in Libros Aristotelis de Anima. Edited by R. Heinze. Berlin: Reimer, 1899.

Thémistius. Commentaire sur le traité de l'âme d'Aristote: Traduction de Guillaume de Moerbeke. Edited by G. Verbeke. Louvain: Publications Universitaires, 1957.

Théry, G. "Averroès et l'Alexandrisme," in Bibliothèque Thomiste. Vol. VII. Kain, Belgium: Revue des sciences philosophique et théologiques, 1926.

Thomas Aquinas. Aristotle's De Anima, in the Version of William of Moerbeke and the Commentary of St. Thomas Aquinas. Translated by K. Foster and S. Humphries. New Haven: Yale University Press, 1954.

--------. Commentarium in Aristotelis Librum de Anima. Edited by P. F. Angeli M. Pirotta. Rome: Marietti Edition, 1948.

--------. De Unitate Intellectus Contra Averroistas. Edited by L. Keeler. Rome: Gregorian University Press, 1946.

--------. On Spiritual Creatures. Translated by M. C. Fitzpatrick and J. J. Wellmuth. Milwaukee: Marquette University Press, 1949.

--------. On the Truth of the Catholic Faith, Summa Contra Gentiles, Book One: God. Translated by A. C. Pegis. New York: Doubleday and Co., Inc., 1962.

--------. On the Truth of the Catholic Faith, Summa Contra Gentiles, Book Two: Creation. Translated by James F. Anderson, New York: Doubleday and Co., Inc., 1956.

--------. On the Unity of the Intellect Against the Averroists. Translated from the Latin with an introduction by Beatrice H. Zedler. Milwaukee: Marquette University Press, 1968.

--------. Opera Omnia. Vols. III and XXVIII. Edited by S. E. Fretté. Paris: Vivès, 1872, 1875.

--------. Opuscula Omnia. Vol. III. Edited by P. Mandonnet. Paris: P. Letheilleux, 1927.

--------. Opuscula Theologica. Vol. II. Edited by R. M. Spiazzi. Rome: Marietti Edition, 1954.

--------. Quaestiones Disputatae et Quaestiones Duodecim Quodlibetales. 2 vols. Rome: Marietti Edition, 1927.

--------. Scriptum Super Libros Sententiarum Magistri Petri Lombardi. Edited by P. Mandonnet and M. F. Moos. 4 vols. Paris: P. Letheilleux, 1929-47.

Thomas Aquinas. The Soul: A Translation of St. Thomas
Aquinas' De Anima, by J. P. Rowan. St. Louis: B.
Herder Book Co., 1949.

--------. Summa Contra Gentiles. Rome: Leonine Edition,
1934.

--------. Summa Theologiae. Latin text and English translation, introduction, notes, appendices, and glossaries. 60 vols. London: Blackfriars, 1964-66.

--------. The Trinity and The Unicity of the Intellect.
Translated by Rose E. Brennan. St. Louis: B.
Herder Book Co., 1946.

Thorndike, Lynn. A History of Magic and Experimental
Science, Vol. V: Sixteenth Century. New York: Columbia University Press, 1941.

Tornay, S.C. "Averroes' Doctrine of the Mind," Philosophic
Review, LII (1943), 270-282.

Tresmontant, Claude. Christian Metaphysics. New York:
Sheed and Ward, 1965.

--------. The Origins of Christian Philosophy. Translated
from the French by Mark Pontifex. New York: Hawthorn Books, 1963.

--------. A Study of Hebrew Thought. New York: Desclée
Company, 1960.

Tritton, A. S. Islam: Belief and Practices. London:
Hutchinson University Press, 1957.

--------. "Man, nafs, rūh, 'aql." Bulletin of the School
of Oriental and African Studies, 34 (1971),
491-495.

Ulken, Hilmi Ziya. La pensée de l'Islam. Istanbul:
Falkulteler Matbaasi, 1953.

Vanderhaar, Gerrard A. "The Status of Scholastic Philosophy in Theology Today," The Catholic Theological
Society of America, Proceedings of the Twenty-First
Annual Convention, XXI (1966), 71-93.

Van Steenberghen, F. Aristotle in the West. Louvain: E.
Nauwelaerts, 1955.

--------. Les oeuvres et la doctrine de Siger de Brabant.
Bruxelles: Palais des Académies, 1938.

--------. Siger de Brabant. Vol. II. Louvain: E. Nauwelaerts, 1942.

--------. Siger de Brabant d'après ses oeuvres inédites.
2 vols. Louvain: Institut Supérieur de Philosophie, 1931-42.

Van Steenberghen F. Siger dans l'histoire de l'Aristotelisme. Louvain: Institut Superieur de Philosophie, 1942.

Verbeke, Gérard. "L'unité de l'homme: saint Thomas contre Averroès," Revue philosophique de Louvain, LVIII (1960), 220-249.

Von Grunebaum, Gustave E. Medieval Islam. Chicago: University of Chicago Press, 1947.

Von Rad, G. Old Testament Theology. 2 vols. New York: Harper and Row, 1962.

Walzer, R. "Islamic Philosophy," in S. Radhakrishnan, ed., History of Philosophy: Eastern and Western. Vol. II. London: George Allen and Unwin Ltd., 1953.

Watt, W. M. Bell's Introduction to the Qur'an. Edinburgh: At the University Press, 1970.

--------. Freewill and Predestination in Early Islam. London: Luzac and Co. Ltd., 1948.

--------. A History of Islamic Spain. Edinburgh: At the University Press, 1967.

--------. Islamic Philosophy and Theology. Edinburgh: At the University Press, 1962.

--------. Islamic Revelation in the Modern World. Edinburgh: At the University Press, 1969.

--------. What is Islam? London: Longmans, Green and Co. Ltd., 1968.

Webb, C. C. J. Studies in the History of Natural Theology. Oxford: At the Clarendon Press, 1915.

Weber, E. H. L'homme en discussion à l'université de Paris en 1270. Paris: J. Vrin, 1970.

Weinberg, Julius R. A Short History of Medieval Philosophy. Princeton: Princeton University Press, 1964.

Wensinck, A. J. The Muslim Creed. London: Frank Cass and Co. Ltd., 1965. First published in 1932.

Whiteley, D. E. H. The Theology of St. Paul. Oxford: Basil Blackwell, 1970.

Wiles, M. The Making of Christian Doctrine. Cambridge: At the University Press, 1967.

Williams, John A. Islam. New York: George Braziller, 1962.

Wolfson, H. A. Crescas' Critique of Aristotle. Cambridge, Mass.: Harvard University Press, 1929.

Wolfson, H. A. "The Double Faith Theory in Clement, Saadia, Averroes and St. Thomas, and its Origin in Aristotle and the Stoics," Jewis Quarterly Review, N. S. XXXIII (1942), 213-264.

--------. "Immortality and Resurrection in the Philosophy of the Church Fathers," in K. Stendahl, ed., Immortality and Resurrection. New York: Macmillan, 1965.

--------. "The Internal Senses in Latin, Arabic and Hebrew Philosophical Texts," Harvard Theological Review, XXVIII (1935), 69-135.

--------. Philo: Foundations of Religious Philosophy in Judaism, Christianity and Islam. 2 vols. Cambridge, Mass.: Harvard University Press, 1948.

--------. The Philosophy of the Church Fathers. Vol. I. Cambridge, Mass.: Harvard University Press, 1956.

--------. "Plan of a Corpus Commentariorum Averrois in Aristotelem," Speculum, VI (1931), 412-427.

--------. Religious Philosophy. Cambridge, Mass.: Harvard University Press, 1961.

--------. "Revised Plan for the Publication of a Corpus Commentariorum Averrois in Aristotelem," Speculum, XXXVII, no. 1 (1963), 88-104.

--------. "The Twice-Revealed Averroes," Speculum, XXXVI, no. 3 (1961), 373-393.

Zedler, B. H. "Arabian Philosophy," in The New Catholic Encyclopedia. Vol. I. New York: McGraw-Hill, 1967.

--------. "Averroes (Ibn Rushd)," in The New Catholic Encylcopedia. Vol. I. New York: McGraw-Hill, 1967.

--------. "Averroes and Immortality," The New Scholasticism, XXVIII (1954), 436-453.

--------. "Averroes on the Possible Intellect," Proceedings of the American Catholic Philosophical Association, XXV (1951), 164-178.

--------. Reviewer of S. Van den Bergh's Averroes' Tahafut al-Tahafut, The Modern Schoolman, XXXIII (1956), 124-127.

--------. "Unity of Intellect," in The New Catholic Encyclopedia. Vol. VII. New York: McGraw-Hill, 1967.

INDEX

Achillini, Alexander, 9
Adelard of Bath, 4
Albert the Great, 4-5
Alexander IV, 4
Alexander of Aphrodisias, 9, 58-59, 89, 96-98
Alexandrists, 9, 50, 141
Alfarabi, 3, 65-67, 127, 140
Algazali, 26, 32, 66-68, 71, 73-74, 77, 105, 109, 141
Allegorical interpretation of Scripture, 26, 61-62, 65-67, 72-74, 141
Alonso, M., 19-20, 142
Anaxagoras, 54, 84
Anfus, 31, 33, 35
Aquinas, 5-9, 12, 15, 21, 23, 25-26, 48-50, 58-59, 82-83, 131, 133-134, 137, 141-142
Arberry, J., 61
Arnaldez, R., 18, 20, 140
Arwāh, 31, 34
Asín y Palacios, M., 15-16, 81, 141
Ash'ari, al-, 62
Ash'arites, 62, 67, 68, 74
Augustine, 48, 64, 136
Averroes
    as fideist, 15, 22, 140
    as rationalist, 16, 22, 140
Averroism, 5, 8, 23
Averroists, 4, 7-10, 12-14, 50, 131, 136, 138
Avicenna, 3, 66, 109, 140

Baconthorp, John, 8
Benedict XII, 50, 139
Bernier of Nivelles, 8
Boethius, 1
Boethius of Dacia, 8
Bonaventure, 4

Calo, Maestro, 11
Calonymos ben David the Elder, 11
Calonymos ben David the Younger, 11
Calonymos, son of Meir, of Arles, 11
Calonymos, Calo, 11
Calvin, J., 50
Consensus, doctrine of (ijma), 72
Contarini, Gaspar, 9
Council of Florence, 8, 50, 139
Courson, Robert, 2
Cullman, O., 43, 51

Death
    as complete unconsciousness, 36, 113
    as sleep, 77, 108, 111, 113, 135-136
    as sleep of souls, 35, 113

195

De Boer, T. J., 63
Democritus, 54
Descartes, 1
Destructio Destructionum, 10-12, 16-17, 24
Dominicans, 6-7
De Vaux, C., 20-21, 142
De Wulf, M., 17, 140

"Eternal life," 37, 53, 66, 104, 113

Fakhry, M., 16-17, 140
falasifa, 63-64, 70
Fasl al-maqal, 15-18, 20, 26, 69-76, 78, 81
Fifth Lateral Council, 9, 50, 140
Frederick II, 3-4

Gabriel, 72
Gatch, M. McM., 50
Gauthier, L., 16-17, 140
Gerard of Cremona, 4
Giles of Rome, 8
Gilson, E., 17-18, 67-68, 83, 141
Gleason, R. W., 51
God, Aristotle's notion of, 67-68
Gonzaga, Hercules, 11
González-Ruiz, J. M., 43
Goswin of La Chapelle, 8
Gregory IX, 2
Gundalissalinus, Dominicus, 4

Herman the German, 4
Hijazi, M. Mahmud, 31
Hourani, G. F., 16, 140

Ibn 'Abbas, 33, 35, 110, 112
Ibn Karram, 62
Ibn Qayyim al-Jawziya, 32
Ibrahim, Mahmud, 31
Intellect
    active, 57-59
    acquired (intellectus adeptus), 126, 128
    agent, 65, 115-129
    characteristics of, 92-95
    in habit, 121-126, 128, 130
    material, 95-98, 100, 103, 115-130
    passible, 101, 103, 117-121, 128-129
    passive, 57-59
    possible, 9
    speculative, 128, 130
    unicity of, 5, 9, 20, 99, 107, 139
Intellection and sensation compared, 92-93
Interim state for the dead, 35-37, 45-46
Irenaeus, 70
Islamic State, 75-76, 81

James of Venice, 1
Jammal, al-, 34
Jawhari, Tantawi, 31
John XXII, 50-51

Index   197

John of Jandun, 8
John of Spain, 4
Justinian, 3

Kashf al-manahidj, 15-17, 19-20, 26, 110
Kindi, al-, 3, 32, 64-65, 70, 79, 140
Knowledge
    habitual, 121-122, 128
    two subjects in, 100, 105, 115, 117-120, 123, 129
    unity of, 5, 99-100, 105
Knowles, D., 48
Freyche, G. F., 49-50
Kunneth, W., 52

Leclerq, J., 47
Logica nova, 1, 3, 48
Logica vetus, 1, 48
Luther, M., 10, 50

Malik ben Anas, 62
Man
    dualistic conception of, 38-40, 51-53, 133-135, 137
    monistic conception of, 36, 38-39, 52-53, 77, 86, 89,
        92, 96, 104, 113, 131, 134-135, 137, 141
    NT view of, 43-45
    OT view of, 41-42
    Thomistic view of, 49-50
    unity of, 13
Mandonnet, P., 15, 17, 24, 140
Maraghi, al-, 34
Marcel, G., 51
Matter, as principle of individuation, 6, 19, 100
Martin, Raymond, 7, 56
Monopsychism, 13, 139
Muhammad, 6, 20, 29, 37, 60, 64, 66, 72, 75
Muller, M. J., 15
Munk, S., 15
Munkar, 36
Mutakallims, 31
Mu'tazilites, 32, 36, 61-63, 74

Nafs, 30-35
Nakir, 36
Neoplatonism, 3, 32, 63, 65-68
New creation, 30, 39, 53, 77, 110, 113, 135
New Testament, 37, 43-46, 59, 134-135, 137, 142
Nifo, Agostino, 9, 11-12
Nogales, S. Gomez, 20, 26, 142
Nufūs, 31

Old Testament, 41-42, 134

Pegis, A. C., 21, 49, 142
Pelikan, J., 47
Petrarch, Francesco, 8
Philosophy, as a demonstrative science, 70, 79, 141
Plato, 1-2, 7, 14-15, 18, 20, 26, 38, 40, 46-51, 56, 58
        63-66, 76-77, 96, 113, 119, 133, 135-136, 139
Plotinus, 3, 64-65

Pomponazzi, Pietro, 9, 12
Proclus, 3
Provincial Council of Paris, 2

Qur'an
    recognizes reason as a way to God, 60-61, 70
    recognizes three avenues to truth, 60-61, 64, 70
    recognizes three classes of men, 61
    recognizes three degrees of knowledge, 60-61
    recognizes three types of argumentation, 16, 61, 70-71, 80

Rahilly, A. J., 24
Rahner, K., 51
Ratzinger, J., 51
Raymond, Archbishop, 3
Razi, al-, 34-35
Renan, E., 15
<u>Republic</u>, 15, 18, 20, 26, 76, 78, 80-81
Resurrection and immortality compared, 52
Revelation, Islamic conception of, 18, 75
Reward and punishment, 24, 77, 91, 104, 114, 128-130, 133, 136, 140
Riordan, J., 21
Robert the Good, 11
Rosenthal, E. I. J., 15, 18, 75, 140
Rūh, 30-35

Scot, Michael, 4
Second creation, 30, 36, 38, 61, 69, 129-130
Shalabi, 'Abd al-Wadud, 33
Shi'ites, 32, 36
Siger de Brabant, 8
Sleep of souls, 35, 50-51, 135
Socrates, 40, 51, 119
Soul
    Aristotle's definition of, 54-55
    cogitative power of, 101-104, 115, 128
    imaginative power of, 101-104
    memorative power of, 101-104
    rational powers of, 101-103
    rational powers of, compared with intellect, 101-103, 106-107
Soul and intellect in Aquinas, 6
Soul, nature of in Aquinas, 6
Sourdel, D., 37, 39
Steinschneider, M., 24
Sweetman, J. Windrow, 19, 37, 141

Tabari, al-, 16
Tabarsi, al-, 34
Tabataba'i, al-, 34
<u>Tahafut al-Tahafut</u>, 7, 10-12, 14-21, 24, 26-27, 77-81, 104-107, 110, 141
Tallon, A., 19, 142
Tatian, 69
Tempier, Etienne, 8
Tertullian, 69
Teske, R., 20, 142

Themistius, 58-59, 128
Theophrastus, 58-59
Thomas of Wilton, 8
Three classes of men, 26, 61, 70, 74, 140
Truth, unity of, 69, 71, 74-75, 79

Umayyad period, 31

Veneto, Paolo, 9
Vernias, Nicoletto, 9
Victorinus, Marius, 1

Watt, M. W., 37-39, 52
Wolfson, H. A., 46

Zamakhshari, al-, 33-35
Zedler, B. H., 21, 26, 142

SR SUPPLEMENTS

1. **FOOTNOTES TO A THEOLOGY**
   The Karl Barth Colloquium of 1972
   Edited and Introduced by Martin Rumscheidt
   1974 / viii + 151 pp.

2. **MARTIN HEIDEGGER'S PHILOSOPHY OF RELIGION**
   John R. Williams
   1977 / x + 190 pp.

3. **MYSTICS AND SCHOLARS**
   The Calgary Conference on Mysticism 1976
   Edited by Harold Coward and Terence Penelhum
   1977 / viii + 121 pp. / OUT OF PRINT

4. **GOD'S INTENTION FOR MAN**
   Essays in Christian Anthropology
   William O. Fennell
   1977 / xii + 56 pp.

5. **"LANGUAGE" IN INDIAN PHILOSOPHY AND RELIGION**
   Edited and Introduced by Harold G. Coward
   1978 / x + 98 pp.

6. **BEYOND MYSTICISM**
   James R. Horne
   1978 / vi + 158 pp.

7. **THE RELIGIOUS DIMENSION OF SOCRATES' THOUGHT**
   James Beckman
   1979 / xii + 276 pp. / OUT OF PRINT

8. **NATIVE RELIGIOUS TRADITIONS**
   Edited by Earle H. Waugh and K. Dad Prithipaul
   1979 / xii + 244 pp. / OUT OF PRINT

9. **DEVELOPMENTS IN BUDDHIST THOUGHT**
   Canadian Contributions to Buddhist Studies
   Edited by Roy C. Amore
   1979 / iv + 196 pp.

10. **THE BODHISATTVA DOCTRINE IN BUDDHISM**
    Edited and Introduced by Leslie S. Kawamura
    1981 / xxii + 274 pp.

11. **POLITICAL THEOLOGY IN THE CANADIAN CONTEXT**
    Edited by Benjamin G. Smillie
    1982 / xii + 260 pp.

12. **TRUTH AND COMPASSION**
    Essays on Judaism and Religion in Memory of Rabbi Dr. Solomon Frank
    Edited by Howard Joseph, Jack N. Lightstone, and Michael D. Oppenheim
    1983 / vi + 217 pp.

13. **CRAVING AND SALVATION**
    A Study in Buddhist Soteriology
    Bruce Matthews
    1983 / xiv + 138 pp.

14. **THE MORAL MYSTIC**
    James R. Horne
    1983 / x + 134 pp.

15. **IGNATIAN SPIRITUALITY IN A SECULAR AGE**
    Edited by George P. Schner
    1984 / viii + 128 pp.

EDITIONS SR

1. **LA LANGUE DE YA'UDI**
   Description et classement de l'ancien parler de Zencircli dans le cadre des langues sémitiques du nord-ouest
   Paul-Eugène Dion, O.P.
   1974 / viii + 511 p.

2. **THE CONCEPTION OF PUNISHMENT IN EARLY INDIAN LITERATURE**
   Terence P. Day
   1982 / iv + 328 pp.

3. **TRADITIONS IN CONTACT AND CHANGE**
   Selected Proceedings of the XIVth Congress of the International Association for the History of Religions
   Edited by Peter Slater and Donald Wiebe with Maurice Boutin and Harold Coward
   1983 / x + 758 pp.

4. **LE MESSIANISME DE LOUIS RIEL**
   Gilles Martel
   1984 / xviii + 484 p.

5. **MYTHOLOGIES AND PHILOSOPHIES OF SALVATION IN THE THEISTIC TRADITIONS OF INDIA**
   Klaus K. Klostermaier
   1984 / xvi + 544 pp.

6. **AVERROES' DOCTRINE OF IMMORTALITY**
   A Matter of Controversy
   Ovey N. Mohammed
   1984 / vi + 202 pp.

STUDIES IN CHRISTIANITY AND JUDAISM / ETUDES SUR LE CHRISTIANISME ET LE JUDAISME

1. **A STUDY IN ANTI-GNOSTIC POLEMICS**
   Irenaeus, Hippolytus, and Epiphanius
   Gérard Vallée
   1981 / xii + 114 pp.

THE STUDY OF RELIGION IN CANADA / SCIENCES RELIGIEUSES AU CANADA

1. **RELIGIOUS STUDIES IN ALBERTA**
   A State-of-the-Art Review
   Ronald W. Neufeldt
   1983 / xiv + 145 pp.

COMPARATIVE ETHICS

1. **MUSLIM ETHICS AND MODERNITY**
   A Comparative Study of the Ethical Thought of Sayyid Ahmad Khan and Mawlana Mawdudi
   Sheila McDonough
   1984 / x + 130 pp.

Also published / Avons aussi publié

RELIGION AND CULTURE IN CANADA / RELIGION ET CULTURE AU CANADA
Edited by / sous la direction de
Peter Slater
1977 / viii + 568 pp. / OUT OF PRINT

Available from / en vente chez:

Wilfrid Laurier University Press
Wilfrid Laurier University
Waterloo, Ontario, Canada   N2L 3C5

Published for the
Canadian Corporation for Studies in Religion/
Corporation Canadienne des Sciences Religieuses
by Wilfrid Laurier University Press